Introducing
Neural
Networks

Alison Carling

SIGMA PRESS – Wilmslow, United Kingdom

First published in 1992 by

Sigma Press, 1 South Oak Lane, Wilmslow, Cheshire SK9 6AR, England.

British Library Cataloguing in Publication Data

A CIP catalogue record for this book is available from the British Library.

ISBN: 1-85058-174-6

Typesetting and design by

Sigma Hi-Tech Services Ltd

Printed in Malta by
Interprint Ltd.

Distributed by

John Wiley & Sons Ltd., Baffins Lane, Chichester, West Sussex, England.

CONTENTS

Special thanks to:

John J. Hopfield, (California Institute of Technology)

Dr. David S. Touretzky, (Research Computer Scientist, Carnegie Mellon University)

Professor Igor Aleksandar, (Professor of Neural Systems Engineering, Imperial College of Science, Technology and Medicine)

Stephen Grossberg

Dr. A. F. Murray, (University of Edinburgh)

Richard J. Evans, (Pattern Processing Group, Plessey Research)

Richard Rohwer, (Centre for Speech Technology Research, University of Edinburgh)

Dr. D. G. Bounds, (Research Initiative in Pattern Recognition, RSRE)

Robert Heicht-Nelson

W. B. Dress, (Oak Ridge National Laboratory)

Demetri Psaltis, (California Institute of Technology)

David Willshaw, (Centre for Cognitive Science, University of Edinburgh)

R. Colin Johnson

1

Introduction

A world controlled by computers – finance, missile control, cars and even washing machines. Our money comes out of a hole in the wall, provided the central computer has not assessed us as being non-credit worthy; our weather predictions are calculated by highly sophisticated computer systems; and the stock market rises and falls on the advice of a machine.

If you take a visit to the hospital, you may find yourself *conversing* with, and being posed questions by, a computer terminal which, incidentally, people tend to be more truthful with more readily than a human inquisitor. Your illness will then be diagnosed by the machine, more accurately in the case of a number of specific complaints, than a group of doctors have been able to achieve. (Bounds and Lloyd, 88)

When you use your credit card and the cashier, or cash point machine, checks your credibility, there is no suprise that it is only a matter of seconds before the information is located and returned from the central computer. Yet consider how many names and numbers had to be searched before yours is located, and there is potentially a large number of other queries taking place simultaneously.

The computer systems currently at our disposal are extremely powerful, able to carry out millions of processing steps per second and we come in contact with this capabilty every day, in one form or another. Even when we put aside the various differences of opinion concerning the definitions of processing speed, the figures are still awesome. With the development of the 80486 Intel chip, which has more than one million working components or transistors on a silicon wafer less than one inch across, even the humble desktop PC has become a machine capable of processing speeds up to 20 million instructions per second (MIPS), and a storage capacity of 100Mb is not unusual, if costly. Japanese companies are currently working on a microprocessor chip which will have up to 16 million transistors.

A great deal of development in this field has taken place since the invention of the microprocessor chip in 1958 by Dr Jack Kirby, and in perhaps only another couple of decades we will see desktop processing power available for a few hundred pounds comparable to the most powerful mainframe currently available, which costs many millions of pounds. We have seen this happen in the past: today we have calculators the size of credit cards, 50 years ago the equivalent technology used valves and filled a large room.

Yet, despite all these impressive feats of modern day technology, in the words of Dr. John Denker of AT & T's Bell Labs: *"Achievements to date have the mental capacity of a slug, but they still can't find their way out of the garden shed"*.

A truly frightening prospect. To imagine that our economic growth may be controlled by a machine with the potential of a slug, and one of lower than average intelligence at that. How can this be justified?

Computer systems such as the ones described above are essentially decision makers, those decisions being based on the application of a very large number of rules to a large base of data or information. Given the correct set of rules and access to enough data, a continuous stream of questions which require a simple YES or NO response can be applied to obtain the final answer or solution to the initial question or situation.

We know the power of a hand-held calculator, the same power which only a few decades ago would have needed a room full of processing equipment to achieve, and we are also well aware that a slug is not a genius at multiplying large numbers together, or any kind of numbers for that matter. Yet our calculator obviously has that potential.

We do not have a difference of opinion, or a mis-assessment of facts. What we have is an inappropriate comparison.

A computer system can be programmed to *know* that a rat is furry, has four legs and a long tail, but if the rat has no tail, does the traditional computer system still recognise it as a rat? Not unless that information was pre-programmed – and the variations are infinite. The rat may be bald, have only three legs, be a strange colour. This means that such systems are only truly efficient when the number of possible permutations are finite and have been previously programmed into the system, held as part of a collection of knowledge – a data base.

Given rigorously defined questions to ask, a conventional computer is perfectly capable of making accurate and extremely fast stock market decisions. A missile can constantly reassess direction and speed to continually update its course given the necessary facts and responses. But pose a question which has no predefined answer, such as: *"How do I find the shed door when I have never seen the shed before?"* And the system flounders.

These systems have their place and are used, with enormous success and accuracy in many applications. A typical such example is that of the previously mentioned medical diagnostics system. The originator of the rules here is a doctor, or many doctors, a pool of resource based on expertise and experience combining to produce a decision maker with all the necessary information available. However, this falls far short of mimicking the simplest, it would seem, of thought processes, whereby our intelligent slug would be a veritable Einstein in comparison.

Fact or Fiction?

Building a robot with human powers of thought and reason has been for some considerable time a *'reality'* as far as Science fiction is concerned. Friendly computers and robots indistinguishable in some cases from the real thing (i.e. a human) are commonplace. The famous HAL in *'2001, A Space Oddessy'*, who could not tell a lie, and who eventually had to shut himself down when ordered to do otherwise; Marvin, in *'A Hitchhikers Guide to the Galaxy'*, with his brain the size of a planet and a thoroughly human streak of gloom and despondancy; the neurotic C3PO in *'Star Wars'*, and the Replicants in *'Bladerunner'* who's search for eternal life and the ability to fall in love and show compassion and fear have become acceptable characteristics in this sort of futuristic presentation. It could be said that we have probably come to expect robots possessing human thoughts and feelings.

Could we actually be expecting and accepting something which is maybe a lot further away in terms of achievement than we initially anticipate? Perhaps we should be asking the question of whether it is a possibility at all. How near are we in mimicking any human faculties, for example speech, visual perception, character recognition, leaving aside concepts such as intuition, emotion and personality?

The brain of any creature is an incredibly complex organ. We can dissect it, put it under a microscope and analyse its composition in terms of cells and chemicals. We can even identify certain parts of it as controlling certain bodily functions such as vision, speech and parts of the body. We know, for example, that the left side of the brain relates in a physical sense to the right side of the body and the right side of the brain relates to the left side of the body. We know that the brain is made up of between 10 billion to 100 billion neurons, each of which is connected to about 10,000 other neurons. We can measure the electrical impulses they emit and identify the chemicals that pass between them. A great deal of useful and interesting information has been collected about the brain. But, are we actually any closer to discovering how it deals with complex and conceptual thought?

The problem we have with the brain is similar to saying that an army is made up of individuals, identifiable by name and that they communicate with each other. We can even note in detail the weapons that each possesses. We notice that this army has motivation and control, but if we do not understand where the instructions are coming from or how each individual deals with those instructions then we can only assess the results of an army in terms of its actions as a whole and the actions of the individuals. In a similar way we can identify the actions or responses initiated by the brain with respect to particular input and we can study the responses of individual neurons to that input and to each other. We can follow the succession of events between input and subsequent output and much work has been carried out to identify the roles of neurons within the brain. However, breaking the process down into individual responses does not seem to have solved the problem of the complex procedures that occur within the brain. There is a big difference, for example, between designing a computer application that can coordinate and control an aircraft and one that can mimic the human brain. The former has been achieved; the latter still eludes us. Why this should be the case may have something to do with the different ways in which brains and computers deal with information?

Perhaps one answer lies in the way in which research has been carried out in the past, using the computer resources available at the time and almost basing models on the way in which those computer systems function. It is true to say that the processing speeds of computer systems are without doubt extremely impressive. Given this conclusion, it is a strange fact that the cells in the brain have never managed to carry out more that a few thousand processing steps per second. Yet people are far more clever than machines. Of course, as mentioned before, this does depend on the definition of the word *clever*. The Oxford Dictionary of Current English defines clever as being 'skilful, talented, quick to understand and learn; adroit, dextrous; ingeneous.' In my opinion, I feel that I am cleverer than a computer. Although I would not, for example, care to compete with the computer in my car to minimise petrol consumption, nor would I feel at all confident in playing a game of chess against a computer, and I certainly cannot multiply large numbers (or even small ones!) together with the accuracy and speed of even a hand-held calculator because machines are simply quicker and more precise. I can understand what someone is saying even if they have a stammer or get the words around the wrong way. I can approach and solve a new problem, simply by drawing on past experiences and I can safely assume that gorillas like bananas because I know that chimpanzees like bananas.

We can identify that people are better than machines at these sort of natural thought processes or cognitive tasks: perceiving objects and noting the relationships between them, understanding language, being able to draw on past experiences to solve problems, retrieving information relating to a given context from memory.

When you look around a strange room, you invariably recognise what you see and can assess distances easily. You can draw on past experiences to build up a range of expectations and to almost fill in the gaps. For example, you would not expect to pull back a curtain and find a brick wall behind it, you would expect to see a window. We can use optical illusions to show how the brain *fills in* gaps for us visually. The same is true for cognitive processes. An example of this was an experiment carried out by Warren (1970) who presented the word *legislature* to a group of people, the s having been replaced by a completely different sound, a click. Although the click was heard in every case, so was the s, and participants were unable to locate the position of the click within the word, hearing it as almost distinct from the word. Our brains do a lot of behind the scenes work for us, based on our experiences and expectations. Experiments of this kind lend an insight into the workings of the brain and help us to analyse how it carries out functions which we take for granted. This is the problem to which Neural Networks relate: to produce coherent patterns of thought and behaviour through the use of computer architectures; to develop an intelligent machine.

However, the burning question is still: *"Why are people, so much cleverer than machines?"* This is such an important question particularly when we know that the brain processes so much slower than a modern day system. It has been determined, that the answer to this particular fact lies not in the speed of processing, but the way in which the processing is carried out.

2

Why is the Brain so much Faster?

As we have seen, current computer architectures are extremely powerful. Systems have been developed which can process in nanoseconds, carrying out many thousands of millions of instructions in the space of a second. Yet the brain actually only processes in terms of milliseconds, thousands of processing steps per second. Somewhere along the development line, an objective has been set and successfully met by researchers, leading to systems which can process at extremely high speeds, but this objective has not taken into account the restrictions imposed by the real life model. The achievement is impressive, but one answer must lie, it seems, not in the processing step capability, which modern day computer systems have exceeded many times over, but in the mode of processing and the method by which those processes are carried out. It simply cannot be a question of arming a system with the necessary information, precision and speed, and then forcing it to follow a predefined program to come to the correct solution. People do not behave like that; people make mistakes, they make shrewd guesses, they make judgements in new situations based on past experiences. People are also a turmoil of emotions and instinct, involving intuition and current needs.

How much do we really know about the brain and how it works? Perhaps the starting point is to look at what we know about the workings of the brain, at how the neurons themselves function. Is this a case of the more we find out the less we realise we know?

What do we know?

This study of the brain is by no means new. Man has possibly always had a fascination with the idea of creating an image of himself and with knowing, understanding, and having control over the functioning of a brain.

In 400 BC, Plato suggested that the brain was controlled by an ethereal spirit which ran through the body, controlling and revitalising the organs. More solid research carried out by Galen in 130 AD, brought to light the differences between motor and sensory nerves. By studying gladiators with damaged spines, he noticed that although they retained the motor functions of their legs, for example, they had lost all feeling. As there were no microscopes at the time, research like this was limited to observations of effects.

Galileo, in 1623, put forward the view that science was only concerned with primary qualities, those of the external world that could be measured and weighed. So called secondary qualities, such as love, beauty, meaning and value were said to lie outside the realm of science. Later Descartes supported this idea by proposing two categories: mind and matter. The matter category related to the physical or extended substance, which can be measured and divided, the mind category being the thinking substances, unextended and indivisible. Consciousness was excluded from the scientific picture of the world which was based upon a geometry of Euclidean spaces defining all as a representation of coordinates, lines and points. The idea of the physical working of the brain was under development, being defined in terms of hydraulic pressures, nerve communications and muscle operation. The concept of any kind of purpose was abandoned; the concern was with *how* not *why*. Newton supported this view of the brain as an automata in his *Rules of Reasoning*.

300 years ago there was no technology available for researchers to be able to really understand the workings of the brain. It has only been fairly recently that we have been able to see and study to discover more.

Galvani, in 1791, started a considerable amount of speculation when he showed that electricity existed as a force within the body, in fact, inside the neurons. He wired up frogs legs and was able to control the motor nerves using electrical currents. These currents were stored in the body in much the same way that a battery works. This gave rise to concepts such as Frankenstein, man creating man by the injection of vast amounts of electricity. In fact this idea still perseveres today – a mindless automata, following strict robot control, is transformed into a thinking, feeling being after receiving a huge amount of current – *'Number 5 is Alive!'*. However, Galvini did not have the technology to measure the currents involved in the body; they were too small. His experiments were later verified by Du Bois-Reymond in 1850, who found that neurons emitted spikes or pulses of electricity, found to be travelling at about 90mph. Purkinje in 1838 found that nerves consisted of two parts, fibres and a nucleus, and described a certain group so accurately that they were later named after him. He saw that plants and animals were also made up of cells, but the technology of the time did not allow him to realise that the neurons were separate. This was discovered by Golgi in 1870 when, using a stain, he identified the axons and dendrites (fibres). The continuous network of billions of neurons which must make up the central nervous system presented a deciphering problem of such enormous complexity that Golgi deduced there were simply too many neurons to make any sense of the riddle. It was established that the neurons in the brain sent information to the motor nerves, and information from the sensory nerves was sent to the brain for analysis.

In the early 1900s Adrian, Gasser and Erlanger, found that the electric pulses within the neurons caused chemicals to be released, the function of which was to send a message to other neurons using the connections between them, and that it took one thousandth of a second for the neuron to recharge after this firing had taken place.

Since those initial discoveries, researchers in neuroscience have discovered much about the physical functions of the brain.

However, as Arbib (1989) says: *"There are no universal statements about the nervous system except for the universal statement that there are no universal statements...."*

Working Together

> *"They weave an ever-changing pattern, never an abiding pattern, the workings of the enchanted loom". – Sherrington, 1906.*

We now know that the human body has between 10 to 100 billion special cells called neurons, each connected to approximately 10 thousand other neurons via fine fibres, to produce a highly complex network. This network is referred to as the central nervous system, the control point being the brain, which is the most complex organ we possess. Most of the neurons in the body actually reside in the brain. Neurons are specialised cells because of the connections that enable them to communicate with other neurons.

Envisaging a network of 100 billion neurons within our bodies is difficult but the individual units are tiny cells, often less than 100 microns in width, a micron being 1 millionth of a metre.

As Arbib (1989) points out, there is: *"No such thing as a typical neuron"* although many thousands of distinct types have been identified. We need to look at what could be considered as the general properties shared by all neurons, a picture which is modified for particular case studies. A neuron which shows these general features is shown in Figure 3.1.

All neurons have common features. From the cell body, the *nucleus* or *soma,* there is one main connector, called the *axon,* which acts as an output channel, passing information from the neuron onto others. The axon is connected to the host neuron at what is called the *axon hillock* and connects to the receiving neuron at points called *endbulbs* or *boutons.* A single axon branches into many parts, this whole area being referred to as the *axonal arborization.* An axon may have endbulbs situated along its length as well as at its end points.

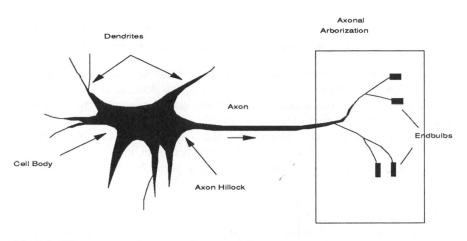

Fig.2.1: The common features of a general neuron.

The information can actually pass either way along an axon but in most cases it is from the axon to the neuron on which it impinges. The axon can also be very long relatively speaking. For example, the neuron which has control of the big toe is in the spinal chord and its axon runs the whole length of the leg. Conversely, in the head, the axons are very small.

The *dendrites,* which are the branches leading to the neuron, not including the axon, act as input channels, gathering information from the endbulbs of other axons and sending it to the neuron. A single neuron may have thousands of these dendrites which are connected to other neurons at what are referred to as synapse points, a microscopic gap between the endbulb and the dendrite.

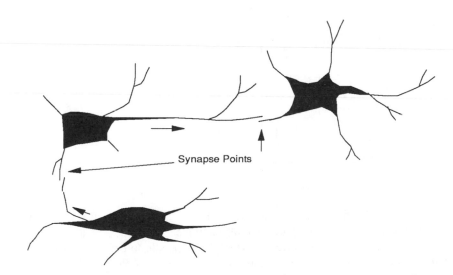

Fig.2.2: Neurons communicate via the synapses.

The membrane on the endbulb is called the *presynaptic membrane*, the membrane of the cell on which synapse acts is called the *postsynaptic membrane*.

The neurons communicate using a combination of electrical and chemical signals. If a cell is activated, a nerve impulse or *action potential* travels down the cell's axon. This signal is passed onto other neurons at the synapse points generally by the use of chemicals in the following way. The nerve impulse reaches the endbulb and causes neurotransmitters to be released through the presynaptic membrane which diffuse across the synaptic gap, to be picked up by the receptors of the target cell through the postsynaptic membrane. The nerve cell membrane is permiable to selected ions, so when in a state of rest there is an electrical potential difference across the membrane. The neurotransmitters cause a change in that the receiving cell becomes more permeable, the result being a change of potential mainly from the influx of sodium and potassium ions. If there is a large enough influx as a result of input from all the synapses, a nerve impulse will be initiated in the receiving cell and so the process continues. This *firing* is a charge which lasts less than one thousandth of a second, being quickly restored by an outflow of potassium ions.

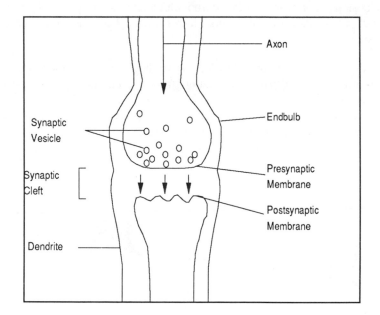

Fig.2.3: A 'typical' synapse point.

Much use has been made of the way that chemicals are used by neurons. Tranquilisers act by modifying the natural chemicals in the gap, and drugs such as LSD cause the chemical to be effected which leads people to perceive ordinary events in a very strange way, for example sounds can be seen as colours. The neurons go a bit berserk and get very confused.

The result of one neuron on another will be either excitatory – a sort of positive reinforcement, or inhibitory – having a dampening effect on the receiving cell. It should be noted that one cannot assume that all the synapses for a neuron will be either all excitatory or all inhibitory as the action depends not only on the transmitter released but also on the receptor structures in the postsynaptic membrane. It has been found recently that some neurons release secondary transmitters that modulate on an extended time scale. Trying to take all this into account makes models very complicated and in general the assumption is made that the effect a neuron has is either completely excitatory or inhibitory and that it fires on some limited time scale.

At an axon hillock a neuron receives input from many other neurons. The receiving neuron then adds all the inputs received at its synapses, and compares this total against some threshold value. If the input is greater than the threshold value and if the axon has recharged itself after the last impulse, the neuron will respond by firing and sending input to other neurons. In this way a pattern of activity is created across the neurons.

Thoughts, stimuli and emotions cause different patterns and reach different neurons. When you consider the billions of neurons and connections, the number of possible patterns that can be created gives some idea of the potential of the brain's power.

The neurons are also all constantly receiving and sending impulses, creating a network of activity much like Sherrington's enchanted loom. Researchers believe that the neurons perform very simple calculations and we know they operate very slowly compared with modern day electronic computers.

As there are so many connections for each cell the action of a single neuron can be widespread and have a very significant effect, perhaps being either very exciting or very frightening. As T.H.Bullock (1985) observed: *"neurons are people"*.

Parallelism

Traditional computer systems were built on the von Neumann, principle which thought of the human brain as being sequential in character – ideas being taken up, replaced, rejected and so on. Perhaps the assumption that this is a discrete process, as though it happened in one long continuous chain, is a misguided one. Given the relatively slow processing speeds of the brain, the problem needed to be approached from an alternative viewpoint. Feldman and Ballard (1982) came to the conclusion that the biological hardware that humans possess, is far too slow for processes to be carried out sequentially as the conventional computer would. The brain would simply be unable to coordinate vision, speech, thought etc. What they suggested is that the procedure is more like a tremendous fan-out effect, with perhaps many thousands of events occurring simultaneously, and fanning in again to provide a unique outcome.

Imagine our army marching to its destination in a single line. Eventually each member reaches the destination but the whole would have to move very quickly to match the army which moved forward together, shoulder to shoulder, in one line spread out across the countryside. A simplistic analogy but the principle is the same. Either vast numbers of very fast steps, or not so many slower steps, but all working at the same time. This is the answer to the enormous power the brain possesses.

Research is showing beyond doubt that it is this ability of the neurons, to function at the same time which is the secret behind the brain's ability to solve complex problems of perception and language in about half a second. This is the principle behind its vast processing potential. A few thousand processing steps per second being carried out simultaneously by thousands of neurons. A parallel processing machine. Compare this to the serial model, which carries out many millions of steps per second, but one after the other and along a single route, and the difference becomes apparent, lending an insight into the enormity of the processing potential under consideration. Now add to this the potential that each member of our army can communicate in some way with thousands of other members of the army. We have not only a very powerful body, but a coordinated one as well.

This method of doing many things at once, referred to as Parallelism, causes a great deal of simultaneous activity to occur within the brain in response to a given problem. This activity is not randomly motivated, but coordinated and coherent, a rational sequence of processes taking place which ultimately converges on a solution which satisfies as many of the problem's requirements as possible. This approach is now widely supported and work is being carried out by computer scientists, using Parallel Distributed Processing or connectionism techniques, by neuroscientists using neural computing, and also psychologists using computational neuroscience, in an effort to provide solutions to the problem of developing a computer system that mimics the brain.

Reductionism

At a cellular and molecular level we now know a great deal about the way that neurons function and can explain the brain in physical terms as cells, chemicals and pulses. However, the relationship between neuron behaviour and the perceptions that are received is a more difficult problem that involves the coordinated activity between many parts of the brain. Concepts such as reasoning and language are even further removed and far more complex. Researchers had hoped that the study of neurophysiology would explain the true nature of consciousness and over the last century the brain has been taken apart bit by bit.

This reductionist strategy has been in use since about 300BC, when Euclid defined the truth about lines, angles, points etc. by logic, in terms of a number of basic elements or axioms. This was thought to encompass all truths about everything, causal connections between objects in the world could be replaced by logical implications in a formal system. Descartes, argued around 1600AD that the only truth that one could really be sure of was the truth of personal perception: *"I think therefore I am"*. So now all reality could be expressed in terms of the *I* and formal definitions. But although the reductionist approach has identified about 60 types of neurotransmitter, mapped the wiring of major nerve pathways, and recorded the impulses of individual neurons, no evidence of consciousness has yet been found. As R. Colin Wilson (1988) points out: *"Geometry pictures the world as points and lines and planes. But these are empty structures when compared to red balls, laser beams and asphalt parking lots"*.

Hebb (1949) determined that more understanding of the physical workings of neurons was not the answer to how the brain functions. If we take a car to pieces we can identify each part – brake pads, pistons, valves and tappets, and we know the function of each. But to understand how the whole functions we have to reassemble it into its constituent parts. In this way also, thought and feelings are not to be found by looking at the cells of the brain. Maybe we should look at the different modules of the brain.

Avenues of research into these problems have been, and still are, numerous and diverse. They encompass the study of the brain at a base organic level, neuroscience and neuropsychology – incorporating the study of cognitive defects arising from brain damage; cognitive science – the study of thought and learning processes; the development of computer hardware that matches the structure of the brain; the development of artificial intelligence systems, machines with human powers of thought and reasoning; the development of mathematical algorithms to explain the thought processes of the brain. An important area of research is that carried out by mathematicians, computer scientists and electrical engineers, those involved in the hardware side of brain study. It is through attempting to emulate the brain using models which involve all of those above that we are making some headway into understanding.

The brain is a physical entity, that is without doubt. With some degree of confidence we can now describe it at its base level in terms of a collection of cells, fibres, chemicals and electrical pulses. The sheer number of neurons involved in the physical makeup of the brain is a stumbling block as far as building a reasonable representation given current technology, but that is not the only problem. We are beginning to understand how the neurons communicate, and the structures involved, but we do not know what they communicate. In terms of chemicals and pulses – yes. In terms of how those represent memories, emotions, language, sight and smell – no.

The need is to find how knowledge and thought are utilised and captured. It is one thing to know what functions different parts of the brain have, another to know how they are carried out. Each area of discipline provides answers to different questions.

Coordination between the fields has been achieved to some extent in recent years and has led to a considerable amount of work being directed towards the development of new computer architectures based on the concept of a massively parallel, highly adaptable system. Conventional systems have been designed based on different principles, the von Neuman principle of serial processing being the original concept of how the brain functioned. Both approaches have their limitations, but the progress made has shown that if a computer system is to be developed as a model of the human brain, a different set of requirements than those originally anticipated, need to be met. Ideally, we need to know how the brain functions at a base neurological level; how the neurons work as it were. Then we need to know how the brain functions at a cognitive level, how it processess ideas, experiences, language and so forth. Then all this information needs to be applied to a highly advanced computer architecture.

Research is carried out at a neuronal level but it is very difficult to separate the functions of the different types of neurons. One example, which hopes to lead on to the development of a neural chip, involves the study of the slug.

The Study of a Slug's Neurons

AT&T Bell Labs has biophysicists and electronic engineers working together, carrying out pioneer work on neural chip developments the aim of which is to develop a system modelled on the nervous system of Limax, the slug. Limax has an easily studied nervous system with large nerves and not too many neurons, only about 20,000. A *"nicely complicated system"*, simple enough for it to be studied and catalogued, yet exhibiting behaviour complex enough to be interesting.

Having catalogued all the neurons in Limax, a circuit has been developed which models taste buds connected to an auto-associative memory similar to Hopfield's model in Chapter 4. In this model there are 4 neurons representing the taste buds and the system works by settling into stable states which represent a solution to the taste problem. The taste pattern is identified as being either nice or nasty and stimulates an eat or flee response.

So we have a slug solution where the same response can be achieved using different taste patterns.

The study of the nerves was carried out by transplanting the actual slug nerves into a bed of liquid nutrient and watching the connections grow and form, not to build a real slug, but just for study. The individual nerves turned out to be a lot more complex than has been imagined. In fact our very simple neuron is now likened to having the capabilities of a hand-held calculator, some of them needing to be able to carry out summing and comparisons of inputs and to *turn down the volume* between a pair of neurons if it was above a certain threshold.

3

Memory and Learning

Some major differences between traditional computer systems, which attempt to emulate some form of intelligence, and the brain itself, have been identified. We have looked at the configuration, the use of parallelism within the brain and that the brain learns from past experiences.

The secret to how the brain carries out these processes must be hidden in the neurons, in the way that they communicate and how they are connected.

How is data stored?

How does the brain store information? Data needs to be retained in order that learning can be said to have taken place, and so that we can learn from experience using the stored information in the form of what we call memories.

"Memories, light the corners of my mind"

Gladys Knight (or was it Barbra Streisand?) was right when she sang these words because it is memories that enable us to literally, shed light on our current experiences. In every experience, we have a multitude of memories to draw on to add texture, colour and understanding.

In the 17th century, Descartes described the brain as being a holder of memories, each of which left a trace. These traces were later renamed *engrams* and the search continued for where in the brain these were stored.

In 1952, Walter Penfield, a brain surgeon, found that he could stimulate past memories in patients by touching electrodes to certain parts of the brain. Furthermore, the same memory could be stimulated again and again by repeatedly touching the same place. Many thought that the engrams had been found.

Lashley (1951) devoted about 30 years of his life to studying and searching for engrams and he eventually said that they did not exist, that memory must be spread throughout the brain rather than being individually located. This idea of *Distributed Representation* within the brain was considered by many to be far too radical and vague, but Lashley made the comment that was to be an insight into how the brain stores data - *"no special cells are reserved for special memories"*. As neurons die on a daily basis, and we do not lose important memories in one fell swoop, this can be seen intuitively to be true. However, although this idea of distributed representation seems to be appropriate, we have still not answered the question about where and how our memories are stored.

In conventional methods of data representation, a pattern is stored in memory and copied when retrieved. This method is used in all desktop PC systems and general commercial computer systems. There is no other way, currently, that data can be retained. The storage medium may be a hard disk internal to the machine, a memory chip, or it may be a floppy disk, a magnetic tape or cartridge tape. The memory of the computer is some medium which stores, in separate locations, each piece of data that may be needed. The ways in which the data is retrieved from the storage medium are numerous, some more efficient than others, but when the computer system needs the data, the point is that it must retrieve it from somewhere. A neural network model, like the brain, does not store the patterns used in the model in the way described above for conventional computers. It would seem that our brains have no memory storage space which we could liken to the memory chip of our desktop PC. But if the memories are not stored in the neurons, where are they stored? This is a puzzle because the brain only seems to be made up of lots of communicating neurons. Have we missed something?

So what happens when we think of something? How do our memories seem to come into play?

The neurons communicate through the synapse points and the strength of the connection, i.e. the amount by which one neuron affects another, varies between neurons and with time. One neuron can cause others to be positively or negatively reinforced depending upon the relationship that exists between them. For a long time it has been thought that this effect may be the key to learning within the brain. To understand why this should be so, we need to think about why these relationships should exist between the neurons at all.

Imagine that each individual neuron or group of neurons is taken to represent some concept, and these are linked to others to which they are related. Some concepts, through experience and learning, will be more strongly related than others, for example, *fish and chips, eggs and bacon, black and white*. We've all played games where you have to say the first word that springs to mind, an association of pairs. The strongest association is the one which dominates. That does not mean that there are no other associations with the word *fish* other than *chips,* if you are a keen fisherman your experience may lead you to say *net* as the strongest association. The point is that associations do exist between the neurons, that the stimulation of one will spark off those to which it is connected, and that the strengths of the connections vary. The reverse is also true, in that some concepts will positively prevent others from being stimulated.

So memory can be thought of as a pattern of activity across the neurons in the brain. Whenever we think of something, this causes a great deal of neural activity, neurons being stimulated and having an excitatory or inhibitory effect on others to which they are connected. A ripple effect which causes other associations to be stimulated.

Whether or not a neuron is stimulated into action will also depend on how much input it receives from other neurons. If it is a great deal then obviously there is a strong relationship in which the neuron is a significant element. Models often refer to the amount of input that a neuron has to receive before it is active as the *threshold* value.

Problems to think about

This idea of neurons or groups of neurons representing related concepts and stimulating each other is only the thin end of the wedge as far as model design is concerned because our memories and experiences are such complex functions.

Even the remembering of a single word carries with it many associations. The word *horse* for example. Let us first consider the spelling which we will store somehow in memory. That in itself is not a simple process, there being many studies on the subject of speech and linguistics, some of which are discussed in more detail further on in the text. A word may be stored in memory as an assembly of letters - the audial stimulation of the word, initiating the correct (hopefully!) pattern of letters. A single letter may be represented by a single neuron, the *horse* pattern then being retrieved from memory by the existence of the strengths between the neurons. The h neuron will be activated, which will then in turn activate the o neuron, this rippling of activation will continue through the neurons representing the remaining letters r, s and e until the whole word is retrieved. Alternatively, a single neuron may represent the complete word *horse*, or other subsets may exist. Of course, this is how the representation may take place in a model. We are as yet ignorant of how the brain itself deals with representations. Although we can say that it is the repeated stimulation of an association through the senses which enables the idea to be stored in memory, different models make different assumptions concerning the actual representation of that association.

The spelling of a word is not the only association that our memories retain - there is also the meaning of the word to consider, and in turn the contextual implications. Imagine hearing the following sentences:

I am not well and I am feeling a little hoarse.

I am a vet and I am feeling a little horse.

Within context, one can sort out without too much difficulty, which spelling of the word to use, *hoarse* or *horse*. Out of context, there are no indications. A linguistics model which attempts to recreate the functions of the brain must take into account the associations that a word has, in terms of meaning. Not only does the brain store the mechanical spelling of a word, it stores a wealth of experiences and associations which are triggered when that data is needed, as in the sentences above. We can demonstrate the power of this kind of associative memory to ourselves by simply sitting and recalling an abstract word, for example, the word *holiday*. Memories, hopes, plans for the future, you can almost feel the activity.

Learning rules in a model

The information which is stored, is in the connections between the integral parts of the pattern, that is, the connections between the units. The pattern can then be recreated at any point when required. The power of using this method is that learning may be achieved in a model by finely tuning the connection strengths between the units. This must done in such a way that existing patterns are not lost or interfered with - they can still be recreated, and new patterns can be incorporated into the design.

The approach which enables learning to take place is to formulate a set of rules - the relations that the model has to remember if you like - in the form of input and associated output patterns. These pattern pairs are then applied to the model which will allow it to associate the input with the output and to extract the rule from the information which can then be used in future examples. (Winston 1975, Chomsky, ACT model of J. R. Anderson 1983) The learning process starts with powerful generalisations and is then expanded by including further sets of rules.

This process can be thought of in terms of a child learning verb construction. A model has in fact been set up by Rumelhart and McClelland (1986a) to demonstrate the learning of past tenses of verbs. When tested it behaved in exactly the same way as a child would when learning, making the same mistakes.

When a child begins to learn the past tenses of verbs, the general form is learnt first, for example, chop and chopped, wash and washed. This would be the first strongly generalised rule to be applied to the model.

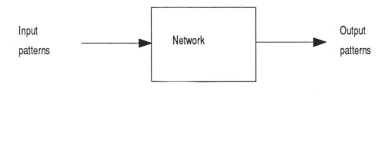

Fig.3.1: The network is given the general rule initially and will apply that rule to all input.

At this stage, as shown in Fig. 3.1, the model would produce the general form for all past tenses, therefore it would produce swing and swinged, come and comed etc. The next stage is to then apply some other rules to the model which take into account the non-general forms, for example, come and came, sing and sang. The model would then adjust the connection strengths to incorporate these forms as shown in the diagram in Figure 3.2.

Strangely enough, the mistake which the model then made, although the form had been presented to it, was typical of children. For example for the verb come, it produced the past tense camed. Because of the parallel with the way in which children learn, this should be taken as an extremely encouraging result. It may be illogical in terms of the accuracy we traditionally expect from a computer, it may be considered to be an inaccurate model definition in terms of tuning the connection strengths so as not to interfere with existing patterns. However, the important thing is that the model mimics what actually does occur. The model allows the units to behave as though the rules are known, even though no explicit rules actually exist and no powerful computations are carried out. The process is achieved by simple connection strengths. This type of model is discussed further in Chapter 19, it is only used here to illustrate how the connections are established.

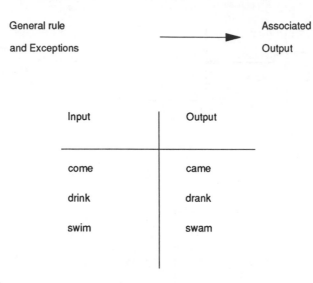

Fig.3.2.The second stage incorpereates non-general forms into the model..

A simple example of such models of learning is that of a *pattern associator* or *autoassociative* model. This model is defined so that the pattern of activity across one set of units will activate an identical pattern across an associated or corresponding set of units. Intervening units do not represent one pattern or the other entirely. An example cited of this is the link bewteen aroma and vision (Rumelhart and McClelland 1986).

The connection strengths for the pattern associator are not put in manually as the system is self teaching through experience. They are adjusted through the repeated processing of pattern pairs. This means that the pattern which represents the vision of a plate of curry is applied as the input (or output) for the vision units, together with the pattern for the aroma which is simultaneously applied as the associated pattern. In this way the model builds up associations between pairs. Of course, the more pattern pairs applied to the system, the more *knowledge* the system will have for assessing new patterns presented to it. It also has to be determined what the *patterns* for a plate of curry would look like!

This is one of the advantages of the pattern associator, i.e. that slight variations of the same pattern may be presented and the model will eventually learn to generalise and ignore the *noise* of the slight discrepency. For example, there are many different types of curry, and many subtle variations in smell, which would, in terms of the model, produce slight variations in pattern. However, we always know that we are smelling a curry because we are able to generalise. The model would be capable of extracting the central tendency and apply that information to produce the result. This is possible because patterns which do not have this type of similarity do not interact in this manner.

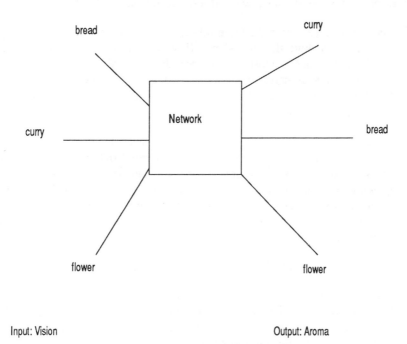

Fig.3.3: *The various visual inputs to the network will be associated by the network with the various aroma outputs.*

How strong are the connections?

The connections between the neurons that transmit the signals from one neuron to the next, have an associated *weight* adjusted according to experience and which modifies the strength of the signal actually sent. This weight enables a bias to be built into the system so that associations, positive or negative, can be built up between the neurons. The strength of the connections between the neurons can be thought of as an indication of the associations that exist between concepts. If a neuron represents a concept (and that is also an area of debate and research) then strongly related concepts will also be strongly connected. This is apparent in people - for example in word association games where we say the word most strongly stimulated by the word we hear. Of course this is based on experience. Quite often a player will choose a really quite bizarre word: it cannot be wrong, just based on personal experience. Exactly how this weighting should be carried out is a central area of research, as is training the network to build up the initial associations. This kind of *Associative Memory* allows the presentation of one piece of data to result in the retrieval of a large amount of information to which it may be related in some way.

The rules for the adjustments which the model makes to the connection strengths play an important role in the usefulness of such a model. One of the first set of rules were those put forward by Hebb which we will look at in Chapter 4.

Learning is taking place within the brain all the time with the meeting of new people, reading a book or watching the television. All these memories, it is said, are retained somewhere. Indeed, under hypnosis, people are able to recall the most obscure details of events which they were hardly aware of observing. That amounts to a great deal of information being stored somewhere in the brain and in such a way that new memories do not wipe out existing ones.

This is an important thing to remember; that as learning is taking place by the synapses adjusting strengths, the process must be carried out in such a way that the new memory or pattern is incorporated into the network of association without interfering with, in a destructive sense, any existing patterns. Existing patterns are modified and new experiences included, and the ability to recreate previous memories is preserved. This idea has many complexities but can be expressed in a very simple way using basic models.

Neural network models basically utilise two sorts of learning:

Associative Learning: The model learns to produce a pattern of activation across one set of units whenever a particular pattern of activation is present across another set. This method is used when it is necessary to store patterns for future retrieval. The relationships between the subpatterns can be stored.

This method is used with what is referred to as a Pattern Associator or Auto-Associator model. The Pattern Associator is used when it is necessary to create an association between patterns over subsets so that connections are established such that when the pattern appears over the first subset, this will stimulate the production of the pattern over the second.

Regularity Discovery: The model learns to respond to the input of patterns, already known and unknown. This is used for feature discovery.

Data Retrieval

Learning can be thought of as an accumulation of memories, an experience being stored as a pattern of activity across a set of neurons which can be recreated when required. A conventional computer memory works in such a way that a piece of data is stored in a specific memory location. That data may then be retrieved by *looking* in the appropriate location. The brain does not function in this manner, no one location being used to store one specific piece of data. The data is stored as a pattern across many neurons.

Of course, storing the data is one thing but it is of no use having a wonderfully efficient memory process if the data cannot be accessed when required. This is information- or data-retrieval. The human brain is extremely powerful, potentially, at information retrieval, being capable of retrieving a piece of information or a memory or stored experience if you like, from, it would appear, the most obscure of clues.

Some people are better at remembering things than others, although it has been said that this is all due to practice. Apparently, the method used by performing memory artistes, when remembering people's names for example, is to build a picture in the mind which is then triggered on seeing that person again.

Retrieving information is content addressability, which for a computer system can be either sequential or indexed. Sequential is similar to looking for a name in a jumbled up telephone directory; every entry would have to be scanned until the correct one was found. Indexed is a similar process except that the telephone book would be in the correct order.

The Artifical Intelligence method of pattern recognition attempts to emulate high-level geometric or liguistic concepts. However, neural networks do not do this. Instead they describe the low-level electrical behaviour of the nerve networks themselves and the high-level tendencies then seem to emerge automatically once a massive enough number of low-level connections have been made. From studies of the brain, it appears that a continuous perception is broken into meaningful parts and then organised into pictures/sounds/tastes/smells/textures groupings. The cells compete for dominance, the winner sending a message to the next level in the cognitive process. The greatest competition occurs at the lower levels - as higher levels are achieved the neurons start to cooperate and get organised.

The problem with a traditional computer memory is that if the clue is wrong there is a good chance that the wrong, or no, information will be retrieved. The system is not immune to error. A neural network model is much more tolerant to errors.

If the model has been trained as we discussed before, and has learnt a number of associations between patterns, then to retrieve that information the model would be presented with a pattern. When this occurs the network will select particular properties, all units with those properties being activated and eventually the most dominant suppressing the others. The dominant units of other properties will also be activated and may not give information which is actually correct. But in general, it can be said that the more similar things are in aspects which are known, the more likely they will be similar in aspects which are unknown.

For example, if an association was present to show that tigers hunt and kill animals for food, the activation of lion would in turn activate other big cat features which would lead to the assumption that they also hunt and kill animals for food. Conversely, as tigers like to swim and wallow in water, one may also assume that lions like to do the same, which would not be correct. This would be updated with experience and ultimately be activated by tigers alone.

If no particular pattern dominates - there may be many units activated nearly cancelling each other out - the model has been found to then retrieve those features which are common to all activated units. For example, animals with stripes may activate tigers and zebras. Perhaps the only common ground is that they live in Africa.

The system will therefore work without the necessity of any special error recovery scheme. This is referred to as *graceful degradation*.

This simplified view of a neural network model, exhibits natural extensions of retrieval which would require very complex computations for more conventional computer systems to achieve.

Defining Memory Types

Memories can be classified in terms of their duration, the shortest being called iconic memories. These are extremely short memories, a fraction of a second - the time necessary to write down a telephone number which you have just been told or looked up. To remember the number long enough to be able to dial it, the short-term memory (STM) is used, which lasts for about 15 seconds. This memory can be extended by reinforcment. To remember the number longer we would usually repeat it a few times. Saying it aloud often seems to be very effective, and eventually the number could be fixed into long-term memory (LTM) when it is associated with something familiar.

Arbib (1989) defines the two very well. He says that STM contains items that may be lost if you are distracted and LTM contains items retained from some earlier period.

Arbib talks of STM and LTM in terms of schemas, a concept we will look at in Chapter 18, but which can be described briefly as a model of the environment. This can be a current model which incorporates the present scene, or alternatively, a view of some past experience. The important thing is that STM can be seen as an adaptable schema linked to a variety of other schemas in LTM which are memories of past events or impressions. In this way we can use our knowledge in LTM to make judgements and valuations of our environment.

STM need not, however, be fleeting images which pass through and are forgotton. Not only can an STM become an LTM if reinforced sufficiently but such a redefined STM may persist in influencing a person's life and actions long after having been incorporated into LTM: an unfulfilled plan or ambition; an unpleasant experience; or something which may even result in a task for the psychoanalyst.

LTM can be seen as corresponding to standard properties of the environment, STM is not, as Arbib puts it, *"a tape-recording"* of recent events, it is the relevance of the world around, relying heavily on input from LTM to fill in the details.

Having tried to outline some of the concepts behind learning and storing data in neural networks, the best way to see how this works is to look at a very basic model of a neural network which incorporates all these principles.

4

Neural Network Models

The biological computation of the brain is so effective it seems obvious that similar properties may be attained by building models based upon the same principles we looked at in previous chapters, namely:

❑ A large number of highly connected simple processing units

❑ Adaptable connections

❑ Parallel processing

Simple models have been built but researchers have a number of difficulties. One significant thing is that neurons are very complex creatures, despite the fact that they are always referred to as being simple, which they most certainly are in comparison with how we envisage a processor these days. However, there is the problem of separating the different processing roles carried out by the neurons. They carry out some functions simply to keep the cell alive, others appear to be vital for the processing cycle. When attempting to create a model of the brain based on the physical way in which neurons interact, and the connections that exist between them, researchers tend to start with a simple idea and then increase the complexity to compensate for any inadequacies.

The models developed to date really bear very little resemblance to any actual biological structure. Nevertheless, even a highly simplified model of a neuron, when networked to other such units, can most certainly offer a whole new meaning to machine computation and can also carry out significant computations which are able to shed new light on some of the brain's mysteries. The general principles of such systems can be discovered even if the details of the basic components are drastically over-simplified in terms of the processing that occurs within the individual units and what happens at the synapses.

One feature that both the biological system and the neural net model have in common is that they both consist of several interacting parts whose state evolves continuously with time. Because the state of the network depends on the effect that one unit has on another, it is not suprising that the behaviour depends critically on the connectivity pattern.

One of the major differences between the brain and a traditional computer system is that the fomer is not programmed. There is no fixed set of processing steps for any one given situation. Learning is nature's substitute for programming. Not much is known about how learning is carried out but the use of the memory must be involved. In trying to emulate the brain, much work has been carried out towards developing systems that are capable of learning from past experiences using the configuration that the brain suggests.

Models of neural networks have basic design features in common, research still being based on the original work carried out by McCulloch and Pitts which provides the framework for the general model. The network may be a model or a simulation, used for speech recognition, pattern recognition or perhaps to model the behaviour of a frog. There are many types of model, often having very different objectives because neural network research has its roots firmly set in many disciplines. The intention may be to study an animal's behaviour patterns, cognitive processes or the suitability of hardware architectures. It could be referred to as Mathematical Biophysics, Cybernetics, Connectionism, PDP, and Neurocomputing. The subject has learnt in the past from advances in fields such as Symbolic Logic, Automata Theory, Information Theory, and Holography.

Model or Simulation?

Research is in a bit of a *Catch 22* situation at the moment. We do not have the technology to build in a physical sense anything which is nearly as complicated as the brain. After all, 64,000 is a drop in the neuron ocean compared to 100 billion, so most of the research into how the brain handles data is carried out as simulations using digital computers. This may not seem to be a problem. After all, they have the processing power and although a realistic speed would not be evident, researchers could study events at given time intervals. The problem is that a simulation is predefined by definition. For example, if you were going to simulate the point at which a glider will stall, you first enter the equation *stall=given physical conditions*. Nothing new is actually discovered. However, if one was to make a model of a glider, put it into a wind tunnel and model the wind conditions, and the glider stalled at some other point then, given all the scales had been correctly determined, this could be taken as an event which occurred in reality. Researchers do not know how the brain deals with representations of ideas, so simulations, although very interesting, have to be based on what is believed may be true. They are not models and so can tell us very little about what is really happening. Having said that, a great deal of very useful research has been done using simulations. Research carried out in this manner cannot be discredited because of this. The assumptions may be correct.

Pitts and McCulloch, influenced by Turing's model of an ideal computing machine, discussed in Chapter 17, put forward the first formal analysis to describe the nervous activity of the brain, a network of formal neuron-like units. Before we look at their model, we will look at what we know about the functioning of neurons in the brain and try to get some of the terminology worked out. There will be some repetition here but this is necessary to relate the physical neurons to the concepts and terminology used in models.

Neurons

Neurons receive and send stimuli thus transmitting patterns of pulse–like activity through the network of the billions of neurons in the brain. When a neuron is active, output is produced in pulse form which travels along paths called axons, to the receivers, called dendrites via an interconnection called a synapse. (See Chapter 2 for details).

The neurons are continuously active, sending and receiving pulses via the synapses, the strength of the pulse being chemically controlled according to the current state of activity of both the sending and receiving neurons.

The actual output which is sent to one neuron from another depends on a weighting factor which determines how much of the available output affects the receiving neuron. If two neurons are only weakly connected, in an association sense, the potential output will be scaled down as it were. This proportion of the output received is adjusted by something called a *weight*.

McCulloch and Pitts developed a simple model to represent the variable synaptic connections, or weights, between the neurons and the activity of the neuron itself. Their adaptable network was based on the explanation of neuron synapse behaviour that the weights affecting the output are able to be changed, and that the activity level for a neuron, that is, whether or not it should fire, is found by summing the total inputs at all the synapses connected to that neuron. This task is carried out by the neuron itself. The model assumes that the output has a value of 1 if the neuron is firing and a value of 0 if it is not. This is a particularly useful definition in computing terms as it relates directly to a two state binary system and can be represented in a diagram by being either black (on) or white (off).

One major disadvantage of this model is that it can only perform functions which are *linearly separable,* a problem which has led to the infamous *parity* problem the network is unable to detect whether the input has an even or odd number of 1s. This is discussed in more detail in Chapter 5.

Nevertheless, the concepts behind the model are easy to grasp and have led to some interesting variations on the general theme. It should be remembered that this is indeed a very simplified model of what was believed to occur between the neurons in the brain, a process which even now we do not fully understand. Therefore this cannot be considered to be a true representation of a real neural network. However, it was a good step in what appears to be the right direction.

Learning in a Model

McCulloch and Pitts only looked at models in which the weights were fixed, a condition which did not allow learning to take place. To utilise a network properly and efficiently, some method needs to be developed which will enable the weights to be adjusted in order to represent some input and required output. There is a variety of problems with this procedure because firstly, existing set-ups must not be disrupted when new ones are presented to the system, a process called *convergence*. Secondly, it is not known precisely how the neurons in the brain receive the information which enables them to adjust weights, so any method of learning is unsubstantiated in real life; we can only judge by results. The actual process of altering the weights to retain or learn an input pattern is referred to as a *learning algorithm*.

Frank Rosenblatt in 1958 incorporated learning into the McCulloch Pitts model, calling his class of models the *Perceptron*. Rosenblatt studied a great number of models which have retained their importance even now. Another major influence was Donald Hebb who, in 1949, expressed an idea which, although it can be traced back to Pavlov and before, had not been previously formulated in such an inspiring manner. This became known as *Hebbian Learning* and enabled the development of learning rules which could be used with the networks described above. His actual words were as follows:

> *"When an axon of a cell A is near enough to excite a cell B and repeatedly or persistently takes place in firing it, some growth process or metabolic change occurs in one or both cells such that A's efficiency, as one of the cells firing B, is increased"*. (Hebb 1949)

Hebb was interested in the idea of a modifiable or dynamic structure and realised the importance of the synapse connections between the neurons. A neuron will not always receive input from all the other neurons to which it is connected. This will only occur if there is some relationship between the pairs at the time, which will depend very much on the circumstances. He developed the above rule of synaptic adaptability and suggested the concept of the existence of assemblies of cells, and the idea of activated units rippling through a connection network of such cells. In other words, that groups of neurons could be activated in a variety of patterns, each of which represented a different memory or experience. It is a matter of considering initially how the neurons represent an idea.

Local or Distributed Models

Some models, called local models, attempt to assign *concepts* to individual units, one unit being defined as representing one pattern. In the case of language processing this may be a word, a letter or maybe a sound. Other models, called distributed models, relate a concept to a pattern of activity over a number of units, the knowledge of a pattern being stored in the connections between the units which are involved in the pattern representation. Whichever model is used, the relationships and associations between the units can then be built up by presenting the units with a given input and required output. The units are then allowed to adjust their connections accordingly. This idea of associated learning is discussed by Hinton and Anderson (1981).

In general, distributed models provide a different account of learning and aquisition than that offered by traditional methods and interestingly enough, even these most simplistic models give quite an insight into the learning process. The simple local learning mechanisms allow generalisations to be made through experience. The performance of such models emerges from the interactions of simple interconnected units, following linguistic rules using a simple, local, connection strength adaption process.

As we saw, neurons can be defined as being either excitatory, or inhibitory. In nature this is determined by the chemicals released by the neuron. An excitatory neuron will switch on and send pulses when the input received is above a certain threshold. An inhibitory neuron will switch on when the input received is below a certain threshold. In models, the excitatory neurons are considered to have a positive effect on other neurons, causing the effect of an input to be increased as it were and to stimulate the activity of the receiving neuron. An inhibitory neuron, on the other hand, can be thought of as having a dampening effect on other neurons, decreasing their state of activity. However, an inhibitory neuron, will have a strengthening effect if the receiving neuron is also inhibitory, increasing and reinforcing the inhibition effect.

Hopfield in 1982 defined the association very well in terms of the following four simple rules:

❑ If an active neuron meets a neuron which is also active there is a strength increase.

❑ If an active neuron meets a neuron which is inactive there is no strength increase.

❑ If an inactive neuron meets a neuron which is active there is no strength increase.

❑ If an inactive neuron meets a neuron which is also inactive there is a strength increase.

This simply means that if a neuron in an excited state, whether excitatory or inhibitory, communicates with a neuron in the same state, the strength of the connection between them is increased. If, for example, you noticed that your cat left the room when you played loud music you may think this was a coincidence. However, if this happened repeatedly the experience would be continuously reinforced until it became an accepted part of your cat's behaviour.

Hebb's rule applied to a model which had a set of input units connected to a set of output units, there being no intermediate or *'hidden'* units as shown in Fig.4.1. below.

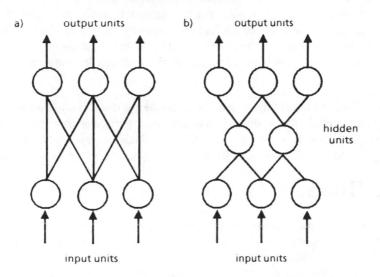

Fig.4.1: The network in a) has a layer of input units connected directly to a layer of output units. The network in b) has a layer of hidden units between the input and output layers.

For the model to produce the correct result for a given input, there were severe limitations on the relations which could or could not exist between the input values (Kohonen 1977). However, if these restrictions were followed the memory model would exhibit perfect recall even if each synapse strength was involved in storing many different patterns.

Developments in computer hardware during these years, enabled computer simulations to become more extensive because of the increases in processing speeds which were available and many researchers began development of models based on Hebbian learning rules. In 1962 Rosenblatt attempted to design a neural network with general adaptive intelligence, and Widrow in 1960 had demonstrated a method of weather prediction using an analogue computer based on neural net principles. Researchers were inspired and work continued throughout the late 1950s and into the 1960s.

However, the potential of such systems remained limited and the enthusiasm for developing neural network applications went into a decline following the publication by Minskey and Papert in 1969 of *Perceptrons*. This formally analysed the very real limitations of such systems, and advocated a Symbol Processing approach which has since been central to Artificial Intelligence work. Minsky and Papert demonstrated that such a single-layer neural network would need a ridiculously large number of elements in order to solve any interesting problems, and they suggested that the inclusion of multiple layers would not increase the processing power by any reasonable degree because of the difficulty of training such a network. This caused many researchers to turn their attention towards AI work although in the field of neural network research the basic principles of the Hebbian learning rules have been maintained.

At this point we will pursue developments no further, but try to build up some idea of how the basic model can be defined and look at a particular example. In the next chapter we will look at some of the problems which are classically unable to be solved by the model and what steps have been taken to overcome these difficulties.

Basic Hopfield Model

Hopfield (1982) defined a model, based on the ideas of Pitts and McCulloch, which is one of the most straightforward of neural network methods and has in turn become the basis for many others. It enables images to be stored or remembered by the network during a learning process, the network then having the ability to retrieve the complete image when presented with an incomplete or corrupted image. It should not be thought of as the general model but as a specific example which is easy to follow and will serve to consolidate the definitions that we will look at for a general model.

The Hopfield model has been put to practical use in a number of ways. For example, A.Baker and C.Windsor have used this method for the classification of defects within steel test welds, using ultrasonic data wave forms. The model was required to classify approximately 80 defects from four categories. The learning procedure involved applying a typical, random selection of the defects to the model. When 50% of the data was used for training, and 50% used for testing, an accuracy of 100% was often achieved. In this model, the number of pixels, or characters used was 84, the number of defect classes stored was 4.

The Hopfield neural network remembers information in binary form - either a 0 or a 1 - which can then be represented as a black and white image. Consider the letters shown in the Fig 4.2 in a 5 by 5 square grid.

```
    X  X  X        X  X  X  X        X  X  X  X     X  X  X  X
 X           X     X           X     X              X           X
 X  X  X  X  X     X  X  X  X  X     X              X           X
 X           X     X           X     X              X           X
 X           X     X     X  X  X  X     X  X  X  X     X  X  X  X
```

Fig.4.2: Each letter is represented by a pattern of crosses on a 5x5 grid.

These can be represented in binary in Fig 4.3, where X is represented by 1, a space by a 0.

```
0  1  1  1  0     1  1  1  1  0     0  1  1  1  1     1  1  1  1  0
1  0  0  0  1     1  0  0  0  1     1  0  0  0  0     1  0  0  0  1
1  1  1  1  1     1  1  1  1  1     1  0  0  0  0     1  0  0  0  1
1  0  0  0  1     1  0  0  0  1     1  0  0  0  0     1  0  0  0  1
1  0  0  0  1     1  1  1  1  0     0  1  1  1  1     1  1  1  1  0
```

Fig.4.3: Each cross in Fig.4.2. has been replaced by a 1 and each space by a 0 to represent the letters.

The model can be thought of as a 5x5 grid, as in this example, with each square representing a neuron in the network. In this way each neuron will receive as input, a particular 0 or 1 from the input pattern. The model is defined with full connectivity, that is, each neuron-like unit, or element of the pattern which makes up the 5x5 grid, is connected to every other, except itself. Each neuron at a given time is either firing (1) or non-firing (0).

The interconnections between the neurons, the synapses, will have variable strengths and it is the strength of these synapses which actually stores the memory.

The representation of the rules for the Hopfield model are given at the end of this chapter, together with a simple program that can be run on any desktop PC to demonstrate the principles. It is not necessary to understand the mathematics behind the rules as it can be explained quite easily, and understood. However, if you do want to generate a simple learning model yoursef, on a PC, it is useful to understand the notation simply because the commands and keywords in Basic vary between machines.

One of the advantages of the Hopfield model is that it has a very simple learning procedure. The learning, as mentioned previously, is carried out by altering the strengths of the synapse connections between the neurons. A pattern is presented to the neurons in the network and each neuron then assumes the state of the pattern, in either an active, firing state, or non-active, non-firing state. The patterns shown in Fig 4.3. are simply strings of 0s and 1s, each represented by a particular neuron on the network. If the value of the neuron is 1 it is active; if the value is 0 it is inactive.

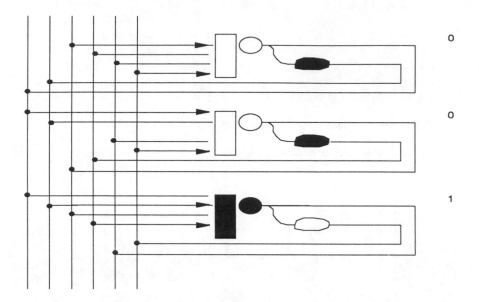

Fig.4.4: In this diagram there are three pairs of excitatory (circles) and inhibitory (ovals) neurons. If a neuron is shaded then it is in an active state, otherwise it is inactive. Each neuron is connected to every other but not to itself, so each will have four input lines. This example shows the pattern 001. Reinforcement occurs where either a non-firing neurons inputs to a non-firing neuron or a firing neuron inputs to a firing neuron. This reinforcement is shown as arrows in the diagram.

If you remember Hopfield's rules for adjusting the strengths between the neurons, and also remember that each neuron is connected to every other, the pattern will cause each neuron to receive input from 24 others. If a firing axon meets a firing axon then growth occurs, and this also happens when a non-firing axon meets another non-firing axon. Otherwise, there is no change. This has the potentially major practical drawback that the model will make no distinction between black on white images, and white on black. It considers the negative version to be the same. This has to be taken into account if the model is such that difficulties may arise.

Each pattern will cause each neuron to have a certain synapse strength pattern which are remembered. To remember multiple patterns, the patterns are applied successively and the resulting synapse strengths are totalled up.

It may be valuable at this point to show this process in a simple example which has just three neurons. In Fig 4.4. and Fig 4.5. the notation used is that as defined by McCulloch and Pitts (1943).

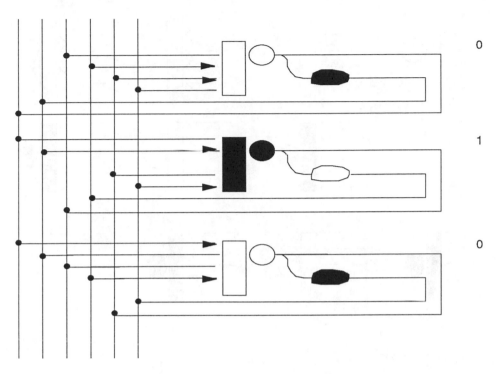

Fig.4.5: This diagram shows the lines of activity for pattern 010. The resulting reinforcements are shown as arrows.

The network in Fig.4.4. consists of three pairs of excitatory and inhibitory neurons, with the axons of each pair connected to every other neuron, but not to itself. The firing neuron is shown as black, the non-firing neuron as white with the lines of activity shown as unbroken lines. The pattern shown here is 001.

The arrows show which synapse strengths are reinforced. Remember that two firing neurons or two non-firing neurons are the combinations which lead to growth. So in Fig.4.5., the synapses are strengthened where a broken line axon is being received by a non-firing (white) neuron, or where an unbroken line axon is being received by a firing (black) neuron.The pattern 010 is shown in Fig.4.5.

To remember both these patterns, we would combine the synapse strengths so that the resulting patterns would be as shown in Fig. 4.6.

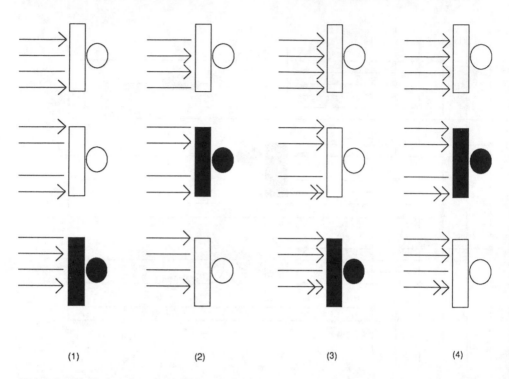

(1)   (2)   (3)   (4)

Fig.4.6: (1) shows the pattern 001, (2) shows the pattern 010. (3) shows the combined reinforcements for both patterns using 001, (4) shows the combination for pattern 010.

In Fig. 4.6., (1) shows the pattern 001, (2) shows the pattern 010. Diagram (3) is then the pattern 001 with the combined synapse strengths for both patterns. Similarly, (4) shows the combined synapse strengths for the pattern 010.

The patterns can be tested for stability by comparing the input for a neuron against a threshold value and checking to see that it does not change state. If the active inputs are greater than or equal to the threshold value then the neuron remains firing, otherwise it becomes non-firing. The threshold for a Hopfield model is defined to be one half of the number of patterns times the number of inputs to each neuron (the number of neurons less one). Here the threshold will be 1/2x3x(3-1)=3. The patterns in the above example are stable under the combination of synapse strengths. For example, the active input (unbroken line) for the third neuron in (3) will be equal to the threshold limit (three synapse arrows), so the neuron will remain active. The input for the second neuron in (3) is below the threshold limit so the neuron will remain inactive.

This is a simple example of the method utilised by the network for storing a number of patterns but it does illustrate the method behind the Hopfield model which can be summarised as follows.

Summary of Hopfield Model

Definition:

❑ A set of nodes such that each node is in one of two states, either on (active or firing), or off (inactive or non-firing). This enables the state of the complete architecture to be defined at any point in time by an ordered list of 0s and 1s.

❑ The potential at any node is taken to be the total of all the inputs received by that node at the current time.

❑ The new state of the node is taken to be on or firing, if the total input for the node is above some threshold value, off or non-firing, if it falls below.

❑ The pattern across the whole network can be updated in a number of ways. One method is to determine a time step and to then update every node, seemingly simultaneously for the current input. An alternative method would be to update the nodes sequentially, either randomly or in some predefined order, so that the new state of each node is then incorporated into the calculation for nodes which it in turn affects. The differing outcomes which these two methods will produce in terms of behaviour of the network will be very significant. The simplest method is to allow the solution to tend towards a stable state, almost like a ball rolling across a bumpy surface and coming to rest in a hollow. This analogy is discussed in depth in Chapter 9.

❑ The training of the network is achieved by a procedure which enables the weights of the network to be updated so that the image becomes a stable pattern within the network.

Definitions for a General Model

Having looked briefly at the Hopfield model, and shown some of the principles inherent in the design, the basic definitions of all models will be easier to understand and relate to. There are many different models of neural networks and it will be useful at this point to try and generalise and to define the principles which lie behind all models.

Such models are not based so much on what has been discovered about the biological functioning of the brain, which, even though much progress has been made, still leaves many questions unanswered, but rather on the method of utilising parallel processing power which has proved to be an excellent representation of human cognitive functioning. It should be said however, that neuroscience discoveries have supported much of the work being carried out.

We can define the basic objective of neural networks as the search for efficient learning procedures which may be applied to networks of many simple processing units, representing neurons, in order that complex internal representations of the environment may be constructed and recalled; the process of learning and relating experiences.

Processing Units

Within a model there will be some number, which we will call N, of processing units; N, because we do not know how many there are and we are trying to consider the rules for a general model. Exactly what the units represent will depend upon the definitions as set up for the individual model. For example, the units may represent some meaningful concept such as features, letters or words, or may be abstract elements over which patterns can be defined.

In general, in a distributed representation, the units tend to be small features over which the pattern as a whole exists at a meaningful level.

In a one-unit-one-concept model, the units tend to represent entire concepts or some kind of meaningful thing.

Which ever kind of model has been set up, it is the units within it which carry out the processing, no central controller being necessary. The units are essentially simple as are the processes which they carry out, being required only to receive input and produce output. The nature of the models require the units to carry out the tasks in parallel with all other units, that is, at any one time, potentially all the units could be receiving input and producing output.

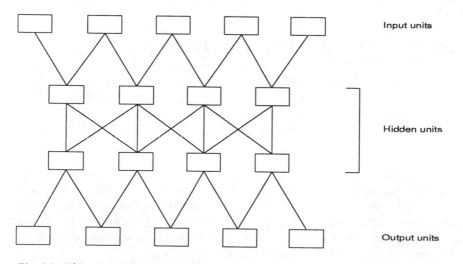

Fig.4.7: This diagram shows one possible configuration for a network with an input layer, hidden layer and an output layer.

The units may be split into three types: input units, which receive input from some external source; hidden units, within the system itself; output units, which send signals externally to the system.

State of Activation

The activation for a unit can be thought of as the amount by which the unit is affected by the input it receives. One could picture a unit vibrating in varying degrees depending on how excited it has become, and different units will be excited, or depressed for that matter, by different stimuli and by differing degrees. Actually defining this state of activation for each unit within a model, and assigning a value to it, is a tricky process because the precision of the model depends on the reaction of the individual units.

Some models use a set of discrete values, that is, one of a finite set of possible values. These are often taken to be 0, 1 or -1. On the other hand, a model may take any value between two limits. This is termed a continuous set of values, because for any two numbers there is always one that you can find that lies between them. Take for example, 1.2243 and 1.2244. A number between these would be 1.22435. In some cases, the model may have no upper or lower limit for the continuous values, but this presents problems, as values can grow to an unmanageable size very quickly.

Output

The output for a unit defines the strength of the connections between the units and will depend upon the activation of the unit at the time. You could think of this in terms of two related concepts, for example, umbrellas and rain. These are strongly connected in that if you see someone under an umbrella, you know it is raining. You can assume this safely, because you know that only in very odd circumstances would someone be sheltering under an umbrella for any other reason, unless they are a little strange. So through experience, these two concepts are strongly related. The umbrella concept could also be related to snow, if other factors support this.

So, if we have units in the model, one representing the umbrella concept, one the rain concept and one the snow, the course of activity would be as follows: An umbrella is present and so the umbrella unit becomes very strongly activated, because this in turn is strongly related to the rain unit; the rain unit will also be strongly activated; the snow unit is only weakly activated, because the connection is not so strong. It is interesting to note at this stage that if further evidence was produced, eg. snow flakes, sledges, a snowman etc., that the feedback of this information would supress the rain unit, and excite the snow unit very strongly. If this were the case the snow unit would eventually dominate and override the rain unit.

Connectivity Pattern

The units within a system need to be connected to other units and this pattern of connectivity is a very important factor with respect to the way in which the system responds.

Once the connectivity pattern is established the connections between the units are weighted. It is usual to have a positive weighting between units which are excitatory (stimulate each other) and a negative weighting between units that are inhibitory (depress each other).

In the example of the umbrella, rain and snow units, all units would be interconnected as there is a relation between them all. The weightings of the connections are a very interesting subject, because they can only depend on the model in question, or, if you like, on past experience. If you live somewhere where there is no snow, the snow unit may not even exist, let alone be stimulated by the sight of an umbrella. If we consider the situation where there is snow, and there is a lot of rain (England, for example!), the weighting on the umbrella-rain connection will be a larger positive value than that for the umbrella-snow connection.

The weightings only act on the current activation, which means that the more activated the original unit, the more of an excitatory or inhibitory signal it is able to send to other units. If you saw a street full of umbrellas, the umbrella unit would be very highly activated and would ripple more strongly to other units, such as the rain unit.

The connectivity pattern for a model is very important and there are issues which may be critical when it comes to system response as the structure plays a vital role in determining how much sequential processing the system will carry out.

For example, how many hidden units should there be? How should the hierarchy of the system be set up; top-down or bottom-up in terms of activation direction? How many levels of units? What kind of fan-in and fan-out? How much information can be stored? In many cases it has indeed been a case of trial and error in order to discover the potential advantages and disadvantages of any configuration.

Fig.4.8. shows two methods by which just eight units can be connected together.

Propagation Rule

A unit will probably have more than one input source, that is, it will be connected to a number of other units and will be receiving input from them possibly simultaneously.

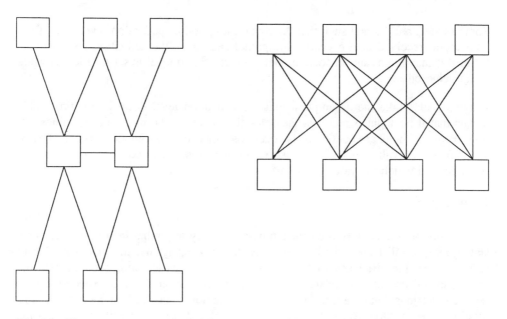

Fig.4.8: These are just two out of the many possible ways in which eight units can be connected.

The total input received by a unit at any given time is referred to as the *net input* for the unit. This is usually taken as the sum of all the inputs, but may be some more complex function.

Activation Rule

When a unit receives input the activation level for the unit will change. As you would expect, the activation level will increase if the input was predominantly excitatory, and decrease if the input was predominantly inhibitory. A lot of research is being carried out to determine the relationship between the inputs and subsequent activation level of the unit. The methods used for specific models are precisely that; they are *tuned* to suit the requirements of a model. There is no evidence to suppose that if we were considering a complete model of the brain and all the functions it carries out, that there would be a uniform *method* by which results are achieved. Rules which are highly suited to visual perception are not necessarily those most suited to speech recognition for example. An integration of all methods would potentially provide the best overall solution. Furthermore, there is no evidence to show that any of the methods used are, if you like, correct, the evidence lies only with achievement.

There is work and research being carried out all the time and described here are some of the more common methods used to determine the activation level for a unit.

Some models are defined such that the maximum possible activation level is 1. If the total inputs received then exceed some predefined value, the activation level will be set to this maximum, and in some models, the activation level is set to 0 if this value is not achieved.

Other models make the assumption that the activation level decays with time. This means that if no input is received the activation level for the unit will be reduced as time passes. If units are continuously receiving input there is generally assumed to be some maximum value preset for the activation level, similar in concept to a saturation point beyond which the value cannot pass.

Learning

The pattern of connectivity used for a model is a very important factor, as previously stated, as this will have a direct bearing on the processing that the model is able to carry out and the efficiency of that processing. As far as learning is concerned, the model should be able to update the network configuration through experience with new connections being added, existing ones removed or the connection strenths modified. Very little research has been carried out in the field as yet, so the implications of how much effect this will have on the ability of a model to meet the requirements is as yet unclear.

All learning rules which are currently used, are basically a variation of Hebb's learning rule detailed in the publication *'Organisation of Behaviour'* (1949). This text is now considered to be a classic study for the student of Neural Networks. The basic principle behind Hebb's learning rule is that if a unit receives input from another, and both units are either in a highly active state, or both inactive, the weight which represents the effect that the second unit has on the first, should be strengthened.

Framework for Neural Network Models

There are many distinct forms of neural network model but the general basic characteristics can be defined as follows in terms of the major features which combine to form the framework

❑ A set of processing units

❑ A state of activation for each unit

❑ An output function assigned to each unit

❑ A connectivity pattern between the units

❑ A propagation rule to determine the patterns of activity through the connections

❑ An activation rule to combine the current activation level of a unit with activation inputs to produce a new activation level for the unit

❑ A learning rule in order that the connectivity patterns can be modified through experience

❑ An environment in which the system can function

❑ An input buffer to enable the model to receive input

Mathematical Notation for the Basic Hopfield Model

Mathematical notation is used to describe the relationships between the various states thus enabling rules to be determined and events to be simulated. This does not necessarily enhance the descriptions previously given in terms of understanding how the models work, from a conceptual point of view, but they are necessary if the reader wishes to set up, for example, a PC-based neural network simulation. This will be done by describing the Hopfield model, although it is important to realise that this example is certainly not the only one in use. However, it has the advantage of clarity and will serve to introduce the terminology used throughout the text.

It is also not necessary to be 'good' at mathematics to be able to use these formulae, but there is a lot of specialised notation used and if you are unfamiliar with such mathematical language you may find it a bit harrowing at first.

Stephen Hawking in his book *'A Brief History of Time'* said that to include one mathematical formula in a book was to cut the readership by one half. I tend to agree with him but feel that nothing is lost in terms of understanding if this section is ignored by the reader.

Input and Output process

Let us first recap on the process which a unit goes through from receiving input, to exciting or inhibiting other units through output. This is shown in Fig.4.9:

Receive input from a number of other units	Activation rule acts on inputs to produce the activation level	Output - a function of the activation level	Output is weighted for each unit connection, and input to that unit.

Fig.4.9.The process of input and output for a unit.

Unit definition

In order to explain the notation, the completely improbable example of three processing units is used, because of the simplicity of the diagram. The connectivity pattern is as shown in Fig.4.10, with each unit connected to every other. This is a two-way connection to illustrate the fact that the first unit may excite the second, but the second may in fact inhibit the first. For example, if the phone rings and you are expecting a call, the concept of that person will be strongly activated by the phone ringing. However, if you see that person, the concept of them ringing you at that moment is going to be totally inhibited.

The units are as shown in Fig.4.10. and will be referred to as U_1, U_2 and U_3.

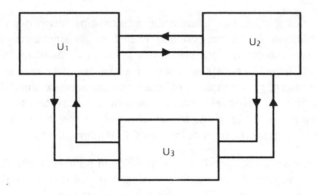

Fig.4.10: Three units U_1, U_2 and U_3 connected together using full connectivity. A general unit is U_i where i = 1, 2 or 3.

Because there will be many hundreds, or even thousands of such units in a viable model and because we want to apply the rules which are written down to each and every one of the units, we will refer to a general unit as U_i, where the i can take any value depending on the number of units. In Fig.4.10., i=1, 2 or 3.

Activation level

Each unit, at any given point in time will have an activation level. This we will call a_1 for unit U_1, a_2 for unit U_2 and a_3 for unit U_3.

In general then, unit U_i has an activation level of a_i.

Now, as said previously, the activation for a unit will change as time changes, so that the activation is related to, and tied to the current moment in time. If we refer to the general time as being t, where t can take any value within the limits of our time scale, the activation level a_i for unit U_i at time t will be written as $a_i(t)$. This will uniquely define the activiation for each moment in time.

To summarise:

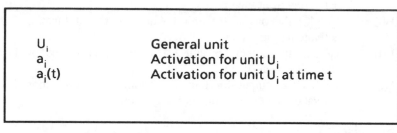

If the activations are included in the diagram this will now look as shown in Fig.4.11.

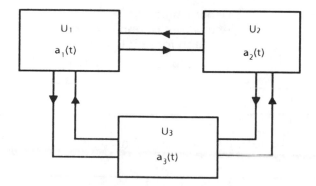

Fig.4.11: The activation levels for the three units at some point in time which we will call t.

Output

The output from each unit will depend on its activation level but the calculation is unlikely to be the same for each. To each unit therefore is assigned an output function which is applied to the activation level to determine the output for the unit. Now this function may well be something like *multiply by 2*, so that the output is then twice the activation level, or it may be something far more complex. Whatever the function is, it will be different for all units, and for all models. We will refer to this unknown function as f and the output which it produces as O.

Then:

Unit U_1 has function f_1 and output $O_1(t)$ at time t
Unit U_2 has function f_2 and output $O_2(t)$ at time t
Unit U_3 has function f_3 and output $O_3(t)$ at time t
Unit U_i has function f_i and output $O_i(t)$ at time t - the general case

The output will change as time changes, and the output $O_i(t)$ is a function f of the activation level $a_i(t)$ for the unit U_i at time t. This is written as follows:

$O_1(t) =$ $f_1(a_1(t))$ the output for unit U_1 at time t is a function f_1 of the activation a_1 at time t

$O_2(t) =$ $f_2(a_2(t))$ the output for unit U_2 at time t is a function f_2 of the activation a_2 at time t

$O_3(t) =$ $f_3(a_3(t))$ the output for unit U_3 at time t is a function f_3 of the activation a_3 at time t

$O_i(t) =$ $f_i(a_i(t))$ the output for unit U_i at time t is a function f_i of the activation a_i at time t, this is the general case

To summarise:

U_i General unit
$a_i(t)$ Activation for unit U_i at time t
f_i Function for unit U_i output
$O_i(t)$ Output for unit U_i at time t

$O_i(t) = f_i(a_i(t))$

The diagram may now be updated to show this information:

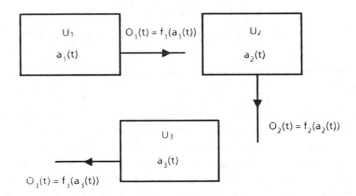

Fig.4.12: The output $O_i(t)$ for each unit is shown as a function f_i of the activation $a_i(t)$. Note: The full connections are not shown for simplicity.

The connections between the units have been shown as arrows. What has yet to be shown is the strength of the connections between the units, this being referred to as the weighting.

Weighting

The weighting will vary between pairs of units so we need to find some way of describing the general form.

Let us call the weight W and represent the weight from unit U_j to unit U_i by W_{ij}. That is, the effect that unit U_j has on unit U_i.

Then:

W_{12} is the effect unit U_2 has on unit U_1
W_{13} is the effect unit U_3 has on unit U_1
W_{21} is the effect unit U_1 has on unit U_2
W_{23} is the effect unit U_3 has on unit U_2
W_{31} is the effect unit U_1 has on unit U_3
W_{32} is the effect unit U_2 has on unit U_3
W_{ij} is the effect unit U_j has on unit U_i

The weighting diagram will be as shown in Fig.4.13.

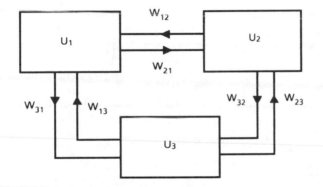

Fig.4.13: The weights between the three units.

The actual effect that U_1 has on unit U_2, for example, will depend upon the output from U_1. This is then modified by the weight value, in this case W_{21}. The result is then the input received by unit U_2 from unit U_1.

The output $O_1(t)$ from unit U_1 is modified by the weight W_{21}.

We can write this as:

$O_1(t)W_{21}$ the input which unit U_2 receives from unit U_1 at time t.

Similarly:

$O_1(t)W_{31}$ the input which unit U_3 receives from unit U_1 at time t.

In general:

$O_1(t)W_{j1}$ the input which unit U_j receives from unit U_1 at time t.

The general form will be as follows between any units U_j and U_i:

$O_i(t)W_{ji}$ the input which unit U_j receives from unit U_i at time t.

This is shown in Fig.4.14.

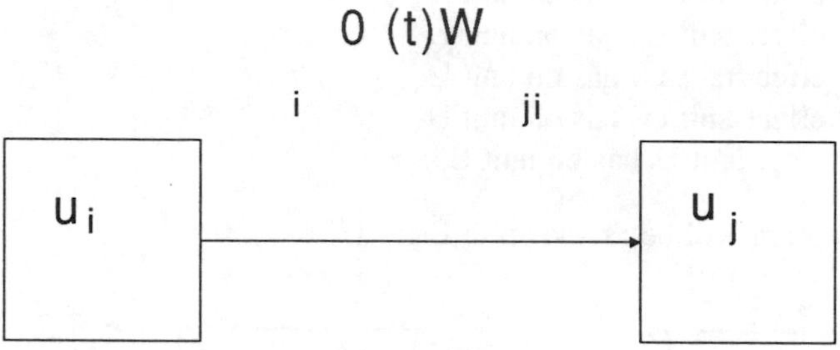

$$O_i(t)W_{ji}$$

Fig.4.14: The input which unit U_j receives from unit U_i at time t.

To summarise:

$O_i(t)$	Output for unit U_i at time t
$O_i(t) = f_i(a_i(t))$	
W_{ji}	The weights between units U_i and U_j. (the effect unit U_i has on unit U_j)
$O_i(t) W_{ji}$	The input received by unit U_j from unit U_i at time t.

Net Input

Unit U_j featured in the diagram above, may well be receiving input from a number of other units at the same time.

For example, unit U_2 in the original example will receive inputs from units U_1 and U_3 as shown in Fig. 4.15.

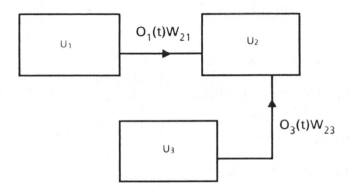

Fig.4.15:The inputs received by unit U_2 from units U_1 and U_3. Note : this diagram is not complete, inputs to U_1 and U_3 are not shown.

The combined, or net input, net_2 received by U_2 is normally taken as the sum of all the inputs received at that particular time. In this example, this will be from U_1 and U_3. The total input for unit U_2 will be as follows:

$$net_2 = O_1(t)W_{21} + O_3(t)W_{23}$$

This can also be written as:

$$net_2 = \Sigma\, O_i(t)W_{2i}$$

The symbol Σ is the Greek letter Sigma and simply means add together all the values obtained when you substitute a value for i into the expression, for all the values of i in the range shown, which here is for the values 1,2 and 3.

Note: a unit will not input to itself so the value for i=2 will be zero.

For example:

$$\sum_{i=1}^{5} 2i$$

This means, for each value in the range i=1 to 5, substitute the value for i into the expression, which is 2 times i, and add all the subsequent values together. i.e. 2+4+6+8+10=30

In a similar way:

The net input for unit U_1 is:

$$net_1 = O_2(t)W_{12} + O_3(t)W_{13}$$
$$= \Sigma\ O_i(t)W_{1i}$$

The net input for unit U_3 is:

$$net_3 = O_1(t)W_{31} + O_2(t)W_{32}$$
$$= \Sigma\ O_i(t)W_{3i}$$

The general case will be:

The net input for unit U_j is:

$$net_j = \Sigma\ O_i(t)W_{ji}$$

To summarise:

$$\sum_i O_i(t)W_{ji} \qquad \text{The net input for unit } U_j \text{ at time t}$$

W_{ji} the weight between unit U_j
and unit U_i

$O_i(t)$ the output from unit U_i at time t

Activation as a Function of input

The activation level $a_i(t)$ for unit U_i at time t depends upon the net input received by the unit, and on its current activation level. This function will possibly be different for all units, and for all models, therefore we need to find a general form. If we call the function F, this will be distinguishable from the previous output function defined as f.

When we set up the model we will need to be able to distinguish between the points in time. We can call successive times, according to the scale chosen for the model, t, t+1, t+2 etc. This is quite feasible because our time interval can be as small as we like. If we have a model with a time interval of 30 seconds, starting at a base time time 0, the values would be as shown in Fig.4.16.

Referred values	Interval from base time (seconds)
t	0
t + 1	30
t + 2	60
t + 3	90
.	.
.	.
t + x	x times 30 seconds

Fig.4.16: In this table, we are working on a time interval of 30 seconds. Starting at 0 seconds and time t, each time step adds 30 seconds to the base time.

The activation for unit U_i will be as shown in Figure 4.17.

The activation for a unit is a function F of the net input for the unit, together with the current activation level of the unit. This sounds complicated, but it could be, for example, 2 times the current activation level, plus the net input which we could write as follows:

Example: new activation = $2a_i(t) + net_i$

Activation	Time
$a_1(t)$	t
$a_1(t + 1)$	t + 1
$a_1(t + 2)$	t + 2
$a_1(t + 3)$	t + 3 etc.

Fig.4.17: The activation for the ith unit at time t is written as $a_i(t)$.

But, we do not know what the function will be, so we will write it in a general form. The actual function can then be substituted:

In general: new activation = $F_i(a_i(t), net_i)$

The final problem we have is that of distinguishing between the new activation level and the old or current activation level. The way we do this is to write it in terms of time. After all, the old activation level will be at time t and the new activation level will occur at the next time interval which will be time t+1.

General form: $a_i(t+1) = F_i(a_i(t), net_i)$

To summarise:

$a_i(t + 1)$	The activation level at time t + 1
net_i	The net input for unit U_i
F_i	The activation function for unit U_i
$a_i(t + 1)$	$F_i(a_i(t), net_i)$

Final Summary

U_i	A General unit, where i can take any allowed value
a_i	Activation for unit U_i
$a_i(t)$	Activation for unit U_i at time t
$O_i(t)$	Output for unit U_i at time t
f_i	Function for unit U_i output
$O_i(t)$	Output for unit U_i at time t
	$= f_i(a_i(t))$
W_{ji}	The weight between units U_j and U_i
	(the effect unit U_i has on unit U_j)
$O_i(t)W_{ji}$	The input received by unit U_j from unit U_i at time t
net_j	The net input for unit U_j at time t
	$= \Sigma O_i(t)W_{ji}$
F_i	The activation function for unit U_i
$a_i(t + 1)$	The activation for unit U_i
	$= F_i(a_i(t), net_i)$

Mathematical Notation for the Hopfield Model

This section aims to provide the mathematical formulae for the Hopfield model, together with the limits which need to be imposed upon the model in order that it will generate the correct pattern from a noisy or partially complete pattern.

The Hopfield model is one of the simplest methods of implementing a neural network, remembering a pattern as a series of binary digits - a pattern of 0s and 1s. If you refer to the letters in Figure 4.2. drawn on a 5x5 grid, each could be represented by a string of 25 0s and 1s. For example, the 'A' in the figure could be written as *0111010001111111111000110001*.

Each pattern is presented to the network, which then adjusts the strengths between the units accordingly. Each unit is connected to every other unit, so that in the 5x5 grid, each character would have input from each of the others, 24 inputs in total. Each character represents a unit and will be firing if the character is a 1, or non-firing if a 0.

To remember more than one pattern, the strengths of the synapses are combined. A simple example of this is shown in Figures 4.4. to 4.6. I do not think that there would be much point in repeating all the details again, so I will explain the formulae behind the Hopfield model and describe how this relates to what was discussed previously.

Base Model

In the model the following definitions will be used:

P   The number of patterns to be stored
N   The number of characters in each pattern
A_{ik} A vector which stores the ith character in the kth pattern

Note: A vector is a single string, in this case, of 0s and 1s. There will be P vectors, one for each pattern, each with N characters. So k will take values from 1 to N. In the vector above, for the letter A, if this is the first pattern then k=1, and we can identify each element by referring to it using the value of i. So that:

$A_{11}=0$, $A_{21}=1$, $A_{31}=1$, $A_{41}=1$, $A_{51}=0$ etc.

T_{ij} This is a matrix which stores the synapse strengths between each unit. There will be N-1 for each of the N units (a neuron does not input to itself).

Note: You can think of a matrix as a block of numbers where each entry can be referred to by a row and column value. For example, T_{ij} will be the character entry in row i column j of the matrix. It is a convenient way of storing values.

Learning Phase

The learning is carried out by presenting each pattern to the network and accumulating the synapse strengths for each neuron in turn using the following formula:

$$T_{ij} = 1/2(1+(2A_{ik}-1)(2A_{jk}-1))$$

This formula states that for each of the P images, the synapse strength T_{ij} is increased by 1 if $A_{ik}=A_{jk}$, and left unchanged otherwise.

Threshold

The threshold is a value against which the accumulated input to the neuron, calculated by E below, is compared. This value must be set to half the number of remembered patterns times the number of neurons less 1 (the input to each neuron). This is written as $P(N-1)/2$.

Recall Phase

An unknown pattern, or partially completed pattern is presented to the network in the form of a vector which we can call A_{is}. The network has already stored the previous patterns in the synapse strengths. A neuron is picked at random, and the threshold sum for that neuron is evaluated using the following formula:

$$E = A_{js}T_{ij}+(1-A_{js})(P-T_{ij})$$

The value for i=j is omitted as a neuron does not input to itself.

This formula sets the threshold value E to T_{ij} if $A_{is}=0$, and to $P-T_{ij}$ if $A_{is}=1$. If the final value for E is greater or equal to the threshold, $P(N-1)/2$, the neuron remains firing and $A_{is}=1$. If it is less than the threshold, the neuron becomes non-firing with $A_{is}=0$.

Restrictions

The patterns remembered by the network may not always turn out to be stable patterns, or attractors, that is, when you apply a partial pattern to the network, the resulting image may not always be one of the stored patterns. The size of the network, in comparison to the number of patterns stored tends to have a large influence on the integrity of the model. In general, a network of N neurons, is able to store 0.15N patterns. This is a little less than a sixth, so if you store no more than N/6 patterns, this should be within the limits.

There may also be problems if the patterns are very similar.

The major problem perhaps, is that the model does not distinguish between black and white, so it may well generate the reverse image of one of the stored patterns. For our example this is just interesting. However for some models, allowances must be made for this otherwise incorrect evaluations may be made.

PC Program for the Hopfield Model

The following program was written using Microsoft Basic, and as such there will be differences with other versions of Basic. The problems will arise using LOCATE, RND and possibly PRINT, in particular. A description is given after the code so that it is quite clear what the program is supposed to do and you can then make any necessary amendments.

An *array* is not the sound heard when a programmer's program works, but a 2-dimensional table of figures. So, for example, if you made out a table of the number of days worked by each of four people over a year, you would perhaps have the 12 months as columns, and a row for each person. The numerical entries would then constitute a 4 by 12 array. Incidentally, each row or column taken individually is called a *vector* (a 1-dimensional array). Most computer languages have special commands to deal with arrays, being a neat way of manipulating numbers.

```
5 CLS: clear the screen
10 PRINT 'HOPFIELD Model'
20 RESTORE.REM start from first DATA statement
30 REM ******set variables***********
40 W=6:REM width of pattern
50 L=5:REM length of pattern
60 P=3:REM number of patterns
70 REM ******define arrays***********
80 DIM A(W*L,P): REM numerical values of characters
90 DIM A$(W*L,P): REM character values of characters for printing
100 DIM T(W*L,W*L):REM synapse values
110 REM *****for each pattern*********
120 FOR K=0 TO P
130 REM ****print title of pattern****
140 READ P$:LOCATE 3,11*k+1:PRINT P$;
150 REM ****read in pattern *********
160 FOR I=1 TO W*L
170 READ A$(I,K)
180 REM **find position and print*****
190 R=INT((I-1)/W):C=I-W*R:REM R=row,C=column
200 LOCATE R+5,C+11*K:PRINT A$(I,K)
210 NEXT I
220 REM *****remember pattern*********
230 PRINT:PRINT "Remember pattern"
240 REM ******check for seed*********
250 IF K=P THEN GOTO 360
```

```
260 FOR J=1 TO W*L
270 FOR I=1 TO W*L
280 REM ***omit neuron to itself******
290 IF I=J THEN GOTO 340
300 REM **find numeric value of A$****
310 A(I,K)=VAL(A$(I,K)):A(J,K)=VAL(A$(J,K))
320 REM *****calculate synapses*******
330 T(I,J)=T(I,J)+(1+(2*A(I,K)-1)*(2*A(J,K)-1))/2
340 NEXT I
350 NEXT J
360 NEXT K
370 REM **generate pattern from seed**
380 PRINT:PRINT"Generate pattern from seed"
390 FOR GEN=1 TO W*L*4 :REM repeated iterations
400 REM ****set threshold sum to 0****
410 E=0
420 REM *****choose random neuron*****
430 RANDOMIZE VAL(RIGHT$(TIME$,2))
440 J=INT(RND*(W*L+1))
450 IF J=0 GOTO 440
460 REM ***calculate threshold sum****
470 FOR I=1 TO W*L
480 IF I=J THEN GOTO 520
490 REM **find numeric value of A$****
500 A(I,P)=VAL(A$(I,P))
510 E=E+(A(I,P)*T(J,I)+(1-A(I,P))*(P-T(J,I)))
520 NEXT I
530 REM **find position for print*****
540 R=INT((J-1)/W):C=J-W*R:REM R=row,C=column
550 LOCATE R+15,C
560 REM ***check E against threshold**
570 IF E <P*(W*L-1)/2 THEN GOTO 590
580 A(J,P)=1: PRINT"X":GOTO 600
590 A(J,P)=0: PRINT"."
600 NEXT GEN
610 LOCATE 22,1:REM move cursor to base of screen
620 PRINT"Pattern complete"
630 DATA "1"
640 DATA 0,1,1,0,0,0
650 DATA 1,0,1,0,0,0
660 DATA 0,0,1,0,0,0
670 DATA 0,0,1,0,0,0
680 DATA 1,1,1,1,1,0
690 DATA "2"
700 DATA 1,1,1,1,1,0
710 DATA 0,0,0,0,0,1
720 DATA 1,1,1,1,1,0
730 DATA 1,0,0,0,0,0
740 DATA 1,1,1,1,1,1
750 DATA "4"
760 DATA 0,0,0,1,0,0
770 DATA 0,0,1,1,0,0
780 DATA 0,1,0,1,0,0
```

```
790 DATA 1,1,1,1,1,1
800 DATA 0,0,0,1,0,0
810 DATA "seed"
820 DATA 0,0,0,1,0,0
830 DATA 0,0,0,1,0,0
840 DATA 0,0,0,1,0,0
850 DATA 0,0,0,1,0,0
860 DATA 0,0,0,1,0,0
```

Details of Basic used

Details of the syntax for the Microsoft Basic commands which may need to be changed if another version of Basic is used are:

RESTORE This allows the DATA statements to be reread from the start.

DIM This defines an array in which all elements have an initial value of 0.

LOCATE R, C Position the cursor at row R column C.

Microsoft Basic	LOCATE R,C:PRINT
BBC Basic	PRINT TAB(C,R)
QL Superbasic	AT R,C:PRINT
Sinclair Spectrum Basic	PRINT AT R,C

PRINT	Print the variable given. Because LOCATE is used to position the cursor each time, punctuation is not relevant.
VAL	To find the numerical value of a string. The program used A$(I,J) to read in the values initially for printing, as printing the numeric value wiped out the previous screen entry. This was then converted to the numeric value A(I,J) for the calculation.
RANDOMIZE	This resets the random number generator, in this case according to a value which is the last two digits of the internal clock value TIME$.
RND	To generate a random number. In Microsoft Basic, to generate a random number between 0 and N the expression is RND*(N+1).

Running the program

When the program is run, the stored patterns are displayed to the screen, as shown in Fig.4.18:

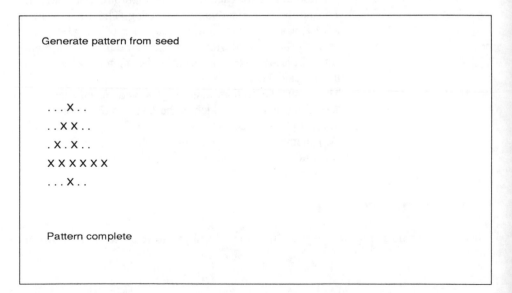

```
Hopfield Model


1                 2                 4                 seed

011000            111110            000100            000100
101000            000001            001100            000100
001000            111110            010100            000100
001000            100000            111111            000100
111110            111111            000100            000100


Remember patterns
```

Fig.4.18. The first screen displays the stored patterns.

The final pattern is the *seed* pattern, the partially completed pattern that will be completely recalled by the model. This pattern is not learnt by the model, simply displayed to the screen.

```
Generate pattern from seed



    . . . X . .
    . . X X . .
    . X . X . .
    X X X X X X
    . . . X . .



Pattern complete
```

Fig.4.19. The second screen displays the pattern generated from the seed.

The next stage will recall the completed pattern. In this case the display will be as shown in Fig.4.19. when the generation is complete.

The examples for the model to learn are very distinct. By using a 5x5 grid and the patterns for numbers 1,2 and 3, the model either converged to a nonsense pattern, one which had not been learnt, or generated a 2 when the seed was a partially completed 3. The 2 and 3 were too much alike, so that the model could only tolerate a slight amount of noisy data. This model will regenerate the 4, when only half the pattern is presented as the seed. Of course, it does also depend on which half you use. It is very interesting to play with this model and see what you can get away with. The seed can be changed by altering the data statements within the code.

If you are going to change the size of the grid, the screen display used will work for a value of W up to 9; you will have to move the text down if you want to change the value of L by more than 1.

5

Problems with the Basic Model

Frank Rosenblatt in the mid 1960s, carried out what was to be at the time the most significant inspiration for neural researchers. He gave his class of models the name of *Perceptron* and during the next few years many variations on his original model were put forward and indeed his ideas are still in use today. He said that his model could carry out more complex functions than digital computers and that it demonstrated the *"feasibility and principle of non-human systems which may embody human cognitive functions"*.

The simplest version of his model was basically equivalent to the model defined by McCulloch and Pitts, but with some extra units called *association units*, whose function was to extract specific features from an input image. The simple perceptron is a model which possesses no short–term memory because the association units are not connected. This general model is shown in Fig.5.1.

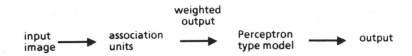

Fig.5.1: The simplest version of Rosenblatts' model was a perceptron type model with additional association units.

Rosenblatt's model was inspired by the discovery by Hubel and Wiesel (1962) that some mechanism exists in the eye of a cat which can determine line directions, eg. vertical or horizontal planes or moving edges. Although he put his model (shown in Fig.5.2) forward as an example of pattern recognition it has many other applications.

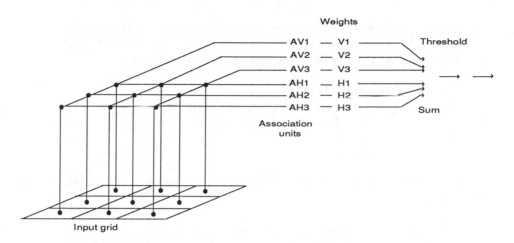

Fig.5.2: Rosenblatts' model showing the vertical (Av) and horizontal (Ah) association units detecting input from a 3X3 grid.

The model shown detects from a 3x3 grid and uses input from the vertical and horizontal association units, Ah and Av respectively, which fire if two out of the three inputs which they all have are active. The association units have weights and the perception is then trained using a learning rule. Fig.5.3 shows two such inputs on a 3x3 grid in the form of the letters T and H.

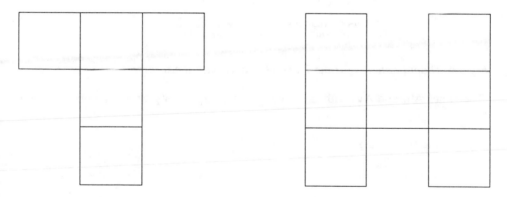

Fig.5.3: Two images which are used in the example of Rosenblatts' model.

The T image on the 3x3 grid will activate Ah_1 and Av_2, whereas H will activate Ah_1, Ah_2, Ah_3, Av_1 and Av_3. Remember that two out of the three inputs for any vertical or horizontal receptor must be active for the receptor itself to be activated. This model has a single output unit, here called F, which can be firing or non-firing depending upon whether or not the input it receives is above some threshold value. This means that F can only distinguish between two images, or classes of patterns. If the output definition is set up in some way so that the T image generates a value which exceeds the threshold, causing the output unit to fire and identify the T, the learning rule will alter the weights H_1 and V_2 so that they tend to have large values. If the H image is associated with the output unit F not firing then H_1, H_2, H_3, V_1 and V_2 will tend to have low values. As H_1 is in both, it will have some middle value.

Let us set the weights as follows:

$H_1 = 0$ $V_1 = -2$
$H_2 = -2$ $V_2 = 2$
$H_3 = -2$ $V_3 = -2$

If the threshold is set at 0, say, the T and H patterns will give the output patterns shown in Fig.5.4.

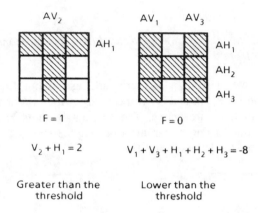

AV_2 AV_1 AV_3

AH_1

AH_1

AH_2

AH_3

F = 1   F = 0

$V_2 + H_1 = 2$ $V_1 + V_3 + H_1 + H_2 + H_3 = -8$

Greater than the   Lower than the
threshold   threshold

Fig.5.4: Output patterns for the T and H images with the threshold set to 0.

T activates Ah_1 and Av_2 with associated weights H_1 and V_2. So the output for T will be:

$$H_1 + V_2 = 0 + 2$$
$$= 2$$

This is greater than the threshold value of zero and so will cause the output unit F to fire and have a value of 1, thus identifying the T image as we wanted.

H activates Ah_1, Ah_2, Ah_3, Av_1 and Av_3 with associated weights H_1, H_2, H_3, V_1 and V_3. So the output for H will be:

$$H_1 + H_2 + H_3 + V_1 + V_3 = 0 + -2 + -2 + -2 + -2$$
$$= -8$$

This is smaller than the threshold value of zero and so will cause the output unit F to remain inactive and have a value of 0, thus identifying the H image as we wanted.

So how does the model cope with corrupted or noisy data? The patterns set out in Fig.5.5 are some versions of the T and H image together with the total output they generate.

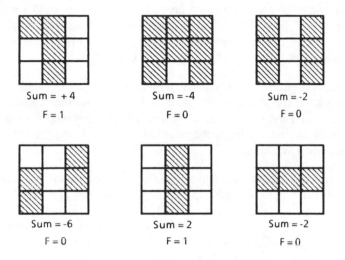

Fig.5.5: This shows six corrupted T and H images and the output that each produces.

Each of these images is able to generate the correct response from the output unit F in order that the model can identify the correct image, T or H.

This is not really an astounding model particularly as it does not deal with more than two shapes, or the shapes being rotated or distorted, but the principle is very important. Rosenblatt knew this and the following is an extract of his views of his model, taken from *Principles of Neurodynamics*,1962.

> *"Perceptrons are not intended to serve as detailed copies of any nervous system. They are simplified networks, designed to permit the study of lawful relationships between the organisation of a nerve net, the organisation of its environment and the 'psychological' performances of which it is capable"*.

He points out that some properties present in the nervous system are exaggerated and some are simplified and stresses that the model is aimed at answering questions. He also said that the model is *"not the terminal result but a starting point for exploratory analysis of behaviour"*.

Perceptron Learning Theorem

Rosenblatt developed a learning theorem for his model (for which there is a good proof by Arbib 1989) which stated that for an elementary perceptron, a given environment, and any problem *"for which a solution exists"*, let the stimuli from the environment occur in any sequence, as long as they occur in some finite time. Then from any initial state, an error correction procedure will always yield a solution to the problem in a limited time. This learning procedure can be stated simply by saying that an active synapse is strengthened if the neuron fails to fire when it should have fired, and weakened if it fired when it should not have fired.

An error correction procedure, which we will look at in some detail further in the text, simply looks at the actual result and compares it with the required result. The weights are then adjusted in order to minimise the error between the two. There are many versions of this rule, perhaps the most widely used being the Widrow-Hoff or Delta rule, described in Chapter 6.

Rosenblatt's learning theorem guarantees that if a set of patterns is learnable by a perceptron, the learning procedure will definitely find the appropriate weight set. However the important thing here is the phrase *"if a set of patterns is learnable"* because this is a linear model and as such can only learn linear patterns, i.e those which can be defined as a straight line (see definitions below and definition of linear separability later in this chapter). This is a severe restriction on the set of patterns which can be used and promoted a lot of criticism.

Linear and Nonlinear

A quick aside about the terms linear and nonlinear which are important and continuing issues in neural models.

A linear system is one for which the output is proportional to the size of the input. Car radios, for example, can be linear systems in which case the reception fades out completely whenever you drive under a motorway bridge because the input reduces and thus so does the output. This problem can be overcome using something called an *automatic-gain-control* device. This enables a car radio to maintain a steady output signal regardless of the strength of the input, creating a highly nonlinear system and better radio performance. Most living systems are a combination of linear and nonlinear. The ear has an automatic-gain-control, a faint sound being perceived just as easily as a loud one if required. The same is true for the eye, reducing or increasing sensitivity to light in response to different conditions.

Rosenblatt's initial attempts produced many problems. He developed a model which could automatically sort an arbitrary set of patterns into groups of similar patterns, using a learning rule based on the perceptron's response and not on the usual teacher correction procedures. Unfortunately, he found that because the weights were unbounded, once one pattern set dominated, it would always dominate. However Rosenblatt was very enthusiastic.

"For the first time we have a machine capable of original ideas".

He considered that the experiments he had carried out could not be achieved using conventional computers but his contemporaries were not at all impressed. Artificial intelligence researchers were adamant and arguments ensued which still persist today because solutions to the questions have still not been found, concerning what the brain can do which computers cannot.

Roseblatt set up a simulation of his model on a digital computer and persisted with the idea that it was not what the brain did, but how it did it which was important. However, as is the case today, people were concerned with producing what the brain did and were not concerned about the methodology behind it. It is a valid point that we need to consider results because we do not know to what extent computer strategies used by the brain must be used to simulate its performance. There is also the view that when we are sure of certain details, such as the physical structure of the brain, this should most certainly be treated seriously. If the aim is to model human intelligence there seems to be little point in starting with the wrong basic design. However, at the time, as indeed still seems to be the case today, highly powerful computers enabled systems to be developed which could process so rapidly that the results justified the lack of comparison with the structure of the brain. Also the digital chip technology was extremely cost effective.

Still developing his retina model, Rosenblatt showed that a 2-layer perceptron could classify 2 to the power of 2^N input patterns each with N binary digits. But the general system needed 2^N units and was severely limited, not generalising well to similar forms occuring in new positions in the retinal field. Unfamiliar background also caused problems.

The results of the full limitations of the perceptron were fully analysed in an extremely rigorous manner by Minsky and Papert in a book entitled Perceptrons, first published in 1969. This was so convincing that the work was abandoned by many who subsequently turned to AI research.

It is interesting to note the following quote from an interview made in 1981.

"I now believe the book was overkill...(being) irritated with Rosenblatt for overclaiming and diverting all those people along a false path...I started to realise that for what you get out of it - the kind of recognition it can do - it is such a simple machine that it would be astounding if nature did not make use of it somewhere". Minsky, The New Yorker, 1981.

It is always important to get things into perspective, although one can understand Minsky's point of view if outrageous claims were being made as often seems to happen. Articles in the popular press these days about neural network developments more often than not, seem to summarise with the notion that in the near future we are all going to be surrounded by talking, thinking machines that are going to do everything for us. Many researchers indicate that this could not be further from the truth and not to trust *shoddy popularisations*! There is much concern over the public not being led up this sort of garden path because it is simply not true that major breakthroughs are just over the horizon. The brain is the most complex known phenomenon in the universe and we know very little about how it functions. However, as far as the publication *Perceptrons* was concerned, a positive criticism from Minsky and Papert would have been more constructive rather than being so damning. The opinion put forward was that the perceptron could never solve any problems of interest, not even if more layers were added. A multi-layer model was said to be of no value, being too unrestricted, and training was not possible. Learning procedures have since been developed for such models.

There were most certainly major problems with the Perceptron and the impression one gets from the majority of articles is that they were the first to point out all these deficiencies. This was not so. Rosenblatt knew about these problems and had developed a great number of other models apart from the simple extension of McCulloch and Pitts' original idea. In his book, *Principles of Neurodynamics*, Rosenblatt looks at a perceptron he calls the *back-coupled perceptron* which was well known as a solution to the linear separability problem, and he also takes a highly critical approach to his own multi-level perceptrons which, as Professor Gail Carpenter (1989) points out: *"puts the lie to the myth that all of these systems were looked at only through rose-colored glasses"*.

However, let us take a break from developments and look in detail at some of these problems that were identified and why the perceptron was unable to deal with them. The importance of these problems is that they have played a major role in the direction that developments have taken, much being done to overcome the difficulties.

Connectedness and Parity Problems

These two issues can be dealt with in the same section because they amount to very similar problems. This is basically the ability to detect the number of separate parts there are in an image. These parts are often referred to as blobs and can take on any sort of shape provided that the shape is continuous. This is more clearly seen in a diagram. In Fig.5.6, the three diagrams each show only one blob, in Fig.5.7 there are 2,3 and 4 blobs respectively.

Connectedness and parity can be defined in terms of these blobs as follows:

Connectedness: The ability to detect if there is just one *blob* in an image.

Parity: The ability to detect an even or odd number of *blobs* in a pattern.

Fig.5.6: These three examples have one blob each, that is a single connected image.

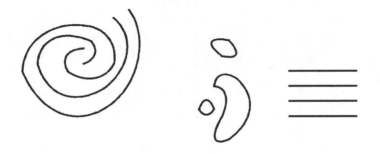

Fig.5.7: These examples have 2,3 and 4 blobs respectively, that is, the number of distinct connected images in each pattern.

Conventional algorithms for computer system have no difficulty in dealing with these sort of problems. If you think of the image as being imposed onto a grid so that each point is identifiable, a conventional computer system will simply be programmed to remove marked points which are next to other marked points until none in that group remains. For the connectedness problem, if none remains then there was just one image. In the parity problem you simply count how many times a group is removed and determine whether there is an even or odd number of groups.

It is easy to show that the parity problem cannot be solved using the McCulloch and Pitts model. Consider the table in Fig.5.8. where the output is 0 if there is an even number of firing units (1s) and 1 if there is an odd number.

Note: think of this model as Rosenblatt's model but with no association units, so each unit has one input only. This is in fact called a 1-order perceptron. In Fig.5.8, we have a perceptron of order 3 as each association unit has three inputs. The order is defined as being the maximum number of inputs to any one unit.

Let us call the weights for the units W_1 for X_1, W_2 for X_2 and W_3 for X_3, and the threshold value T.

The output unit will fire if the combination of weights is greater than the threshold. That is if:

$$W_1X_1 + W_2X_2 + W_3X_3 > T$$

Units					Line
X_1	X_2	X_3	Output		
0	0	0	0	even	a
0	0	1	1	odd	b
0	1	0	1	odd	c
0	1	1	0	even	d
1	0	0	1	odd	e
1	0	1	0	even	f
1	1	0	0	even	g
1	1	1	1	odd	h

Fig.5.8: This table shows the required result of a parity test for inputs from units X_1, X_2 and X_3. The output should be 0 if there is an even number of 1's in the input and a 1 if there is an odd number of 1's in the input.

The table in Fig.5.8 shows the output that we require for the activity levels of the units. So we now need to find some values for the weights which will satisfy the constraints we have defined.

So from Fig.5.8, substituting values of 0 and 1 for the units X_1, X_2 and X_3, we can write down the following statements:

$W_2 > T$ because the output unit is firing and the only input is W_2X_2, $X_2=1$, $X_1=X_3=0$. (line c)

$W_1 > T$ because the output unit is firing and the only input is W_1X_1, $X_1=1$, $X_2=X_3=0$. (line e)

$W_1 + W_2 < T$ because the output unit is not firing and the input is W_1X_1, $X_1=1$ and W_2X_2, $X_2=1$, $X_3=0$. (line g)

So from the first two inequalities, both W_1 and W_2 have to be greater than T, and yet the sum of W_1 and W_2 must be less than T. This is impossible for positive values and for the perceptron because the parity function is not linearly separable. (See definition later in the text).

Although the simple models provide useful solutions to a variety of problems, essentially they can only map similar input patterns to similar output patterns. This leads to an inability for the network to learn certain input to output mappings if they are very different because of the lack of internal representation. However, this can be overcome using hidden units, that is, units which are between the input and the output layers and which allow changes to the representation of the input pattern to be made before it hits the output units.

XOR

A classic example is the XOR or exclusive-or problem. For those of you unfamiliar with this, the definition is, given that there are two inputs X_1 and X_2 which can take the values 0 or 1, the output will be 1 if either one or the other but not both inputs is 1.

We can show this in the truth table in Fig.5.9. where the inputs are X_1 and X_2, the output is F.

X_1	0	0	1	1	XOR table
X_2	0	1	0	1	
F	0	1	1	0	

Fig.5.9: This table shows the XOR relationship for input units X_1 and X_2, output unit F. F is 1 if either X_1 or X_2 but not both are 1 and 0 otherwise.

The output here is 1 if either X_1 or X_2 is 1, and 0 if both or neither are 1.

The reason that this does not work becomes clear if you think of the values for X_1 and X_2 being plotted as the coordinates of a square. The vertices will thus be (0,0),(0,1),(1,0) and (1,1) as shown in Fig 5.10.

The output can be represented as two regions divided by a straight line drawn across the square. Each region represents the activity level of the unit, that is one side of the line for 0 output, the other side for 1 as shown.

In terms of these coordinates, the outcomes for the XOR problem will be 0 for (0,0) and (1,1), and 1 for (0,1) and (1,0).

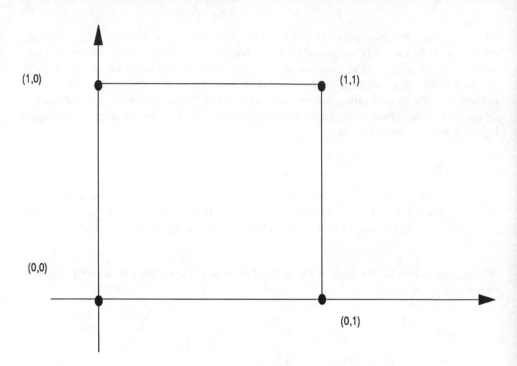

Fig.5.10.This shows the input values for X_1 and X_2 plotted as the coordinates of a square.

Now try to draw a line with (0,0),(1,1) on one side and (0,1),(1,0) on the other; you will soon find it impossible. This is another example of the problem of linear separability.

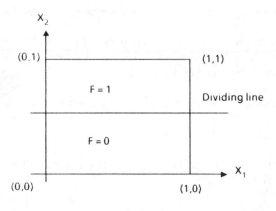
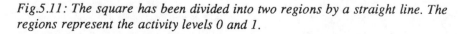

Fig.5.11: The square has been divided into two regions by a straight line. The regions represent the activity levels 0 and 1.

Linear Separability

The *linear separability* problem which has been turning up all through this chapter, is one which occurs for a single layer perceptron, no matter how many input units there are. For the XOR problem there were two units and we were able to look at why this could not be solved using a 2-dimensional figure. If there were N units we would have to look at an N-dimensional figure.

The problem can be visualised in 3 dimensions by thinking of a cube with the neuron-like units situated at the 8 vertices or corners as shown in the Figure 5.12.

If the neighbouring vertices of one of the given neurons are firing, and those far away are not, this implies that the specified neuron must also fire. For example, if the vertices (1,0,0), (0,1,1) and (0,1,0) are firing and none of the others are, this implies that (0,0,0) should also fire. This means that a function that this arrangement could perform successfully would need to be expressable as a plane which cuts the cube. This is a severe limitation as such definitions will not usually generate nice smooth planes such as the one shown in Fig 5.13.

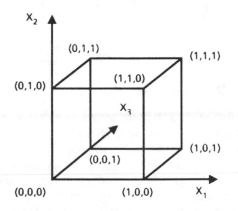

Fig.5.12: This diagram shows the activity levels for three units X_1, X_2 and X_3 plotted as a three dimensional cube.

In 2 dimensions, the function would have to generate a line, as we saw for the XOR problem and in n dimensions, an n-dimensional hyperplane which cuts the n-dimensional hypercube.

The perceptron of order 3 can solve the parity problem if there exists an association unit which detects parity on input, but as Minsky and Papert point out, the order of the perceptron required to carry out this would have to always be at least N, the number of inputs. This is going to be a ridiculously large value for the N which would be present in normal image processing. Hence the model is limited to solving only simple problems. This same principle also applies to the connectedness problem.

Mask Perceptron

Just a quick comment about this type of model which is described by Aleksander (1990) as being the perceptron best suited to the parity problem. The model has one weight associated with each of the four possible combinations of 0s and 1s that can be input i.e. (0,0), (0,1), (1,0) and (1,1). Association units detect these units and fire only if a particular pattern is input. This type of association unit which responds to an input pair is called a *mask*, hence the term *mask perceptron*.

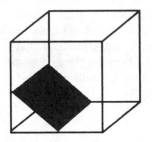

Fig.5.13: This shows the cube being cut by a plane.

Diameter-Limited perceptron

Let us briefly look at this definition. The initial stages of vision in mammals is known to be dealt with by *fixed-logic* cells, these being cells which are diameter limited. This means that any inputs to a cell have to be within some given distance D of each other in the image. This is the same principle as applied to the association units of the diameter-limited perceptron: associations between the inputs to the image must be such that one lies within a circle of diameter D, with the other as its centre. The whole problem with this model reduces again to the parity problem as the differences that need to be detected between patterns in order to classify them as connected or not, will not always be in the same place on the diagram. Hence it is not possible to classify a pair of patterns correctly without messing it up, as it were, for a third pattern. There is no solution which is linear.

Conclusion

Most of the problems with the McCulloch and Pitts model and the simple perceptron boil down to the idea of linear separability, which tends to be an unavoidable feature arising from the very simplicity of the model. There are two very real problems with making things more complicated: one is the physical impracticality of hard wiring a lot of components together, particularly as it was shown that an enormous number would be needed to solve any interesting problems. The other is the sheer cost involved which could be totally prohibitive.

At the time various attempts were made to solve these problems using simple models. For example, the problem of parity was solved by introducing a model which comprised several basic McCulloch and Pitts models connected together to the same inputs. Two such units can be used to perform any logic function but not, unfortunately, the diameter-limited connectedness problem. There seemed to be some severe limitation on all these modifications.

The realisation dawned that the single layer perceptron was really not going to be particularly useful, which, after all, Rosenblatt never claimed it would be, describing it as a starting point. There was now a serious need for the few that remained, who had not turned to AI research, to try and solve some of the huge obstacles that seemed to be in the way. Rosenblatt had already carried out much analysis on other models but the relevance of his work seemed to be lost in the general exodus. As mentioned before, these problems are no longer seen as being insurmountable, all things are possible, and they simply pose rather interesting problems for the developers.

In addition to developing more powerful learning rules to drive the systems, the idea of introducing a feedback element into the networks was also considered. Rather than input travelling straight through the network in a forward manner to the output layer, connections were introduced which enabled a unit to communicate with other units in previous layers. These are called *recurrent networks* and are discussed in Chapter 14.

In Chapter 8 we will look at the steps taken to overcome the problems identified for the basic single-layer perceptron model. Before we look at how these problems were solved, we will look in Chapter 6 at a very important learning rule, the Delta rule, which is worth following carefully as the principles outlined form the basis of many other rules which have since developed.

A brief outline of the aims and achievements of artificial intelligence research is given in Chapter 7, highlighting the difference between this and neural network research.

6

The Delta Rule

In Chapter 4 we looked at the definition for synapse adaptability, the learning rule put forward by Hebb (1949). This rule has formed the basis of opinion upon which further learning rules have been based, namely that the connection between two neurons is strengthened if they are connected and firing simultaneously.

Hebb suggested that concepts or ideas are represented as patterns of activity across the neurons rather than a memory being stored in a single place. After all, neurons are dying every day and not being replaced, which would mean that every day we would lose a memory of something potentially important, our names maybe. This does not happen. Hebb's idea has to date been pure speculation as it has been difficult to get direct evidence. However, recent work shows a learning rule similar to Hebb's may actually be there. This has been described as Long Term Potentiation (LTP) and was discovered in the mammalian hippocampus.

One important point concerning the adjustment of connective strengths is that the information needed to make the adjustments is held locally at the connections, that is, it is not necessary for a programmer to set the rules.

A limitation of the Hebb rule is that learning is only possible if the patterns are totally unrelated; remember linear separability. More sophisticated rules have since had to be developed to allow the existence of multiple patterns.

An expansion of the simple rules expressed by Hebb was introduced in 1962 by Bernard Widrow. Referred to as the *Widrow-Hoff*, *Delta* or *Least Mean Squares* rule, this transformed Rosenblatt's version of Hebb's learning rule into a working model for machine design. It describes competitive learning rules and rules for learning in stochastic parallel models, the connections being adjusted according to rules held locally at the connections which are readily available to the unit. Using this rule, learning is a fairly simple process in that there is no requirement for overall supervision.

In this chapter we will look at the Delta rule, a learning rule for a single layer perceptron type model, and how it works. Then go through a simple example which shows how the rule deals with the weight adjustments. Finally the mathematics of the rule, are given at the end of the chapter.

The Delta Rule

The weights in a network cannot be determined in advance, but a system of error correction can be used to finely adjust the network until it produces the required result. The Delta rule uses this method by comparing the actual result at the output with the desired result and then either strengthening or weakening the weights which have firing inputs, by some amount proportional to the size of the error. This is intended to reduce the error and ultimately eliminate it completely. What usually happens is that the weights are juggled around, so that the output becomes closer and closer to the actual solution. This is called *convergence*.

The process is sometimes referred to as *Least Mean Squares* because it aims to reduce the overall error for the whole network, using a well established mathematical process of least mean squares. This looks at the sum of all the differences between the desired outputs and the actual outputs, and then reduces this error using a process referred to as *gradient descent* – a bit like allowing the value to slip down a slope.

Remember we are aiming to attain the desired state and the actual state will most certainly be different to the value we require. So we need to compare the desired state with the actual state and then change the weights in some way to bring the two closer together.

In visual terms, we can think of the error for the whole network as a multi-dimensional space which has one axis corresponding to each weight value (this is easy to imagine for 2 weights, in 2 dimensions). Then we add another axis which represents the amount of error.

For each different value of the weights, the value for the error will change, sometimes larger, sometimes smaller. All these error values form what is called an *error surface*. If we add some random values we could construct an error surface. For each pair of values for the two weights, there will be a value for the error and if these are plotted onto the graph it may look like Fig.6.1.

For a model such as the one we are looking at, which has no hidden units, and linear output units, the error surface will always look like the bowl shape. Looking down on it will be like looking at an ellipse, and if you cut it vertically, it will look like a parabola or U shape (see Figs. 6.2 and 6.3). The important thing to note about this is that the error surface has only one minimum, although this could in fact be the whole space.

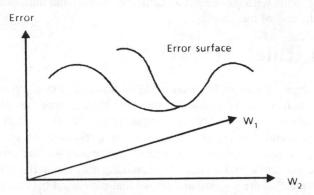

Fig.6.1: The weights W_1 and W_2 together with the error for the network can be plotted in 3-dimensional space to form a surface. This is referred to as an error surface.

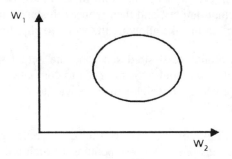

Fig. 6.2: Looking down on the error surface.

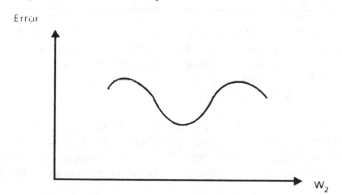

Fig.6.3: Cross section of the error surface.

There are two ways of applying changes to the weights: The first is apply all the inputs and outputs to the network, save up all the changes and then update all the weights at the end. The second, referred to as the *on-line* version and used by the Delta rule, is to update the weights after each input/output pass.

So what do we do with this total network error value, and how do we calculate it given there will be many output units?

The network will have input units directly connected to output units such that the activity level for a unit is determined from the input it receives from the others. This is weighted and compared against a threshold value. A unit will fire when the inputs received exceed some threshold value.

The amount of error is found by looking at the output for a given input pattern, then comparing this actual value against the desired value to give us a value for the error. The Delta rule adds a little bit more to this, usually referred to as e, so that the error will not only be corrected but will also be cleared. The error value after adjustment using e, is then multiplied by a constant d and the result is called the *correction factor*. This means that we do not take off all the error, just an amount relative to d, which represents the proportion of the error to be removed. There are no hard-and-fast rules for the values of e and d; it is simply a matter of trial and error to see which values cause the corrections to converge onto the required solution the most rapidly.

The Delta rule works in the following way: If, for an output unit, the actual output value is not equal to the desired output value then adjust the weights as follows:

❑ Find the error for the output unit – the difference between the actual and desired value.

❑ Find the correction factor – (E+e)d

❑ Adjust the weights for any input units that are firing according to the following rule:
      a. If the output unit is 0 and the required value is 1, increase the weights.
      b. If the output unit is 1 and the required value is 0, decrease the weights.

We shall now look at an example with two input units and one output unit to demonstrate the principles behind the Delta rule.

Example Using the Delta Rule

Consider the two input units U_1 and U_2, connected to output unit F, as shown below.

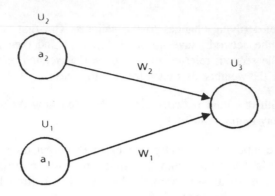

Fig.6.4: Units U_1 and U_2 are connected to unit U_3 with activity levels a_1 and a_2, and weights W_1 and W_2 respectively.

The two units are shown to have weights W_1 and W_2 both affecting output unit F, and activity levels a_1 and a_2.

Let us say that the weights, threshold value T, e and d are as follows:

$W_1 = 0.2$	weight for unit U_1
$W_2 = -0.5$	weight for unit U_2
$T = 0.1$	threshold value
$e = 0.1$	error value
$d = 0.5$	proportional correction

Let us define the activity levels for the units to be either 0 if the unit is not firing and 1 if the unit is firing. Then we can work out the activity levels for the units and the subsequent output.

Remember that the input to output unit U_3 is calculated as $a_1W_1+a_2W_2$ and that the output unit (call this F) will only fire (be equal to 1) if this total is greater than the threshold value T. This will be as follows:

$$a_1W_1+a_2W_2 > T$$

which can be rewritten as:

$$a_1W_1+a_2W_2-T > 0$$

We can consider this to be of the form:

$$a_1W_1+a_2W_2+a_3W_3 > 0$$

where $a_3 = 1$ and $W_3=-T$

In this way we can deal with the threshold in the same way as we do the weights, enabling us to finely tune the threshold as well, which is always considered as being firing.

Activity levels

We can calculate the activity levels, and the output for all possible combinations of the two units U_1 and U_2, with the weights W_1 and W_2 as follows. These are summarised in Figure 6.5.

1. U_1 not firing (0), U_2 not firing (0), so

$$W_1U_1 + W_2U_2 > T \text{ becomes} \quad 0 \quad + \quad 0 \quad > \quad 0.1$$

$$0 \quad > \quad 0.1$$

This is false, so the output unit F, will not fire, and have the value 0.

2. U_1 not firing (0), U_2 firing (1), so

$$W_1U_1 + W_2U_2 > T \text{ becomes} \quad 0 \quad + \quad -0.5 > \quad 0.1$$

$$-0.5 > \quad 0.1$$

This is false, so the output unit F, will not fire, and have the value 0.

3. U_1 firing (1), U_2 not firing (0), so

$$W_1U_1 + W_2U_2 > T \text{ becomes} \quad 0.2 + \quad 0 \quad > \quad 0.1$$

$$0.2 \quad > \quad 0.1$$

This is true, so the output unit F, will fire, and have the value 1.

4. U_1 firing (1), U_2 firing (1), so

$$W_1U_1 + W_2U_2 > T \text{ becomes} \quad 0.2 + \quad -0.5 > \quad 0.1$$

$$-0.3 > \quad 0.1$$

This is false, so the output unit F, will not fire, and have the value 0.

The truth table for this information may be set out as follows:

Activity levels				
a_1	0	0	1	1
a_2	0	1	0	1
a_3	1	1	1	1
Actual output F	0	0	1	0

Fig.6.5: The actual values are found from the activity levels calculated above. Remember that the threshold weight a_3 is always firing.

Now, let us say that the output we require, the desired output, is as shown in the figure below. The values required for F are shown on the last line.

Desired output F	1	1	1	0

Fig.6.6: Desired Values Table..

We now want to apply the Delta rule to the actual output values in Figure 6.5 and adjust the weights in order the produce our table of desired outputs.

Remember the rules for the adjustments:

❑ If the actual output value for F is not equal to the desired output value then adjust the weights as follows:

❑ Find the error E_j for the output unit U_j. The difference between the actual and desired value, this will be a positive value.

❑ Find the correction factor : $(E_j+e)d$

❑ Adjust the weights for any input units firing (=1) according to the following rule:

  If F is 0 and the required value is 1, increase the weights.
  If F is 1 and the required value is 0, decrease the weights.

We will go through the iterations (repeated applications of the above rules to each column of the table in turn) in some detail and then display them in tabular form.

Iteration 1

For $a_1=0$, $a_2=0$ from the table in Figure 6.5: The actual value for F is 0, the required value is 1. So for these values we need to adjust the weights, increasing them by the error correction amount. Remember $W_3=-T$

Error E_j	=	$0-(a_1W_1+a_2W_2+a_3W_3)$	
	=	$0-(0 + 0 + (-0.1))$	
	=	0.1	$E_j= 0.1$ (distance from zero)

Correction	=	$(E_j+e)d$
	=	$(0.1+0.1)0.5$
	=	0.2×0.5
	=	0.1

There are no units firing, so the adjustment is applied only to the threshold weight W_3. Increase W_3 by 0.1.

New W_3 = $-0.1 + 0.1 = 0$

New output values for $W_1=0.2$, $W_2=-0.5$ and $W_3=0$ are as follows:

Activity levels				
a_1	0	0	1	1
a_2	0	1	0	1
a_3	1	1	1	1
Actual output F	0	0	1	0

Fig. 6.7: The output is found from the new values for the weight; first iteration.

Iteration 2

Taking the next column in the table, $a_1=0$, $a_2=1$ from Figure 6.7. The actual value for F is 0, the required value is 1. So for these values we need to adjust the weights, increasing them by the error correction amount.

Error E_j	=	$0-(a_1W_1+a_2W_2+a_3W_3)$	
	=	$0-(0 + -0.5 + 0)$	
	=	0.5	$E_j= 0.5$ (distance from zero)

Correction   = $(E_j+e)d$
             = $(0.5+0.1)0.5$
             = 0.6×0.5
             = 0.3

Only unit a_2 is firing, so the adjustment is applied to W_2 and the threshold weight W_3. Increase W_2 and W_3 by 0.3.

New W_2 = $-0.5 + 0.3 = -0.2$
New W_3 = $0 \ \ \ + 0.3 = 0.3$

New output values for $W_1=0.2$, $W_2=-0.2$ and $W_3=0.3$ are shown in Fig.6.8:

Activity levels				
a_1	0	0	1	1
a_2	0	1	0	1
a_3	1	1	1	0
Actual output F	1	1	1	1

Fig.6.8: Iteration 2.

Iteration 3

Taking the next column in the table, $a_1=1$, $a_2=0$ from Figure 6.8. The actual value for F is 1, the required value is 1. So for these values we need not adjust the weights.

Taking the next column in the table, $a_1=1$, $a_2=1$ in Figure 6.8. The actual value for F is 1, the required value is 0. So for these values we need to adjust the weights, decreasing them by the error correction amount.

Error E_j = $0-(a_1W_1+a_2W_2+a_3W_3)$
             = $0-(0.2 + -0.2 + 0.3)$
             = -0.3 $E_j= 0.3$ (distance from zero)

Correction   = $(E_j+e)d$
             = $(0.3+0.1)0.5$
             = 0.4×0.5
             = 0.2

Activity levels				
a_1	0	0	1	1
a_2	0	1	0	1
a_3	1	1	1	1
Actual output F	1	0	1	0

Fig.6.9: Iteration 3

Units a_1 and a_2 are firing, so the adjustment is applied to W_1, W_2 and the threshold weight. Decrease W_1, W_2 and W_3 by 0.2.

New W_1 =   0.2 -   0.2 =   0
New W_2 =   -0.2 -   0.2 =   -0.4
New W_3 =   0.3 -   0.2 =   0.1

New output values for W_1=0, W_2=-0.4 and W_3=0.1 are as shown in Fig.6.9.

Iteration 4

Taking the next column in the table, back to the first column again, a_1=0, a_2=0 in Figure 6.9. The actual value for F is 1, the required value is 1. So for these values we need not adjust the weights.

Taking the next column in the table, a_1=0, a_2=1 in Figure 6.9. The actual value for F is 0, the required value is 1. So for these values we need to adjust the weights, increasing them by the error correction amount.

Error E_j = $0-(a_1W_1+a_2W_2+a_3W_3)$
         = $0-(0 + -0.4 + 0.1)$
         =   0.3 E_j= 0.3 (distance from zero)

Correction = $(E_j+e)d$
         = $(0.3+0.1)0.5$
         =   0.4x0.5
         =   0.2

Unit a_2 is firing, so the adjustment is applied to W_2 and the threshold weight W_3. Increase W_2 and W_3 by 0.2.

New W_2 =   -0.4 + 0.2 = -0.2
New W_3 =   0.1 + 0.2 = 0.3

New output values for $W_1=0$, $W_2=-0.2$ and $W_3=0.3$ are shown in Figure 6.10.

Iteration 5

Taking the next column in the table, $a_1=1$, $a_2=0$ in Figure 6.10. The actual value for F is 1, the required value is 1. So for these values we need not adjust the weights.

Taking the next column in the table, $a_1=1$, $a_2=1$ in Figure 6.10. The actual value for F is 1, the required value is 0. So for these values we need to adjust the weights, decreasing them by the error correction amount.

Error E_j = $0-(a_1W_1+a_2W_2+a_3W_3)$
            = $0-(0 + -0.2 + 0.3)$
            =   -0.1 E_j= 0.1 (distance from zero)

Correction   = $(E_j+e)d$
            = $(0.1+0.1)0.5$
            =   0.2x0.5
            =   0.1

Activity levels				
a_1	0	0	1	1
a_2	0	1	0	1
a_3	1	1	1	1
Actual output F	1	1	1	1

Fig.6.10: Iteration 4.

Units a_1 and a_2 are firing, so the adjustment is applied to W_1, W_2 and the threshold weight W_3. Decrease W_1, W_2 and W_3 by 0.1.

New W_1 =   0   -   0.1 = -0.1
New W_2 =   -0.2 -   0.1 = -0.3

New W_3 =   0.3 - 0.1 = 0.2

New output values for W_1=-0.1, W_2=-0.3 and W_3=0.2 are shown in Figure 6.11.

Activity levels				
a_1	0	0	1	1
a_2	0	1	0	1
a_3	1	1	1	1
Actual output F	1	0	1	0

Fig.6.11:– Iteration 5.

Iteration 6

Taking the next column in the table, a_1=0, a_2=0 in Figure 6.11: The actual value for F is 1, the required value is 1. So for these values we need not adjust the weights.

Taking the next column in the table, a_1=0, a_2=1 in Figure 6.11: The actual value for F is 0, the required value is 1. So for these values we need to adjust the weights, increasing them by the error correction amount.

Error E_j = $0-(a_1W_1+a_2W_2+a_3W_3)$
             =   0-(0 + -0.3 + 0.2)
             =   0.1 E_j= 0.1 (distance from zero)

Correction = $(E_j+e)d$
             =   (0.1+0.1)0.5
             =   0.2x0.5
             =   0.1

Unit a_2 is firing, so the adjustment is applied to W_2 and the threshold weight W_3. Increase W_2 and W_3 by 0.1.

New W_2 =   -0.3 + 0.1 = -0.2
New W_3 =   0.2 + 0.1 = 0.3

New output values for W_1=-0.1, W_2=-0.2 and W_3=0.3 are as shown in Fig.6.12:

Activity levels				
a_1	0	0	1	1
a_2	0	1	0	1
a_3	1	1	1	1
Actual output F	1	1	1	0

Fig.6.12: Iteration 6.

Fig 6.12. shows the output we require. We can check that this is indeed correct by substituting the values for W_1, W_2 and W_3 in our equation:

$$W_1a_1+W_2a_2+W_3a_3 > 0$$

with values for a_1, a_2 and a_3 from the truth table above.

$a_1=0,a_2=0,a_3=1$	0.3	>	0	true	1
$a_1=0,a_2=1,a_3=1$	-0.2+0.3	>	0		
	i.e. 0.1	>	0	true	1
$a_1=1,a_2=0,a_3=1$	-0.1+0.3	>	0		
	i.e. 0.2	>	0	true	1
$a_1=1,a_2=1,a_3=1$	-0.1-0.2+0.3>		0		
	i.e. 0	>	0	false	0

Giving the correct output.

This method can take many more iterations than shown in this example but the Delta rule illustrates an important principle upon which many learning algorithms are based. Let us summarise these calculations in Fig.6.13.

As we will discover later, the Delta rule is used in many applications but needs to be enhanced for use with models which are more complex than the perceptron type arrangement.

	Activity	Weights			E	(E+e)d	F Actual	F Required	New F Values
		W_1	W_2	W_3					
1	001	0.2	-0.5	-0.1	0.1	0.1	0	1	0010
				0					
2	011	0.2	-0.5	0	0.5	0.3	0	1	1111
			-0.2	0.3					
3	111	0.2	-0.2	0.3	0.3	0.2	1	0	1010
		0	-0.4	0.1					
4	011	0	-0.4	0.1	0.3	0.2	0	1	1111
		0	-0.2	0.3					
5	111	0	-0.2	0.3	0.1	0.1	1	0	1010
		-0.1	-0.3	0.2					
6	011	-0.1	-0.3	0.2	0.1	0.1	0	1	1110
		-0.1	-0.2	0.3					

Fig.6.13: This table summarises the process of the previous example.

Summary of the Delta Rule

The Delta rule is an example of a Simple Supervised Learning procedure which can be summarised as follows:

❑ The network has input units directly connected to output units.

❑ The network is trained to produce output states for particular input states.

❑ The error between the actual output and desired output is minimised.

One of the deficiences of this class of learning procedures is that such simple models can only solve essentially simple problems, as we looked at earlier. In addition, it can sometimes take a very long time for the rule to actually converge onto a solution, as I discovered when I was trying to find some values to use for my example. Methods have been developed, such as the recursive least squares, which will speed up the process (Widrow and Stearns, 1985) and alternative learning algorithms have been developed for more complex models which we will look at in later chapters. We will not go into convergence solutions here; for the purposes of this text, it is more important to understand the basic principles behind the rule.

Mathematics of the Delta rule

For a network with input units directly connected to output units, make the following definitions, in line with the terminology we used for the Hopfield model in Chapter 4:

U_i the ith unit in the network
W_{ij} the weight, or effect, that unit U_j has on unit U_i
a_i the current state of activity for unit U_i

a_j is the actual state of activity for output unit U_j
d_j is the desired state of activity for unit U_j

To minimise the error, the desired and actual output values are compared. The value we look at for each node is:

$a_j - d_j$ Difference between the actual and desired output for node j.
                 This is taken to be a positive value, the absolute value.

The error for the whole network, which is usually called E, can be written as:

$$E = 1/2 \sum (d_p - a_p)^2$$

where:
         p is a pattern
         d_p is the desired output pattern
         a_p is the actual output pattern

So you are looking at a value which is half the difference between the required and actual output, squared and summed for each pattern in the set.

This is a well known mathematical formula which can be minimised using the *gradient descent* process, which comes into the following description of the Delta rule. There is no need to understand the entirety of what this means, proof-wise, but it should be noted that there is a conventional mathematical process for minimising the error.

For the whole network, this measure of how poorly the network is performing with the current set of weights, referred to as E, can be calculated as follows:

$$E = 1/2 \sum (a_j - d_j)^2 \text{ this is calculated for every input pattern.}$$

This is a standard and well known mathematical term using the method of least squares.

A unit will fire when the inputs received by that unit exceed some threshold value. Let us define the threshold value as:

T   the threshold value

Given that each input unit U_i is connected to each output unit U_j, the following formula is used to determine whether or not output unit U_j will be activated, that is, fire. There are N units in total.

$$a_1 W_{j1} + a_2 W_{j2} + a_3 W_{j3} + ... + a_N W_{jN} > T$$

That is, the sum of all the inputs received by unit U_j has to be greater than the threshold T before it will fire.

This will determine the activity, a_j of output unit U_j.

We now look at the difference between the actual value and the desired value of the output unit. If these are not equal it means that the weights for the actual value need to be adjusted so that the total input from all the input units is either greater than or less than the threshold – whichever it needs to be to satisfy the firing condition. When the weights are multiplied by the activity levels of the units, the error E_j, for unit U_j, is taken as the difference between the threshold value and the resultant total input. To deal with this we can rewrite the weights equation as follows:

$$a_1 W_{j1} + a_2 W_{j2} + a_3 W_{j3} + ... + a_N W_{jN} - T > 0$$

The amount of error will be the amount by which the above equation differs from zero. Having found this, the Delta rule adds a little bit more so that the error will not only be corrected but will also be cleared. This is e. This sum is then multiplied by a constant d and the result is called the *correction factor*. The values of e and d are selected (using guesswork) to converge rapidly onto the required solution. So we have now defined:

E_j $0 - (a_1 W_{j1} + a_2 W_{j2} + a_3 W_{j3} + ... + a_N W_{jN} - T)$ the error
e   the small amount added to the error we have found
$(E_j+e)d$ the correction factor
d   the proportion of the error to be removed

The process is as follows:

1. Find $E_j = 0-(a_1 W_{j1}+a_2 W_{j2}+a_3 W_{j3}+...+a_N W_{jN}-T)$ error
2. Find $(E_j+e)d$ correction
3. For firing units:
     If $a_j=0$, and $d_j=1$ then $W_i=W_i+(E_j+e)d$
     If $a_j=1$, and $d_j=0$ then $W_i=W_i-(E_j+e)d$
4. Recalculate output values.

7

Artificial Intelligence

With the publication of *Perceptrons*, many researchers were disallusioned with neural networks and turned their attention towards artificial intelligence (AI) projects. Over the last few years these have gained a great deal of credibility and success, in particular, with the development of *expert systems*. Certain areas of neural network research are in direct competition with these AI developments and there must be a considerable amount of rivalry between the camps.

It is difficult to see the difference between AI systems and neural networks particularly when one considers that the aim of AI is to create a machine with *human-level intelligence*, which is the same basic objective of neural networks. If both disciplines are striving to achieve the same outcome, that is, the development of the *Thinking Machine,* why is it that the two fields are so very diverse?

Background

The concept of simulating a thinking machine was initially proposed by Alan Turing in 1950 and his now famous *Turing test* was the criteria against which such attempts should be measured. The test stated that if a human interacting with a computer was under the illusion that the interaction was taking place with another human rather than a machine, we should consider the computer in question to be intelligent. Suffice to say that no clues or details were given concerning how this was to be accomplished.

Turing's definition is very thought provoking in itself, and certainly seems on the face of things to be a very valid test for human-level intelligence in a machine. That is a discussion which is taken up further in this chapter. Let us first look at some of the differences between AI and neural networks.

Perhaps the key differences can be highlighted in quotes from an interview with Dr. John McCarthy (1989), professor of Computer Science at Stanford. He talks of developing an *"intelligent computer program"*, for example, one controlling a robot, and also states that the development of *expert systems* has been a *"significant advance"* in AI techniques in the last 10-20 years. To decide on the implications of these statements let us look at what AI research has achieved, and more importantly perhaps, how it has been accomplished.

AI Systems

Artificial Intelligence systems are traditionally based on a system of symbol manipulation and early research involved the development of games such as chess and checkers. To the credit of AI in general, chess games now exist which can beat 95% of the population with absolute ease. Chess is an extremely complex game to learn, let alone to master, and anyone who has ever played it will appreciate not only the variety of moves and players involved, but also the strategy and forward planning that takes place. Each move is dependent upon that of the opponent and so not only does such a program have to assess the moves of the other player and select an appropriate and near optimal response, it also has to develop a plan of action and choose from a great number of possible options. The development of such a game is a great achievement towards the common goal.

In order that we can move some way towards really appreciating the implications of such systems, it would be a good exercise to develop a very simple expert system ourselves. Like the neural network, the basic idea is quite straightforward.

Expert Systems

An expert system is basically a computer program which repeatedly poses different questions each with a yes or no answer. These questions are of the form IF(condition)..THEN(action). For example, IF(you are not interested in this chapter) THEN(turn to the next). This process is almost like following through a maze which has many left or right turns. Eventually, if the correct answer is given to the question *"Do I turn right here?"*, answer *YES* or *NO*, you will ultimately reach the centre, as long as your initial information is correct.

Starting with a small base of information, such as the classification of a group of five animals, we could instruct the computer, via a program, to pose questions which will lead it to *"guess"* the correct animal that the user has in mind. In the following example, the group of animals are cat, chicken, snake, monkey and elephant. The information the computer is programmed to have access to can be set out as shown in Fig.7.1:

Animal	Classification			
	has legs	has wings	has a trunk	lives in a tree
Snake	N	N	N	Y
Chicken	Y	Y	N	N
Elephant	Y	N	Y	N
Cat	Y	N	N	N
Monkey	Y	N	N	Y

Fig.7.1: This table shows how the animals in the example are to be classified.

The answers given to the information above could undoubtedly be disputed, but for our purposes let us take the answers to be *yes* or *no, maybe* not being allowed, and work from these conditions. This then will be sufficient to classify each animal.

The process carried out by the computer program in this case will be to pose this information in question form to the person at the keyboard. This can be shown in the flow diagram in Fig.7.2.

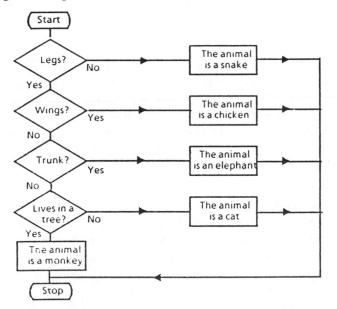

Fig.7.2: The flow of logic used to classify the animals in the example.

The path through the flow diagram is controlled by the responses to the questions. If the answer to *Has the animal got legs?* is NO, then in our example, the animal must be a snake. If the answer was YES then further questions are posed to classify the animal. It is important to note at this stage that the system simply checks whether the answer is YES or NO and takes the appropriate response we have defined as being correct. The system would not consider that an animal without legs could also be a worm for example, because we have not included that information in the knowledge base. It has not been put into the program.

It would not then be too large a step to turn this into a computer program using a simple language like BASIC.

The following program is written in Microsoft BASIC and can easily be adapted for any version. The only problem may arise when using the INPUT statement.

```
10 PRINT "WHICH ANIMAL ARE YOU THINKING OF?"
20 PRINT
30 INPUT "Does your animal have legs? Answer Y or N.";A$
40 IF A$="Y" THEN GOTO 70
50 IF A$="N" THEN PRINT "You are thinking of a snake.":GOTO 200
60 GOTO 30 : REM input not Y or N
70 INPUT "Does your animal have a trunk? Answer Y or N.";A$
80 IF A$="Y" THEN PRINT "You are thinking of an elephant.":GOTO 200
90 IF A$="N" THEN GOTO 110
100 GOTO 70 : REM input not Y or N
110 INPUT "Does your animal have wings? Answer Y or N.";A$
120 IF A$="Y" THEN PRINT "You are thinking of a chicken.":GOTO 200
130 IF A$="N" THEN GOTO 150
140 GOTO 110 : REM input not Y or N
150 INPUT "Does your animal live in trees? Answer Y or N.";A$
160 IF A$="Y" THEN PRINT "You are thinking of a monkey.":GOTO 200
170 IF A$="N" THEN GOTO 190
180 GOTO 150 : REM input not Y or N
190 PRINT "You are thinking of a cat."
200 STOP
```

It would take an extremely large number of questions to classify every animal that exists using this method and we would need to enter into a great deal of specialist detail if we wished the program to be accurate. Clearly at this current time it is not, not even for this small set. However, accuracy is not the point of the example shown above, the point being that it can be done and in really quite a simple way. The condition is that the programmer has included all the necessary information within the program in the form of simple decisions that the system can then act upon.

AI techniques have made considerable advancements over the past few years enabling highly sophisticated systems to be developed. In particular, programming languages such as LISP and PROLOG have been designed specifically for the task of symbol manipulation, enabling a great deal of the *hard work* to be taken out of the job of presenting information, access and selection according to certain criteria. Let us consider the main problems which AI systems have to tackle.

AI Basics

AI systems are like humans in that they need to represent knowledge and to access and use that knowledge in order to solve problems. Humans generally take these actions for granted, expecting to be able to store events or facts in long term memory and to be able to recall those facts quickly, easily and at will into some kind of short-term memory. People are able to solve problems by applying conditions, logic, hunches and intuition to what would appear to be a massive base of stored knowledge, in order to reach a decision. The outcome may not be the perfect solution but it will be one of the best possible given the information and the facts available at the time. Translating this process into some kind of computer program is a task which requires a number of different techniques and, as our knowledge of the functioning of the brain is still far from extensive, techniques are based upon observations of results rather than how we envisage the brain to handle data.

AI programs differ from conventional computer programs in that they access a knowledge database rather than dealing with specific numbers in a database. That knowledge base comprises all the information necessary for the particular subject of the program. Not only are all the necessary facts held, but the knowledge base will also contain the relations and rules which exist between those facts, in a way that is understood by the program. Knowledge is represented in the language of logic, in terms of associations between data items.

This symbolic representation of data or knowledge is the primary concept upon which AI systems are based.

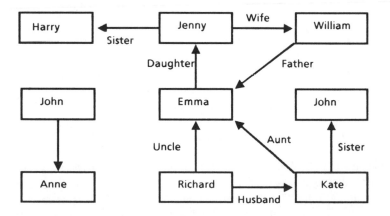

Fig.7.3: The relationships which may be stored between associated data pairs.

The data may be contained simply within the program, as in the BASIC program above, or it may be a separate entity that the AI program is able to search for solutions. Whichever the method used, the knowledge base itself poses quite a problem, not only in that it is likely to be very large, (consider the case of a medical diagnostics system), but the actual process of collecting and collating all the necessary data is a lengthy and costly business. The most obvious method is to sit down with the required human experts, to conduct interviews and glean all the knowledge from them. Other methods have been utilised whereby the system is given vast amounts of data and, using statistical techniques, extracts the general rules from the information. This works well enough but is not a particularly reliable method. A combination of the two would probably be the most efficient in terms of cost and time. The general rules are determined initially and the base is then manually modified using human expertise. The data must also be entered onto the system in such a way that the AI program will be able to access it efficiently and the people entering the data are able to understand it easily.

Having obtained the necessary knowledge, it has to be remembered that this is unlikely to be static data. Changes in medicine are ocurring every day, so it is necessary that the knowledge base can be updated easily and efficiently without corrupting existing data. In addition to this, mistakes in the original knowledge base may need to be corrected. Neither of these tasks is easy to accomplish because of the interrelations that need to exist between the data sets. New data has to be incorporated into the existing knowledge base in such a way that it is valid and reflects the responses required by the system. Even adding another condition and animal definition to the Basic program would require a number of changes which would have to be thought through very carefully.

Once the knowledge base is available, and that knowledge is represented in some way that is meaningful to the computer program and to the people entering and updating it, pattern matching algorithms need to be developed in order that the system can recognise and make use of relevant pieces of the data. This process is referred to as *unification*, and works directly with the methods used to store and code the data relationships in order to enable problems to be analysed and solved.

The actual location of relevant data by the AI program can be a very complex process and languages such as PROLOG use a method of backward searching to rule out selections which may later prove to be uninteresting. The process of searching for a solution is goal orientated, which means the system will not produce answers which, though related to the problem, are irrelevant to the solution. An advanced expert system is also able to deduce facts which are not specifically held within the knowledge base. For example, if the following facts were stored, namely that *Jack has a brother called John* and *Jack has a sister called Jill*, but no other relationships between the people were available, the system could deduce that *John has a sister called Jill*. There is of course some kind of identifier which will distinguish this particular John, Jack and Jill from all others.

Search methods used need to allow not only all possible options to be considered, but also to enable the system to produce a solution which is the best solution under the circumstances.

One searching method is based on hierarchies. Initially the system deals with a very general condition which allows sound basic options to be selected. This process then becomes more and more specific as suboptions and issues are taken into account.

Another search method, heuristic search, estimates how far the system is from achieving its goal. As more of the space is searched, this estimate should improve when increasing numbers of options are brought into play. Evaluation is used to guide the search along routes which appear to be the most beneficial. Of course the system could also search for specific facts known about the knowledge base which would considerably speed up the process as this would eliminate a stage where many options would need to be taken into account and/or eliminated.

AI systems are implemented using conventional digital hardware and one of the problems in the past has been that digital computer systems deal only with exact values. The idea of an answer being nearly correct, or the best possible solution for a given set of conditions, has not been a possibility. Because of this, computer systems often waste time searching for an exact answer when an approximation would be sufficient. There is a trade off point between time and exactness reducing to cost and efficiency, which is optimal for successfully solving a problem. In fact it could be said that accuracy can actually impede a systems ability to perform and control a process.

A method called *fuzzy logic* was introduced in order to overcome some of these problems. This enables more than a simple *yes* and *no* to be incorporated into the logic of a system, and degrees of closeness to the ultimate solution can be established to give a range for acceptable solutions.

This idea of a system which produces an answer which may not be quite exact, or which may, in some cases, even be wrong, is a feature of AI and indeed neural networks which certainly mimics human thought processes, but which is at the same time a difficult concept for people to accept. We have in the past always considered computer systems as ones which come up with an exact answer. The idea of them being not quite right, is considered by many as being wrong. A miss is as good as a mile. If a system requires a high degree of accuracy this is certainly justified. The developer of a missile guidance system would be a bit iresponsible to think in terms of blasting an enemy tank, or perhaps something in the near vicinity. However, there are most certainly situations where a good answer is preferable to the best solution which may take hours to find.

Applications

There are more than 1,000 expert systems commercially available which exist in applications such as medicine, chemistry, engineering and configuration diagnosis. The actual commercial success of these systems has come as quite a suprise, because the whole principle of AI research has been, until fairly recently, viewed as an esoteric subject with little or no practical applications. The practical advantages are obvious - the 24 hour availability of such an expert to a specific site. Although the initial cost of such a system may be quite high, the cost of an expert in the field can quickly justify the initial outlay.

Expert systems are the most successful of current AI systems in terms of being commercially acceptable and of practical use. Other applications are used but are possibly of a more specific nature. These days, AI can be divided into three main development areas; expert systems, natural language processors and robotics.

Natural Language Processors

Natural language processors are AI systems which understand, process or produce natural languages; by this we mean English, not a machine-based language. This should not be confused with speech recognition techniques, but is a system which is used, for example, in translating written text from one language to another. This task was initially done by translating a language word for word - not particularly effective when one considers that the translation of *Sacre bleu* would be *Sacred blue!* More advanced methods consider the context and meaning of phrases but still require manual editing, although obviously, not so many amendments would be necessary. *Cyrus* was one such dedicated natural language system which searched the information system for details about the US Secretary of State, Cyrus Vance. This was presumably to streamline his social appointments as the system was able to deduce that his wife had probably met the Israeli Prime Minister's wife as the two men had previously attended the same state banquet!

Natural language processors are also able to generate user manuals, product descriptions and simple fairy tales. This is not as simple as it sounds. It is a difficult task to know when, for example, to end sentences and how to construct them effectively without too much repetition. They are also used as interfaces between the user and database systems in the form of question and answer facilities, and as a method of querying the database.

Natural language processors also have applications in hardware and have automated a great deal of the work involved in such tasks, for example in the design and testing of chips and computer systems. The system is presented with the specification and has available the manual concepts, algorithms and tools to enable the design to be achieved. For example, a system used by AT&T Bell Labs called *Synapse,* carries out the complete design from start to finish. Such systems need to be tested and this has the facility of provable correctness being achieved by the initial specification being defined as a mathematical formula in common algebraic notation. The system degenerates this formula progressively until it has been broken down into recognisable components using stored rules. In this way the original formula is not corrupted in any way.

Another hardware application is that of designing computer systems to match customer requirements. The system XCON or R1 (A.Brug et al., 1986) developed by DEC and John McDermott at Carnegie Mellon University, configures VAX-11/780 systems for customers. The input comprises the order, the output is a graphical representation of the layout of the system in terms of which components are required and where they are to be located in the cabinets. The information also includes details of assembly for the engineers, connections, power supplies and floor placings. The system uses a set of IF(pattern) THEN(action) rules and aims for efficient use of space. A feasible though not necessarily optimal solution is looked for.

In fault diagnostics, there is an AI system called DART (diagnostic assistance reference tool) (J.F.Gilmore. 1987) which diagnoses faults within the teleprocessing subsystem of IBM 370 machines. The system is able to determine how critical a fault is and how likely it is that the existence of a fault will lead to a system malfunction.

This is not intended to be a list of AI systems which have practical uses, but it is interesting to cite a few examples which can serve to show the usefulness of research to date. Another avenue of research which is most interesting is that of robotics, the control of movement and perception within a machine.

Robotics

Robotics have been used for some time in industry. Initially such robotic systems were completely task dedicated, using what was called hard automation, so that if there was a minor change to the set pattern of actions to be carried out, the systems had to be shut down and the physical changes updated and tested accordingly. These days, requirements are becoming far more sophisticated and the need is for flexible automated systems which can carry out a variety of tasks, and deal with changing environments.

If such a flexible system needs to be altered it is a matter of simply changing the control software, a process which is far more cost effective than physical updates, and avoids lengthy shutdowns because the software updates can be developed and tested elsewhere.

A lot of robots which are able to move around a factory area follow some kind of trail such as a wire, chemical marking or magnetic tape which is embedded into the floor. This presents many problems because changes involve ripping up floors and if the method used is easier to update, such as a chemical trail or tape, this tends to get dirty and has to be replaced fairly frequently. Such a system really needs to be able to cope with any environment without the need of preset guidelines. This *motion planning* is a problem not unique to artificial intelligence systems. The way that it is dealt with in this particular branch of the research, is to give the robot a description of the environment and the required start and finish positions. It is then able to take a path which avoids collisions, assuming no one has parked a fork lift truck in the aisle in the meantime. Because of the problem with changing environment it is desirable that the system can detect obstacles and avoid them.

The University of Southern California (G.A.Bekey, 1989) has been carrying out this sort of research for nearly a decade being involved in robotic vision, teleoperator control, multi-fingered end effectors (hands!), robot skill acquisition and sensor development. Further projects include image understanding and interpretation, parallel computer implementation of control algorithms, robot languages and applications of neural nets to computations of dynamics. Quite a list, with a great deal in common with neural network research.

The difference lies in the approach which is taken to the problem. A system described by Bekey called EARSA (expert assisted robot skill assessment), is concerned with the transference of skills from some kind of human expert to a robotic system. Basically, the procedure builds up a knowledge base and is able to construct new rules from experience and initiate a discovery process. The learning part is rule-based and written in Lisp, being able to generate new rules.

The systems are highly sophisticated and are fulfilling many commercial needs. In 1988, AI hardware sales were $317 million, software was $351 and services $224 million. A firm called *DataQuest* which analyses future technology trends anticipates that by 1992 these figures will have ballooned to $1.9 billion, $1.7 billion and $1.1 billion respectively. Companies such as General Motors have led the way, being very actively committed to expert systems development and machine intelligence (Jarosh,J. 1989). It seems likely that over the next few years we will see AI being incorporated more and more into conventional systems although each will have to be tailor-made as a company's methods will have to be incorporated into the software design.

The AI Approach

Dr. John McCarthy says that AI research can be seen as taking two approaches. The first is the biological aspect, in that studying humans in the psychological or neurophysiological sense may enable us to learn something about how intelligence is represented. The second is the computer science method which contemplates the aspects of computer systems. Dr.McCarthy recognises that an intelligent system needs to have some kind of general view of the world which would have to be based on what we understand about knowledge. He points out that current classes of expert systems are unable to handle general information or to draw general conclusions and that to endow them with such features would require significant scientific advances. At the moment a diagnostics system is a bit like the farmer whose cow was ill and asked his friend for advice. His friend said that when his cow had the same symptoms he gave it some brown medicine. So the farmer did the same and the next day he told his friend that his cow had died, and his friend said, "Thats funny, so did mine!" The point of this appalling tale is that an expert system can diagnose a patient and that patient could die, but until its knowledge base is updated it will carry on with the same diagnosis, it knows nothing about what it is really doing. It does not understand.

Dr. McCarthy says that expert systems have been a *"significant advance"* in AI developments, and yet they have less understanding than my cat has when I get out the tin opener. Here we have a Pavlov's dog situation in that a response can be triggered by certain stimuli, but does the creature actually understand? It is certainly a topic for debate and most cat and dog owners will insist that Spot/Fido/Tiddles *"understands my every word"*. Intelligence of this type, which is way above the intelligence exhibited by expert systems and the like, can be compared to a man with a German phrase book and a Spanish phrase book, who speaks only English. He can be given a phrase in German and translate in into Spanish, and with practice could become familiar enough with both languages to convince people that he knows what he is talking about. This analogy was put forward by philosopher John Searle who says that the point is that the translator hasn't got a clue what he is saying in either language but can give a very good impression that he does. Developing a machine that gives the impression of intelligence is as far as we can aim at this present time until we can devise some means of actually defining how intelligence, understanding and consciousness can be measured.

AI Limitations

When research in AI initially began to show such promising results there were many highly optimistic claims made concerning achievements in the near future. Very few of these have actually been realised but the work carried out has helped enormously towards a better understanding of human intelligence, in terms of understanding cognition and developing problem solving and searching techniques.

There are many successes in this field of research but there are still major limitations which need to be overcome before further steps can be taken towards developing a thinking machine.

The first consideration is the problem of the initial accumulation and subsequent modification of the knowledge base. This is a huge task in itself and needs to be more automated if it is to be realistically applied.

Another major problem is that of developing systems applicable to more than one specific problem. In essence this leads to a system with access to more than one knowledge base which may quite conceivably be governed by different rules and access methods. This is currently not possible using conventional computer methods. In addition, when a system becomes very large, in terms of the knowledge base, there are serious problems with response times. If a limit is imposed on the time for a system to find a solution to a problem then this may lead to either a completely inappropriate result, or no result at all. Reliability becomes very dubious.

Another criticism is that AI systems could not currently be considered for real time applications, for example, an airline booking system, simply because of the problem of updating information quickly and efficiently. The process is far too complex. Also, AI systems do not produce exact answers, they produce near optimal answers. There are many applications currently carried out very efficiently by existing systems and it is unreasonable to expect a system which is required to mimic human thought, to be able to carry out this type of processing. Some of the research being carried out on AI systems is currently in order to adapt these systems more to real-time applications, but perhaps the outcome would be a system ill-suited to either objective.

Artificial Intelligence has the objective of producing computer systems like brains and comprise digital computer systems with an expert knowledge base. The systems carry out the same kind of reasoning done by the experts involved. However, is this what is looked for in an intelligent system? The one crucial difference is the numerical precision of digital computers. The accuracy can actually impede a system's performance. It may be stuck in a loop as it were, searching for an exact solution when a near approximation would be sufficient. Von Neumann (1951, 1956, 1966) foresaw the dominance of digital systems and warned that it would force computers into an area of least developed mathematical theory, that is, discrete mathematics. The most highly developed being the realm of continuous mathematics. fuzzy logic is an attempt to bridge the two and to get around the problem of accuracy.

But even so, people are not programmed, they learn by experience.

Conclusion

This is not a thorough explanation of AI program techniques; there are many excellent texts on the subject, some of which are given as references at the end of this chapter. This is intended simply to give a brief taste of the techniques and features and to highlight the differences between these and Neural Network systems.

Because the main objective of the two avenues of research is essentially the same, the differences initially occur with respect to the ways in which that objective is met. Neural Network systems work from what we know about the structure of the brain; that it is a network of communicating and essentially fairly basic processors. This could be considered to be a *bottom-up* approach to the problem, working from what we can glean from neuroscience. AI systems work from the premise that the brain handles data symbolically, and builds up vast knowledge bases to represent that data. Is this to be considered a *top-down* approach?

Von Neumann believed that any attempt to describe the functioning of the brain would end in unfathomable complexities and implied that the network of the brain is its best description. Any attempt to break it down into simpler parts, such as AI systems attempt to do, is an incorrect approach. As we build machines by defining certain parts as having certain functions it is difficult to see how we can build something as complex as the brain out of something essentially as simple as a few billion communicating neurons. It is a strange fact though, that by building such a simple structure, properties such as associative memory and fault tolerance emerge naturally. As we learn more other features may become apparent.

Neural Networks are not programmed. There is no central controlling program as there is in AI systems, the flow of activity across a neural network being generated by the relationships which exist between the neuron units. From what we know about neurons in the brain, they have no central control either and the relationships are activated by chemicals released between the neurons.

People are not programmed, they learn from experience. Although AI systems are able to incorporate new knowledge into a base which has been assembled by experts, and can automate the process of reasoning to use that knowledge, they are unable to learn anything new by themselves. Neural networks are able to learn. Examples are presented to the network which is able to extract the relationships and build up the necessary patterns to represent those relationships. In this way the system can deal with new problems by drawing on past experiences.

AI systems cannot be condemned in any way at all, there is a place for all systems. It just depends on the objective. AI has had a great deal of commercial success and is proving to be excellent for many tasks. However, we return to the objective which neural networks and AI systems have in common, the thinking machine.

Researchers agree that the thinking machine is a long way away and some will even say that it is an impossibility. AI researchers themselves have been quoted as saying (Baer,J., 1988.) that by programming a computer to do anything, you essentially remove the function that causes real thought. Dr.Hofstader, an AI researcher, refers to expert systems simply as *"artificial expertise"* with *"no flexibility or adaptability or tolerance for errors"*.

An expert system called *Doctor,* developed by Joseph Weizenbaum at MIT, as a bit of a joke, caused him a lot of embarrassment when it was taken extremely seriously as a theraputic aid. Apparently the system asks questions and the patients interact with it using a keyboard. It works using keywords and a simple analysis method, responding with things like *"What does that suggest to you?"* to encourage what Weizenbaum describes as really a *one-sided conversation.* However, here we have a machine which appears to be intelligent and which has fooled many people into believing that it really understands them. Some have requested to *speak* to it privately! Mind you, if it helps, don't knock it. The only problem is when this is considered to demonstrate machine intelligence, in Turing's view, it does indeed.

Howard Gardener in his book, *The Mind's New Science,* believes AI to be the major contributing factor in discovering how humans think. However, he comes down firmly on the side of von Neumann's original fears concerning digital systems by saying that computer science may currently only be demonstrating how we *do not think.* Gardener defines what he calls the *computational paradox.* He says that humans do not approach a complex task in a logical or orderly fashion, or using any method that entails step-by-step symbolic processing. He describes the idea of the brain operating in a parallel fashion.

Machines are being developed which also support this view, such as the *'Connection Machine'* (Hillis, 1987) from the Thinking Machines Corporation. This uses 65,536 processors operating in parallel, and although, as W.Daniel Hillis, co-founder of the company points out: *"it seems a bit silly to build a machine by analogy to something (the brain) we don't understand. Fortunately the machine works".* The Connection Machine has been used for artificial intelligence work, building up multiple relations between the information stored in the knowledge base. As we do not understand the brain, it is difficult to say that symbol processing is not the method used. In any event, at this moment in time, any contribution which can shed more light on the workings of the brain cannot be ruled out. However, the reason that the previously mentioned chess game was unable to beat the remaining 5% of the population is because people who are masters at the game are unable to define why they make a particular move at a particular time. If this information cannot be specified, an AI system cannot be programmed to *know* it.

If we are aiming to achieve Turing's definition of an intelligent machine, that is, it just has to convince the people interacting with it that it is intelligent, then this objective has been met in AI research. However, as with *Doctor* and our friend with the two phrase books, is this really a definition of intelligence? According to Turing, it could be, but hesitation about the objective must exist, because of the very difficult interpretation of what really is intelligence. The basics here have surely got to be what we know about the physical make-up of the brain. It does not operate like a digital computer, nor like a parallel computer made up of digital elements. It does not have a fixed knowledge base, or a central controlling program. The principles of symbolic manipulation may well be correct, but the implementation is not an analogy of the brain.

AI research has led to the development of many highly successful systems which fulfill a need and are the best models for the task; this is currently undisputed. The only dispute is whether they accurately model the brain. Perhaps they are, truly, very artificially intelligent.

John Hopfield (Personal communication) makes the observation that there are very different tasks that need to be done by an intelligent system. The first can be described by logic and precision, a sort of maximum use or investigation of a small amount of information - a task which rule-based AI systems carry out and which present-day digital sytems are excellent at implementing. The second is exemplified by recognising the face of a friend, recognising words in speech or driving a car. A massive amount of highly imprecise data must be processed very quickly to get decisions in real time. By the time a digital system had worked out the optimum way of steering a car around a corner, you would be well into the farmer's field! The issue here is the unreliability and massiveness of the data involved, both of which can be dealt with by biological or nonbiological neural networks.

Hopfield goes on to say that higher levels of cognition require a combination of both these sorts of tasks and it will generally be true that the neural-net approach is a good *front end* to many cognitive processes, but that the *back end*, which does logical reasoning is best left to digital systems. Hopfield summarised by saying:

"I see neural nets as an important adjunct to AI. and a significant coprocessor in an intelligent machine, where massive pattern recognition or associative memory must be done, and rapid but sloppy preliminary analysis of 'features' found".

Response to Problems

We looked at Minsky and Papert's comments that there did not exist a learning rule powerful enough to generate the representations required to create a neural network which could solve interesting problems. Which, at the time of course, there didn't.

The following is an extract from their book *Perceptrons*, 1969.

> *"The perceptron has shown itself worthy of study despite (and even because of!) severe limitations. It has many features that attract attention ... There is no reason to suppose that any of these virtues carry over to the multi layered version. Nevertheless, we consider it to be an important research project to elucidate (or reject) our intuitive judgement that the extension is sterile. Perhaps some powerful convergence theorem will be discovered, or some profound reason for the failure to produce an interesting "learning theorem" for the multilayered machine will be found".* P.231-232

Response to this has taken three main forms:

❑ Develop a learning rule capable of internal representation

❑ Assume an internal representation

❑ Competitive learning

Develop a learning rule capable of internal representation

Boltzmann Solution

This method is used for a network with hidden units and uses a stochastic function to calculate the probabilities of the actual value being equal to the required value. See Chapter 10.

Back Propagation

This method is used for a network with hidden units and uses a two-stage learning procedure. During the forward pass, the input units are clamped to the required values. The second pass works backwards from the output layer looking at the error between the actual and expected values and changing the weights to minimise the total error to bring the solution closer to the required value. See Chapter 11. It is interesting to note that this rule is the same as the Delta rule if no hidden units are included.

It should be noted that neither the Boltzmann machine or error back-propagation are meant as literal models of real neural circuitry. They are also quite different from each other. The Boltzmann using binary stochastic units in a symmetric network, back-propagation using real-valued units in a feedforward net. Both have learning algorithms that use gradient descent.

Internal Representation

In this method the values for the hidden units are assumed to be an internal representation which seems to be reasonable. For example, the *'word perception'* model of McClelland and Rumelhart (1986) and verb learning. See Chapter 19.

Competitive Learning

In this method, simple unsupervised learning procedures are used to develop useful hidden units. No external force exists to ensure that the correct mapping is developed. See Chapter 12.

Research

In Chapter 5, we looked at research up until the perceptron and the severe limitations outlined by Minsky and Papert which caused enthusiasm to wane somewhat. We will continue the story and see what happened next.

Minsky and Papert showed in 1969 that a network with a layer of hidden units could solve the problems, and that with a large enough set of hidden units, a representation for any mapping could always be found. They also said that the number of units required would be unfeasible and that no learning rule existed powerful enough to deal with multi-layer networks.

The late 1960s and early 70s saw research using serial processing techniques based on the von Neumann principles of processing. Cognitive Scientists developed theories of information processing during a time when the work on neural networks had fallen into a decline, and as such, the relevance of such work had become of little importance. The modes of computation which we now consider most highly suited to neural systems, were not taken into account at all. Processing power was the prime objective, and traditional computer methods were used to carry out the intensive processing required.

At much the same time, unaffected by developments in the field of cognitive science, neurobiological research teams, mostly at a cellular level, using simple invertebrate nervous systems or tissue culture preparations (Rosenzwerg and Bennett 1976) carried out studies that strongly supported the basis of neural network research – the view that a learning procedure involved the modification and adaptability of synapses (Lynch 1984) within the brain.

There was at this time, little or no coordination between the different fields of research, each group finding other avenues of research interesting, but not seeing the relevance that it may have for their own work.

Another group of researchers were, however, using models which were to be the foundation of future developments. These were based on the original ideas of a network of adaptable processing units, which could communicate, a memory being represented by a pattern of activity across the units. Anderson (1973,1977), supported the use of this type of distributed representation and showed the relevance of neurally inspired models for theories of conceptual learning. Grossberg (1976), realised the relevance of mechanisms which were also inspired by neural studies. He was one of the first to analyse the properties of a competitive learning machine and he put forward an inspired mathematical analysis of neural networks which was later experienced through simulation. McClelland developed the Cascade Model in 1977, moving from serial processing to distributed processing; Marr and Poggio in 1976, developed a model of stereoscope depth perception; and the HEARSAY speech understanding system, whose architecture was too demanding for the resources currently available inspired Rumelhart's (1977) interactive models of reading and later word recognition (1986). Many references are given at the end of the book for further reading. Researchers were beginning to recognise that hardware which mimicked the configuration of the brain was a powerful tool.

Towards the end of the 1970s, the idea of a parallel processor was being developed more fully and in 1982, Hopfield developed a learning model with multiple layers that inspired new interest in artificial neural networks. Hopfield greatly impressed the scientific element of research with his in-depth analysis of the subject, and with the fact that powerful features such as error tolerance and associative memory are natural properties of a network of connected units. Some of his ideas are discussed in Chapter 9. This interest was further strengthened by Wilshaw and Littley whose studies and analysis of Adaptive Highly Interconnected Systems were being carried out utilising the mathematical techniques used in physics. At this point, many cognitive psychologists began to realise that the computational capabilities of currently used systems did not efficiently meet the requirements of neural networks. A new approach had to be found. Unfortunately, the limitations anticipated by

Minsky and Papert were still causing some doubt about the true value of neural networks.

The output of the McCulloch and Pitts neuron could only take values of 0 or 1, an all-or-nothing action. This does not take into account the *graded* response of neurons, expressable as an average rate of firing. Further developments took this into account.

The major breakthrough was made in 1984 when Geoffrey Hinton was able to show, through the use of a model called the *Boltzmann Machine*, see Chapter 10, that these problems could be overcome. Hinton together with Anderson were able to bring together research into neural networks and cognitive science by demonstrating that neural networks are well suited to pattern recognition and data retrieval from partially complete data sets.

The Boltzmann machine is a direct extension of the simple perceptron introduced by Rosenblatt, the difference being that whereas the original model had an input layer directly connected to an output layer, the new version included layers of hidden units between the input and output layers and full connectivity between the nodes. The learning algorithm for this model took the form of a sigmoid function, one which used the idea of a neuron having a probability of firing, rather than taking a 0 or 1 value.

Introducing hidden units as Hinton, Sejnowski and Williams did with their Boltzmann machine increases the power of the network as each hidden unit can partition the space in a different way. This enables solutions to be found to problems which simple networks are unable to solve. Their model was an important theoretical model but software simulation was too slow for it to be of any real practical application.

Hidden units introduce stability into a network and are vital towards the solution of the so called hard learning problems of Chapter 5, a single layer between input and output being sufficient to perform any transformation (Palm 79). However, the number of hidden units required may be very large. In practise, a subset of the possible transformations is all that is needed and only a relatively small number of hidden units are used in a model.

Hidden units in multi–layered networks need training algorithms and much research has been carried out to develop generalised learning procedures. One possibility is to allow the network to discover the proper features without supervision from a teacher. Several of these *unsupervised learning* procedures have been developed that can automatically model from the environment. Kohonen (1984), Grossgerg (1976), Rumelhart and Zipser (85), Pearlmutter and Hinton (1986). We will look at some of these methods under the title of competitive learning in Chapter 12. The drawback is that all the hidden units may discover the same features. Competition through mutual inhibition is one solution that forces the hidden units to select different patterns to represent (Feldman 1982). Another problem is that the structure in the inputs may not be relevant for the solution of the particular problem. In this case feedback is needed, which we will look at in Chapter 14.

Supervised learning procedures have also been developed, one example using reinforcement signals from a teacher in order to tell the network whether or not the output is correct. This *reinforcement learning* is looked at in Chapter 13. The method provides the minimum amount of information that the network needs but leads to a hesitant and slowly moving system.

The cognitive scientists had been working using traditional sequential computer processing techniques, which do not lend themselves to easily producing the powerful features that the Boltzmann machine was capable of achieving. The neural network approach was able to offer a method of analysing cognition far more effectively, and naturally, than had been previously utilised.

Two such cognitive scientists, Rumelhart and McClelland, were very impressed with ideas put forward and began work using *parallel distributed processing* systems (PDP) as they had already developed an interactive model of reading, which incorporated a number of the features which neural networks could offer. Rumelhart, Hinton and Williams (1986) also asked the question of whether or not all the units need to be fully connected in order to solve the problems that the Boltzmann machine could. They suggested an alternative network with hidden units as a solution. This network is often referred to as a *Multilayer Perceptron* and a great deal of recent research work is based on the model. The principle behind PDP systems in general is that of a few hundred processing steps being carried out simultaneously by many thousands of processing units. These systems enable a better understanding of human cognition to be achieved and although research is very much in the infancy stage, many of the models tending to be highly simplified, numerous very interesting and significant features are being identified. Rumelhart and McClellands *Parallel Distributed Processing*, Volumes 1 and 2, are an excellent and thorough documentation of the work and research being carried out using these techniques.

Another major contribution made by Rumelhart et al., and independently discovered by Werbos (1974), Le Cun (1985) and Parker (1985), was the development of an algorithm called the *Generalised Delta Rule* or the method of *Back-Propagation* which has become a favourite amongst researchers. See Chapter 11.

The fundamental principles of PDP or *connectionism* as it is now more often referred to, were laid down in 1982 by Fieldmann and Ballard and since that time much work has been carried out using models of neural networks, consisting of interconnected layers of simple neuron-like units. The models vary a great deal in patterns of connectivity, learning rules or training techniques and objective. They may be simulated on a powerful mainframe computer, on a desktop PC or developed using the hardware resources available. For example, David Wallace, professor of physics at the University of Edinburgh, until quite recently carried out research using the ICL

Distributed Array Processor, with 4,000 separate processing units and capable of parallel processing. He is now looking to use the currently most powerful computer in Britain, produced by Meiko and based on a parallel, communicating array of over 1,000 transputers – the computer-on-a-chip produced by Inmos.

So, up until quite recently, research routes have indeed been quite diverse with each distinct group struggling to identify with the others in terms of the validity or relevence of the work being carried out in their own field. Cognitive scientists studying the theory of thought processes at a conceptual level could not appreciate the value or relevence of taking into account work being carried out in neuroscience concerning the low level basic functions of communicating neurons in the brain. Similarly, the development, by artificial intelligence researchers, of computer systems capable of extremely high processing speeds, had set what would seem to be an unecessary objective in the light of what is known concerning the level of processing carried out by the brain.

Current research recognises the need for integration and the very real value of each field of research in the development process. This spirit of cooperation together with the advances made in computer technology enabling systems to be developed to match requirements, rather than models being specified to suit the restrictions of computer architectures, pave the way for exciting future developments.

Defining Areas of Research

Neural network research has grown up out of so many different disciplines, points of view and objectives and it is difficult to actually say that one area of research is called one thing and another is called something else. Throughout the rest of this book I deliberately try and avoid calling it anything but *Neural Network Research*. It seems that everyone has their own ideas about what they are doing and exactly what it's called, with each text book, research paper and researcher giving subtley different definitions. Now these differences may in some cases be so minor that they could be ignored, but it would be incorrect to classify an area of research into something which is not strictly appropriate.

We have already seen some definitions, for example, PDP, connectionism, neural computing, cognitive science, pattern recognition to name but a few. These are the definations received from Dr.David Touretzky and Prof.Igor Aleksander.

Dr.D.Touretzky (Personal communication) splits neural network research into the three main areas:

The first is pattern recognition in which a variety of networks such as back propagation and competitive learning, are applied to a number of pattern recognition problems. Sometimes better results are produced by these than by other pattern recognition techniques; in some cases, the results are not so good. An example of this class of models is the ALVINN autonomous vehicle navigation system developed by Dean Pomerleau. As Dr.Touretzky points out, these systems do not work even remotely like a brain, the only common feature being that the units are modelled, in a very abstract and shallow way, on real neurons.

The second area is called computational neuroscience. Researchers attempt to build physiologically accurate models of real neural circuits – for example, the simple computations such as those which occur in the sea slug Aplysia, or in the early stages of the mammalian visual system. This low-level circuit modelling has nothing to do with cognition but can produce some very interesting results.

The third major area is cognitive modelling, PDP or connectionism as it is sometimes called – a less well developed area than the other two fields. The area is in direct competition with AI research, and, incidentally, currently far behind what can be accomplished using symbolic AI systems. This deals with the problems of language and knowledge representation in neural networks, a subject about which virtually nothing is known. As Dr.Touretzky says, unlike the computational neuroscience group, connectionists cannot stick electrodes into people's heads to discover the representation of a noun; it is unknown where such things reside, or how they are encoded. He also says that it's not clear if noun phrases even exist in the brain – perhaps they are only in the imaginings of linguists.

Professor Igor Aleksander (Personal communication) makes the comment that to classify net research into pattern recognition, computational neural science and connectionism or cognitive modelling is: *"somewhat arbitrary and idiosyncratic."* He suggests that a clearer distinction is appearing between those who work purely on mathematical theory, those trying to make machines and those performing very close modelling of biological systems. Words like connectionism and pattern recognition do not map easily into these divisions and he finds that knowledge of Hopfield Nets are required in all three. (Boltzmann Machines and Hopfield Nets being what Hinton defined as connectionism). So he does not feel there are any clear distinctions although there is a lot of: *"jockeying around amongst authors to try and make their own interpretations of these definitions stick."*

Aleksander goes on to say that there is: *"a lot of politics in this business altogether and I only wish that authors and research workers would collaborate a little more and stop throwing mud at each other's work".*

In the next chapter we will look at the contribution that Hopfield made to the rekindling of interest in neural networks.

Hopfield's Contribution

In 1982, John Hopfield, of the California Institute of Technology, and a consultant to AT&T Bell Labs, inspired researchers with his work on neural networks. Hopfield worked with interconnected units, in simple non-linear devices, and the reason his work became so important was that he drew attention to the associative properties involved. He showed without doubt that networks of this type have *emergent* features. This means that when a network is built using the basic simple highly connected units defined by the brain, there are certain important things which occur simply as a result of this configuration, namely, associative memory and error correction.

Although his model has now been superseded by more powerful models containing hidden units, his ideas were an important milestone, particularly appealing to theoretical physicists because Hopfield used methods developed in statistical mechanics, for example, spin-glass models. (Wallace,D.J., 1988)

Before we can look at Hopfield's ideas of associative memory, we need to clarify the useful concept of an *energy minima*.

We saw in the example of the basic Hopfield model, that the network would generally produce one of the patterns it had been presented with, or learned, previously. These patterns can be thought of as stable states in that the network will settle into one of them and then not leave. Hopfield showed that the system would always enter one of these states given a particular input, and that the states can be created by changing the interconnection strengths between the units. We need to look at what this means, and a good analogy which is often used, is that of the *bumpy ball*.

Hopfield's model in Chapter 4 is very straightforward but has certain features that are not typical of most network models.

Symmetry: The weights in the network are symmetric. That is, $W_{ij}=W_{ji}$. We noted that this could lead to the negative of a black and white pattern being equivalent to the original input.

Update: The method used to adjust the weights is an asynchronous updating rule whereby a unit is picked at random and the sum of the weights on the connections is found. If this is greater than the threshold the unit is turned on, otherwise it is turned off.

Bumpy ball

Hopfield looked at the similarities and differences between biological processes and electronic computations and concluded that the brain is a biocomputer that performs collective computations, a view which is in opposition to the reductionist view of expressing everything in terms of its smallest components. Hopfield wanted to model real neural networks and so he looked to the brain as a model.

There are many ways to keep a computer on the correct path; conventional computers are directed using programs but this is not the case with neural networks. Such a collective system itself determines the overall path, not using a program, but by the structure and strength of the connections between the units. To explain how this can be, try to visualise that at any one time each neuron in the network will have an activity level, the sum of all these being the total energy level of the whole configuration. There will be times when there is a lot of activity going on, with many units all firing. There will also be times when very little is happening, with not many units firing. If we think of this in terms of the total activity or energy level for the whole network we could plot this on a graph and it may look like the diagram in Fig.9.1. Initially there will be a lot of activity in the network until it converges onto a solution and only a few units are firing.

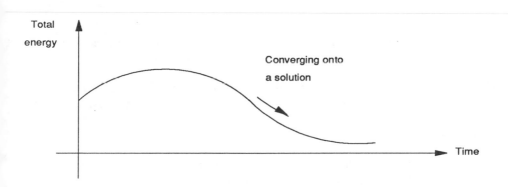

Fig.9.1: Converging onto a solution.

The network channels the decision path by pushing the overall activity level of the network back to a nearby valley in the computational energy, by minimising the activity level for the whole network. If you imagine a ball rolling across a bumpy surface and then coming to rest in one of the hollows, this is the way the system relaxes into a solution which is an energy minima.

It is the notion of the energy minima which provides a picture of how memory in the model is dealt with, where the valleys correspond to stored sets of associated information. This could represent an associative memory, which will be explained in more detail later, where the valleys correspond to stored sets of associated information. An item can be recalled by specifying just enough of the pattern so that the state of the network tends towards the complete minima, almost like placing the ball on the edge of a hollow and then allowing it to naturally roll the rest of the way down. If the circuit starts out with approximate or incomplete information the route is taken to the nearest valley which represents the complete information. This property also exhibits the natural error tolerance property of the network because if data is corrupted or noisy, we will still have partial input which will lead to the complete solution being recalled.

Each point on our bumpy surface represents an activity state for the whole network as shown in Fig.9.2.

Fig.9.2: The energy of the network, represented by the ball, settles into a local minima.

The point of this image, is that the hollows represent solutions to a problem, that is, the correct output for a given input, which is some point where the total activity for the network is at a minimum. By rolling into one of the hollows, the ball has found a solution, and tends to stay there.

An important feature of Hopfield's model was that the connections were symmetric, meaning that the connection between any two neurons in the network is equally strong in either direction. It is this symmetry which gives the network most of its decision making power.

Hopfield found that if the connections were symmetric, the computational energy surface would have well defined peaks and valleys. If the connections are not symmetric the paths taken by the system are not so well defined, because the peaks and valleys are not so clear. The ball is just rolling around on what could be thought of as a slightly wobbly surface, not going anywhere particularly useful and behaving in a generally random manner.

Basically, what Hopfield said, and was able to prove, was that a network structured according to his design would change state in such a manner that it never returned to a previous state. He demonstrated that the network as a whole possesses an energy level based on the activity levels of the individual neurons and that when the network changes state, the total activity remains the same or takes on a lower value. The total activity for the network cannot increase, but eventually finds some value below which it cannot fall, an energy minima. Hence the idea of a ball rolling along a bumpy surface; it settles or relaxes into a hollow which represents a stable state of lowest energy. There is a very good explanation and proof of this in Professor I.Aleksander's book (1990). It is possible to use this method to model large problems which have many solutions. For example AT&T Bell have developed a long distance telephone routing system.

There is one problem with this which needs to be overcome, which is shown in Fig.9.3.

Fig.9.3: The ball may not settle into the best minima

Fig.9.3 shows a ball which has come to rest in the nearest hollow, a stable state or energy minima. The only problem is that just a few bounces away is a deeper hollow, which represents a lower place for the ball to settle, and a better one, if the lowest level is the objective. Now if we say that the lower the state that the ball settles the better the solution to the problem, this could be a major drawback to Hopfield's idea. We have a solution, but it is not the best one and as we want to get as close to the optimal solution as possible the potential that the network will settle into a local minima as opposed to the best global minima, is something which needs a lot of thought. After all, we could end up with a situation like the one shown in Fig.9.4.

One way of getting around this problem is to introduce a bit of *noise* into the network. You can think of this as giving the ball a litle jiggle as it rolls around, almost like giving it more minimas to consider before settling.

Methods towards solving this problem have been researched by Geoffrey Hinton and Terry Sejnowski (1986) using a Boltzmann machine described in Chapter 10.

Fig.9.4: This is a situation which is highly undesirable.

As Professor Aleksander points out, a network is only going to be useful if the stable states that exist can be selected or *created* in some way. This can be carried out in two ways: The first is to calculate the connection strengths necessary in order to achieve the desired stable states. The second method is to train the network, in which case it is the network itself which, with the use of an appropriate learning rule, makes the necessary adjustments to the weights in order to achieve the stable states that the trainer requires.

The problem with manually calculating the weight requirements for stable states is that there may be other stable states which have not been anticipated and which may be equally likely to occur. Hopfield did not originally discuss any solution to this problem which has been looked into by Hinton.

Hopfield also noticed that correct conclusions within a network could be achieved with only partial input. This cannot be achieved using traditional digital systems and he concluded that valid neural network systems may not be strongly linked with Boole's ideas of logic at all. This idea of the network being able to cope with errors in the input data, is what is called an emergent feature of the net. In other words, it is not deliberately built into the design, but arises out of the basic design itself. Another such emergent feature is *associative memory*.

Associative Memory

Much of the great interest in Hopfield's work came from the realisation that such networks had a natural feature, called an *emergent feature* of associative memory. So let us look at what this means.

Associative memory, or content addressable memory, is a useful application for collective systems and differs quite significantly from conventional methods of storing data. A conventional computer stores data in physical locations, on a disk for example, and the method of access is to use an address which tells the processor where the information is stored but tells nothing about the data itself. When you are staggering through the card index system in the local library, the location of the book is indexed under author and sometimes subject as well if you are lucky. If you just know that the book was published in 1983 and you are not sure of the author's name, there is generally very little, far short of looking through every entry, that you can do to find the book. A far better system exists in the Library of Congress in Washington DC. All that was necessary was to type in a word, say *neural networks,* and the system would throw up an index of every publication including magazine and newspaper articles, research papers and books, which made any reference at all to the keyword. Then you could actually view the article on screen, or get the location, usually on microfiche, and take a hard copy. There followed a very interesting debate about this system because the library receives 500 new items each day, and we wondered how many hundreds of people must be kept busy keeping this incredible system up to date. Our memories work in a similar manner to the Library of Congress system (although perhaps not so efficiently!) in that we can retrieve complete information from partially complete data, using information as addresses, being associated to other bits of information. Fruit flies and garden slugs have associative memories, and as these creatures only possess very simple nervous systems this implies that the feature is a spontaneous result of the connected neurons themselves.

The difference between the system at the Library of Congress and the one used by our brains is that the former is a purpose designed associative memory. Someone has to laboriously sit down, type in all the keywords and cross reference all the indicators, and the system has been designed and programmed in order to display the responses that it does. This is not the case with a brain; the feature of being able to extract complete data when only presented with a part of it, and to display the properties of associative memory emerge naturally from the design of the brain. In the same way, neural networks use associative memory and are also tolerant of noisy or even faulty data, error correction being an automatic process, or emergent feature. Hopfield encouraged engineers to look into these emergent properties as many creators of systems are naturally suspicious of features which are present but have not been specifically put there.

It was found in 1984 that these sorts of networks are very adept at solving optimisation problems where a large number of constraints have to be satisfied simultaneously. One classic example of this is the travelling salesman problem which involves a salesman who has to visit a number of cities. The network has to find the best route for him to take given that he visits each city once and returns to his starting point (Hopfield 1985). This was carried out using a simulation of an assembly of 100-1000 interconnected neurons.

The simulation showed that a simple network of 900 neurons could find a good solution to a problem involving 30 cities in a single convergence, the time taken being about 0.2 seconds. Although the network did not find the absolutely optimal solution, it always found one in the top $1/10^{23}$, which is one of 10^7 out of a possible 10^{30} solutions. We can compare this result to a microcomputer which may be operating about 10^5 times faster than this simple network and containing 100,000 more transistors, which would come up with a comparable result in a similar time space. Hopfield does not say how long it would take the microcomputer to come up with the best solution, which could take longer. This may no really be relevant; for a simple network which simply adjusts connections we have a good solution which can be applied to problems of perception where a vast amount of information is processed very rapidly to give us an impression of what is happening.

James Anderson and Teuvo Kohonen (1976) developed mathematical models of associative memory, the requirement being to find the best possible solution for a set of information. For example, descriptions of all your friends may include hair colour, height, habits, sex etc. A person's associative memory will produce the best solution for the information available, as with the patterns used in the Hopfield model in Chapter 4. The associative memories developed required only local information about two related units, in order to modify the strength of the connections between them. A principle which coincides with the idea of Hebbs that memory is stored in the synapses and changes are effected at a local not global level.

Problems

One of the problems with Hopfield's model was that of false minima, energy wells that have crept in and are not wanted. This can be avoided by specifying further conditions on the network, but involves an impractical number if the model is going to be of a reasonable size. For a 100 neuron net you would need to have 2^{100}, and that is not a very large network (Aleksander 1990).

Hopfield also did not say much about the network being able to learn the stable states through training. The Delta rule is an example of a learning rule which creates stable states and reduces the energy of a state to its minimum.

Another problem is that of storage capacity. Abu-Mustafa and St.Jaques have deduced that a Hopfield net of N nodes can store a maximum of N N-bit patterns as stable wells. This is quite low and is a direct consequence of the ability of the net to correct errors. There is always a price to be paid. Hopfield's net also cannot achieve solutions to the problems we looked at in Chapter 5. All these problems are serious but able to be overcome by the use of hidden units.

In the next chapter we will look at how the Boltzmann machine was used to overcome some of the problems cited here.

Dreaming

Because the brain is a finite system, there is a need to optimise the available storage, and dreaming is thought to be used in humans to sift through the events of the day and literally sort it all out – maximising the efficient use of the storage and keeping the memory organised and free of superfluous information.

With this in mind, Hopfield and Tank (1987) noticed that some circuits also required this periodic *cleaning-up* process. Special memory circuits were being used which mimicked association processors, numbers being stored as stable energy states in a network of artificial neurons and the network being able to recall a 10-digit number from a partial input of just two. It was found that the memory began to take different times to recall different numbers, the more recently trained numbers being recalled more rapidly than previously trained values. The more values presented for training to the network, the more time it was taking to recall values and in addition, the network was beginning to throw up spurious values which it had not learnt. It was starting to make them up. It was found that by mapping the surface with minima which had not been learnt by the network, and adding a small amount of extra energy into the circuit in order to juggle it around a bit and bombard it with associations that it was not programmed to retrieve, the network would settle into a deep energy minimisation. Once this had been done the network responded properly with no spurious memories, and with equal time responses. This process was likened to dreaming. By inducing random memories into the network it enabled sleep to be simulated and for the network to clean-up its memories.

Similarily Carlos Tapang (Johnson, 1990) of Systonics Systems says of his chips that: *"they must sleep"*, needing about eight hours sleep after being active for 24 hours in order to refresh. The sleep is simulated by allowing it to run with no input. A special circuit on the chip senses the need to *dream* and triggers the sleep mode. Tapang says he is wary of the comparison with sleep and dreaming because his circuits are so much simpler than real neural networks in the brain.

The Boltzmann Machine

Relaxation

In the last chapter we discussed how the total activity for a network can be thought of as settling into a stable state which is a solution to the problem under consideration. This is Hopfield's notion of energy minima, and can be represented by thinking of a ball rolling across a bumpy surface and coming to rest in one of the hollows. This is an emergent feature of the design of the net itself, not something that has to be specified by the designer. One of the major drawbacks of such a concept is that the ball may settle into a hollow which is not the best one; there may be a deeper hollow representing a better solution. One way of overcoming this problem was to introduce a bit of noise into the network, giving the ball an extra push so that it is more likely to find the best hollow in which to come to rest.

This method is also referred to as *relaxation*, specifically applying to a situation where many weak constraints need to be satisfied simultaneously.

It was Hinton, Sejnowski and Williams, working on artificial vision problems in 1986, who came up with this very solution to the problem, calling their model the Boltzmann machine. It uses binary processing units which are updated using probabilities. The internal state of the machine tends to fluctuate even for constant input, this being controlled by a temperature parameter. It is these fluctuations which allow the system to escape from any local minima. The units are symmetrically connected which enables an energy state for the system to be defined and also ensures that the system will relax into a state of equilibrium which minimises the energy, as in Hopfield's model.

Probability

It may be just as well to make a quick detour here for those who are not familiar with the idea of a probability. Basically, when we talk of probability, this is a numerical value which represents the chance of something happening. For example, when you toss a coin you would expect it to land either heads or tails (let us say that there is such a small chance of it landing on its side that this possibility can be ignored). For a fair coin, the chance of either of these events occurring is equal. Now, the total probabilities for all the possible outcomes for an event adds up to 1. So if we write the probability of a head showing as being P(H) and for a tail showing as P(T) we can say that:

P(H) + P(T) = 1   all possible outcomes sum to 1
P(H) = P(T)   if the coin is fair or unbiased
P(H) = P(T) = 0.5 both are equal and add up to 1

Boltzmann

Ludwig Boltzmann, at the end of the 19th century, found that gas molecules have random motion, and that the energy they possess is directly related to temperature. This has also been found to be true for any electronic circuitry which carries a current – the higher the temperature, the more *noise* or energy is introduced into the circuitry. Think of the hiss found on a radio; if reception is good the wave form will be smooth, if it is poor a certain amount of wiggle is apparent and the result is the radio program, but accompanied by a hiss.

Fig.10.1. Smooth wave form and wave form with noise.

Hinton used the name Boltzmann because of the similarity in concepts and called the amount of wiggle introduced into the network, the *temperature*, in line with Boltzmann's theory. If the temperature is zero, we have a network which is the same as Hopfield's model. If the temperature is increased an amount of uncertainty will be introduced into the activation function. The point of this is that the ball bounces away from the local minima. However when things are carried out like this the ball bounces around but does not settle because it is full of energy. To overcome this, Hinton suggested *cooling* the network while it was running; in this way the ball bounces about quite energetically and is brought to a halt by diminishing its energy so that it will settle into a hollow.

This concept of starting with a high energy level or temperature and then reducing it so that the network will gradually find a suitable state to settle into is called *simulated annealing*.

The *annealing* part is a term used in metallurgy where a metal is heated until it is nearly at melting point. The temperature is then reduced, which serves to erradicate any local stresses due to high energy, which may later lead to metal failure. Similarly, the annealing concept used with the network serves to get rid of the possibility of the network settling into a local rather than an optimal mimima.

It is interesting to note that this is the same as a Perceptron with symmetrical weights if there are no hidden units and the temperature is reduced to zero.

Noise in a Hopfield Net

In the Hopfield model in Chapter 4, a unit had an activation level found by summing the total input received from all the other units. The unit would then fire if that total was above a certain threshold limit, otherwise it would become, or remain inactive.

The way noise is introduced into this model is to make the firing mechanism a little less clear cut, not so precise if you like. Hinton suggested that an element of probability should be introduced so that the unit had a probabilty of firing when the input was within a given range, rather than the process being an absolute certainty. The two methods could be as shown in Fig.10.2 In the model the unit takes on binary values of 0 if it is not firing, 1 if it is.

In Fig.10.2, a slope has been introduced into the graph. As the amount of input received nears the threshold value, there is a probability that the unit will fire. Hinton likened this to a function which had emerged as a result of Boltmann's physics, which possesed the same properties as shown. The mathematics of this function is explained at the end of this chapter and can be avoided if required.

The Boltzmann firing probability function allows a jump **UP** in the energy values to be achieved. If you recall, Hopfield's model only allowed the network to jiggle into a state which was equal to or less than the current energy state. This function now allows us to give it a little shake and climb a few small obstacles before settling. Strictly speaking, the function has the property that the larger the difference between the current energy state and a lower one, the larger the probability that the network will dive into the lower state. Also, the larger the difference between the current energy state and a higher one, the smaller the probability that the network will jump up into the higher state. So the higher the jump up, the less likely it will do it, the further the jump down, the more likely it is.

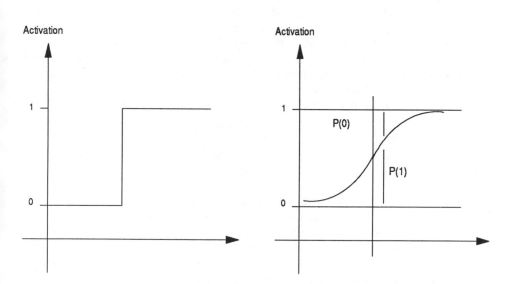

Fig.10.2: The left hand graph shows the activation level changing instantly from 0 to 1 when the threshold value is reached. The right hand graph has an element of probability. P(1) is the probability that the activation level will be 1, P(0) is the probability that the activation level will be 0. There are no absolute certainties, however at a given point it may be more likely that the activation level will be either 0 or 1.

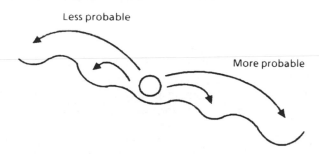

Fig.10.3: The ball is less likely to roll upwards than it is to roll downwards into an energy minima which could be an optimal solution.

The probabilty of the network being in any particular state at any particular time can be worked out using a Markov Chain, which is simply a table of the probabilities showing all the possible outcomes – a very useful method of analysing neural networks. Once this has been accomplished it is possible to show what happens once the temperature (not actual temperature, but energy level) of the network is reduced –

the annealing process. Hinton defined *thermal equilibrium* as being a state the network has reached when, although the units still change state, there is very little change in the probabilities calculated using the Markov Chain technique. The state of the network will only change when the temperature changes, so when it has fully cooled, i.e. reached a stable state, there will be no more changes. It was shown that if the Boltzmann function is applied repeatedly to the units, the system will reach this state of equilibrium. When this cooling is complete, the network will have settled into one of the stable states, the probability of which state it has settled into depending on the energy of the states. Now, as the lowest state (the best solution) will have the lowest energy state, it is most probable that the network will settle into this, the optimal state. It was also shown that the higher the initial temperature then the faster the network will approach a state of equilibrium.

It is really quite a remarkable thing that our hypothetical ball rolling around, and being given little pushes now and then, is actually going to end up in the deepest hollow. Of course, this is not a certainty, but it does have the highest probability of occurring. The chances are that if it does not end up in the best hollow, it will find its way to a hollow which is not quite as deep but not far off, a solution for the network which is not optimal, but which nevertheless is a good solution.

Unfortunately this method does not get rid of all the spurious local minima which may have been introduced accidentally into the network when the connections and weights were being adjusted during training. This means that during training, as the probability of ending up in one of these local minima depends upon the energy levels involved, careful control must be exercised over the energy states of the minima in the system.

Hidden Units

Minsky and Papert pointed out the deficiencies of the one-layer perceptron in no uncertain terms, but they also said that a perceptron which had a layer of hidden units could solve problems with difficult learning if only it could be worked out how to train them. Fig.10.4 is an example of a network with hidden units.

Hidden units are used in a network to represent complex relationships which may not be expressable, as in the case of a model with no hidden units, in terms of the pairs of connections which exist between input and output units. The visible units are used to specify the input and output patterns and during training, the model will build up its own internal representations of the training input within the hidden units. Having hidden units is obviously going to increase the power of a model simply because of the number of alternatives that will then be available to the training process, rather than a one-to-one mapping directly between input and output units.

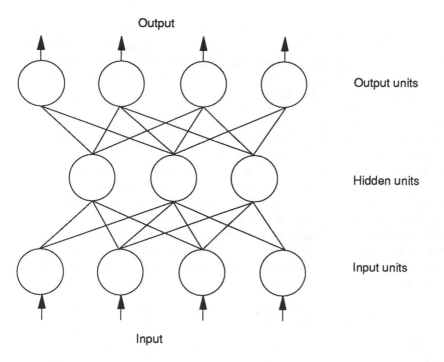

Output

Output units

Hidden units

Input units

Input

Fig.10.4: This is one possible network configuration with a single layer of hidden units between the input and output layers.

The problem with hidden units is that they are literally hidden between the input and output units. You can present a network with an input pattern and see what the result is in terms of an output pattern, but what goes on in the hidden units is a mystery. The only way of carrying out any kind of analysis at all was simply to assess whether or not the output was as required.

Training the Boltzmann Machine

Hinton and Sejnowski used hidden units in their Boltzmann machine and got around the problem of training by defining that not all the units needed to be in the training set, only the visible ones; the hidden ones could be omitted. They defined that the way to achieve the correct result for a given input was to control the energy levels of the states of the network in order that they are the same as the probability of their occurrence during training. In other words, the desired probabilities are equal to the actual probabilities.

For the Boltzmann machine, the training patterns were defined in terms of the visible units only, the hidden units not being specified. The training set can be viewed as an *environment* which must be absorbed by the network in order that, when it is running freely, it is able to reproduce it at its visible units. Hidden units give an extra parameter which can be involved in the generation of such an environment. The tuning of a network to produce the correct results is very tricky to actually carry out, after all there will be a lot of combinations and subtle adjustments which can make a lot of difference to the final outcome. Which change to opt for can be a matter of trial and error – the results of any amendment will by definition ripple through the network and cause many other alterations.

Hinton and Sejnowski tackled this problem by looking at the difference between the actual probabilities and the desired probabilities of the network during training and defined a measure of the distance between the pairs of values, which could be thought of as an error. When the two values are the same this error will be zero, much like the thinking behind the Delta rule in Chapter 6. The input to the network, achieved by clamping input units to some particular value, was not a deterministic mapping but a probability function in that if a unit received many positive inputs there would be a high probability of it firing. There was also no simple one-to-one mapping for input and output, as in some models where the network is presented with the input and the desired output and the weights are then adjusted to ensure that the two are linked and can be duplicated later.

Learning was a complex two-phase process. In the first phase, the patterns were randomly presented to the network, by clamping both input and output units to the required values, and a simple Hebbian learning rule used to adjust the weights accordingly.

i.e. $\Delta W_{ij} = da_i a_j$

Δ is called *delta* and signifies a small change

d is the amount of change to be made

As the activity levels take on only the values 0 for non-firing and 1 for firing, the weight is only incremented by an amount d when both a_i and a_j are firing, otherwise it is left unchanged.

In the second phase the network is allowed to run freely and the annealing process then enables it to approach thermal equilibrium. The system is run for a fixed time at thermal equilibrium with no inputs at all, in which case some units will continue to fire because of the stochastic nature of the system. An anti-Hebbian learning rule is then used:

i.e. $\Delta W_{ij} = -da_i a_j$

which states that those units which fire most often are supressed and become less likely to fire. This in essence, removes the effect that the connections have and leaves only the performance due to the environment on the network.

This turns out to be a powerful learning procedure which enables partial patterns to be completed and retrieved by the network.

An important result of their definition was that in order to reduce this error value, which is the difference between the required and actual values, only the weights which are local to the unit need to be known and updated. The changes to the weights are then made in such a way as to reduce the error. When the error is zero for every pair in the network it has been trained successfully. This method of changing the weights in order to minimise the error was found to be a *gradient descent* optimisation problem, which means that as the weights are changed, you literally slide towards a value such that the error difference can be minimised. One drawback is that the method may also create spurious local minima, although it will, having created them, reduce the possibility that they will have lower energies than the trained ones and so the network will be less likely to slide into them.

Applications

This learning procedure, using simple pairwise connections has been used for speech recognition (Prager, Harrison & Fallside, 1986), but it is considerably slower than the popular back propagation learning rule, described in Chapter 11, because of the time that the network takes to reach a state of equilibrium. However, a special purpose VLSI chip has been designed to speed up the learning process (Alspector & Allen, 1988). There are also problems with the network which can be likened to the effect demonstrated if sand is sprinkled onto a sheet of metal and a violin bow drawn across it. The sand clusters into patterns at the places where the metal vibrates the least. In a similar way the network tends to develop units which are either always off or always on. In vision, a major problem is that of interpreting a 2-dimensional image in terms of its 3-dimensional actual image. This is a problem which needs additional constraints to determine the depth and orientation, a task which the human visual system is very adept at carrying out. The Boltzmann machine has been used for a number of constraint satisfaction problems in vision. For example, ground separation analysis (Sejnowski and Hinton, 1987; Kienker et al., 1986) generalisations have been successfully applied to image restoration (Geman & Geman, 1984) and it has been used in binocular depth perception (Divko & Schulten, 1986).

Hardware

One advantage of the Boltzmann machine, and an interesting feature is that it is very straightforward, relatively speaking to apply it to a chip with dedicated hardware connections. The annealing process can be carried out very rapidly using analog circuitry and research is being carried out into the development of a chip which is expected to run about 1 million times faster than a simulation on a VAX. This is really going to make a difference in terms of practical applications.

Mathematics of Noise in a Hopfield

Just to recap:

U_i a general unit, where i can take any allowed value
$a_i(t)$ activation for unit U_i at time t
f_i function for unit U_i output
$O_i(t)$ output for unit U_i at time t = $f_i(a_i(t))$
W_{ji} the weight between units U_j and U_i (the effect unit U_i has on unit U_j)
$O_i(t)W_{ji}$ the input received by unit U_j from unit U_i at time t
net_j the net input for unit U_j at time t = $\Sigma\, O_i(t)W_{ji}$
F_i the activation function for unit U_i
$a_i(t+1)$ the activation for unit U_i = $F_i(a_i(t),net_i)$
T_i the threshold for unit U_i

Activity levels

The output for unit U_i is 1 if:

$$\Sigma W_{ij}a_j > T_i \text{ summed over j}$$

otherwise it is 0

We will define the activation level, A_i, for unit U_i as:

$$A_i = \Sigma\, W_{ij}a_j - T_i \text{ summed over j}$$

Boltzmann Probability Function

The Boltzmann probability function for unit U_i will give the probability of the unit firing. This will depend on the activation level and is written as follows:

$$1/(1+e^{-A_i/T_i})$$

This is really quite straightforward if we look at what it all means.

The constant e is a special mathematical shorthand term which is usually referred to in the language Basic as EXP or something very similar.

EXP(x) in Basic means the value e^x, whatever x may be.

This function has certain properties, namely that as x gets larger, the value of e^x starts to get very large very quickly and tends towards infinity. This is an exponential fuction.

A good analogy to this is compound interest, or an unrestricted rabbit population!

e^{-x} is the same as $1/e^x$

This is true for all numbers, so, for example, $2^{-1} = 1/2$, or $3^{-2} = 1/3^2 = 1/9$.

e^{-x} is known as an asymptotic function – which means that as x gets larger, the value tends towards zero.

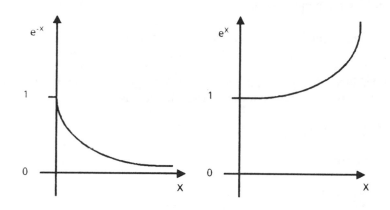

Fig.10.5: The left hand graph shows x plotted against e^{-x}. This is an asymptotic function, as x gets larger then e^{-x} tends towards zero. The right hand graph shows x plotted against e^x. This is an exponential function, as x gets larger, e^x gets very large very quickly and tends towards infinity.

In the Boltzmann function, x in e^{-x} takes the value of A_i/T_i and is written as:

e^{-A_i/T_i}

If $A_i=6$ and $T_i=3$, this would be $e^{-6/3}$, i.e. e^{-2}. The logarithm of this 0.1353.

The Boltzmann function is used to calculate P(1), the probability of a unit firing, and P(0), the probability of a unit not firing. This is from the unit's activation and threshold values.

$P(1)_i = 1/(1+e^{-A_i/T_i})$ The probability that unit U_i will fire – have a value of 1.
$P(0)_i = 1 - P(1)_i$ The probability that unit U_i will not fire – have a value of 0.

The equation for P(0) can be seen to be true as any unit can only be in one of two states, 0 or 1, so the total of the probabilities must be 1.

Probability of a Unit Changing

Because only one node can change at any one time, if there are N nodes the probability of node U_i changing will be:

$P(1)_i/N$ The probability unit U_i will fire.

$P(0)_i/N$ The probability unit U_i will not fire.

This can be written more formally as:

$$[a_iP(1)_i+(1-a_i)P(0)_i]/N \;\; = \;\; P(1)_i/N \quad \text{when} \;\; a_i = 1$$
$$= \;\; P(0)_i/N \quad \text{when} \;\; a_i = 0$$

The probability of a particular unit U_i not changing is what is left after all the changes have been accounted for and can be written as:

$$1- \sum [a_iP(1)_i+(1-a_i)P(0)_i]/N$$

Let us make some more definitions:

V   The number of visible units.

S_n One of N training patterns. The set of which is:
            $S_1,S_2,...S_n,...S_N$
            The probabilities that the network will be in state S_i at time t is $P_i(t)$.

$P^+(S_n)$ The desired probabilities for the training patterns. The set of which will be:
            $P^+(S_1),P^+(S_2),...P^+(S_n),...P^+(S_N)$

$P^-(S_n)$ The actual probabilities for the training patterns. The set of which will be:
            $P^-(S_1),P^-(S_2),...P^-(S_n),...P^-(S_N)$

When the network has been correctly trained for the set of training patterns, the actual probabilities will be the same as the desired probabilities. That is, $P^+(S_n)=P^-(S_n)$ for all values of n from 1 to N.

Measure of error

The measure of the error for the whole network is given as:

$G = \quad \sum P^+(S_a)\ln[P^+(S_a)/P^-(S_a)]$

> In this, ln means the natural logarithm and has the property that $\ln(1)=0$. This means that if the actual and desired values are the same the quantity within the brackets will be equal to 1 and as $\ln(1)=0$ that pair will contribute 0 to the total error of G.

The first quantity $P^+(S_a)$ which multiplies the ln value will ensure that the most frequently occurring states will have a greater effect on G.

G >=0   At all times.

G=0   When the actual value is the desired value and the network has been trained.

So the idea is to minimise the value of G.

Rate of change

The rate of change C, of G when a weight is changed is given as:

$$C = -1/T[P^+_{ij} - P^-_{ij}]$$

where: T   is the temperature

P^+_{ij} is the average probability of the units on eachside of W_{ij} both firing with a 1 when the net is being trained

P^-_{ij} is the average probability of the units on each side of W_{ij} both firing with a 1 when the net is free running

Note: It is important to note from this that all we need is local information.

If C>0   The weight is increased.
If C<0   The weight is decreased.

Important things

In order to reduce the value of G, which is the error we calculated for the whole net, we only need to know local information in order to alter a particular weight. We are aiming for G to be zero in which case the net has learned the set of input patterns.

This process also applies to both visible and hidden units.

A summary of the training procedure is as follows:

❑ Clamp pattern at visible units onto input and output units, one by one according to the probabilities that they will occur when the net is free runnning.

❑ During clamping, noting the probabilities that both ends of the net are 1.

❑ Let the net run free, again note the probabilities that both ends of the net are 1.

❑ Compare the last two results and adjust the weights to bring the results closer together.

❑ Repeat until the actual values are the same as the desired values i.e. G=0. Hinton's theory shows how to reduce the weights. This has been shown to be a gradient descent optimisation problem and is the major difficulty in the machine. Although the process controls the energy of a given set of states, it does not remove any extra local minima but simply reduces the possibility that they have lower energies than the required minima.

11

Back Propagation

Simple two-layer associative networks with no hidden units were by now well understood and have proved to be useful in a variety of applications such as those which require the mapping of similar input patterns onto similar output patterns. This enables such networks to make pretty good generalisations and to classify new patterns fairly well.

The problem arises when the input and output patterns are very different so that such networks, with no hidden units which enable an internal representation of the input pattern to be made, are unable to cope. In the XOR example, it was the patterns which overlap the least which were supposed to generate the same output pattern.

The perceptron convergence rule, or the variation of this called the Delta rule, described in Chapter 6, provided a guaranteed learning rule which could be used with simple networks, but no such rule existed for models with hidden units.

One response to this (and for others see Chapter 8) was the development of the Generalised Delta Rule, or method of Back propagation (Rumelhart et al.,1986) - the most popular learning algorithm today. This algorithm applied to a loop-free network, that is, no feed back, and hidden units.

The rule was formally described by Rumelhart, Hinton and Williams who said that the problem with the perceptron was that it lacked layers and so had to rely on the external input for similarities, whereas with internal units, these similarities can be identified and represented by the network. Similar methods were almost simultaneously defined by David Parker in 1985 as *learning-logic,* and Yann Le Cun, also in 1985.

The rule repeatedly adjusts the weights in order to minimise the error between the actual and required output. Hidden units, which are not included in the training set, in that they are not input or output, then represent the important features in the training set and any regularities are represented in their interactions. If there are no hidden units it is interesting to note that the rule reduces to the Delta rule. We will look at the mathematics behind the rule, but before we do, we will look at exactly how it works and some of the outstanding serious problems it has been capable of overcoming. Remember, these were the problems which led to the demise of neural networks as a serious contender for neural research in the eyes of many after the publication of Perceptrons in 1969.

General model for simple form

The simplest form of the learning rule is for a layered feed-forward network, which looks like a multi-layered perceptron network. The input units comprise the first layer; there are then a number of intermediate layers containing hidden units, the final layer being the output layer. The number of layers is not important, the important thing is that every unit can only send output to units in layers above its own, and receive input from units which are in layers below its own. One version of the network is set out in Fig.11.1. Remember that this is not the only solution, there are many possible connectivity patterns.

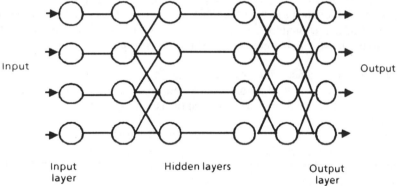

Input   Output

Input   Hidden layers   Output
layer   layer

Fig.11.1: A layered feed–forward network.

There are no connections within the layers and connections between can skip a layer.

The rule has the same principles as the Delta rule in that we will have an actual and desired output value. We will also have an error value for the whole network calculated for all the set of input patterns.

The activity level for a unit is determined from the input it receives from the other units. This is weighted and compared against a threshold value. A unit will fire when the inputs received by that unit exceed some threshold value.

The amount of error is found by looking at the output for a given input pattern, then comparing this actual value against the desired value. This will give us a value for the error for that particular pattern. These are combined to find the total error for the network.

The rule has a two-stage learning process involving two passes: a forward one and a backward one.

Forward Pass

For each input/output pair, the input pattern is applied by setting the states of the input units. A forward route is taken through the network and the total input to a unit is defined as usual to be the total of all the inputs from the other units. The activity levels for all the units in the network are calculated in turn using the computed activity levels of units in previous levels. As there are no connections within layers, all units in a layer can have their states updated in parallel. The layers are dealt with in sequential order, that is, one after the other, and the output for each unit is calculated and then used as input for subsequent units in the next layer. Finally, at the output layer we have a result which, in the majority of cases, will not be the one we are looking for. Next comes the backward pass through the network, phase two.

Backward pass

In phase two, the process is reversed, starting at the output layer and, armed with the actual and required output patterns, an error value can be found for each output unit. The procedure is worked backwards through the layers and the error is used to apply the appropriate weight changes to each unit in the network, the same sort of principle as used for the Delta rule. As the units in a layer send output only to the units in the layer above, the weights can be re-adjusted and the changes rippled back through the network.

The hidden units act as partial definers of the input data before the output layer makes a final decision, and are said to create *internal representations* of the data. It should be stressed that the hidden units are thus not trained by the *teacher* but make their own patterns, the result of which can only be seen by the response of the output units. A bit like the brain really, we know what goes in and what comes out but what happens in the middle is quite a puzzling mystery.

So to summarise the process. On the first time through, the forward pass, the inputs produce an output, the second phase. The backward pass then looks at the errors and adjusts the weights in order to bring the result closer to the desired output.

Gradient Descent

The total error for the whole network can be minimised using a method called *gradient descent,* (not to be confused with the Hopfield energy minima), which involves applying a computation to each weight in the network in turn from the bottom up as described above. The simplest method is to change the weights by an amount proportional to the accumulated error as you go through the backward pass. This method will not converge as rapidly as the alternative which is to save up all the changes as you go, and then change the weights at the end. The former method is easier to use and to implement on parallel hardware, no memory being required to remember the accumulated values.

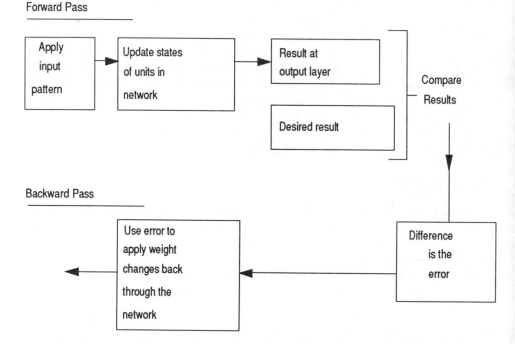

Fig.11.2: This shows the stages of the forward and backward pass for the method of back propagation.

Being a hill descending procedure, like Hopfield's net, this can also become stuck in local minima which do not provide the solution to the problem. To avoid confusion with our Hopfield bumpy ball analogy, I will refer to this as the *ravine and donkey* analogy. This particular problem can be overcome if the problem is restarted for different initial weight values so that the correct solution will eventually emerge as being dominant. Of this problem, Rumelhart et al. said that experience with many tasks has shown that the network very rarely gets stuck in poor local minima that are significantly worse than the global minimum. So the solution may not be the best, but it will be a good one.

Learning rate

Another ravine problem is exactly that, because for a number of applications, rather than having neat little hollows representing solutions, we end up with long, deep, gradually sloping ravines. These have an optimal point, that is, a lowest point which represents the best solution and it is a matter of deciding which way to take to get there. Do we push the donkey straight over the edge taking small, tenuous steps towards the lowest point, or do we head for the bottom and gallop along the flatter base, taking the risk that our donkey may career up one of the sides and disappear into another ravine? A compromise of the two is to head for the valley bottom, which is optimal because we can move faster using larger steps, and increase our speed as we go. However, we must keep a firm check on the speed of the donkey, each time only increasing speed by a smaller amount than the time before. The size of the steps taken is referred to as the *learning rate* and needs to be chosen in such a way that ensures the most rapid learning without the values oscillating wildly. One way to accomplish this is to include what is called a *momentum term* which is our check to make sure the donkey is not increasing speed too much at one time.

There is also the problem, inherent in any system, of how long it will take for learning to take place and whether or not it can occur in a reasonable time. These are questions which can be answered to some extent by looking at simulations which have been carried out.

The mathematics involved in this are at the end of this chapter. It is worth noting that some of the weights can be fixed so that their values do not change during the backward pass.

Problems solved

Simulations

Rumelhart et al.(1986) used simulations with an activation rule similar to the one used for the Boltzmann machine, which they call a *logical* activation function - a continuous nonlinear function. A value similar to a threshold is also included which they call a *bias*.

In most of the simulations the momentum term was set to be 0.9 although they did find that the same results could be obtained by setting the momentum term to 0 and reducing the size of the learning rate. So having a donkey which takes large steps but under quite tight control, is equivalent to having the donkey take small steps with no control. However, the difference is that the system learns faster when the values for both are larger, so it is indeed quicker to have good control over a galloping donkey.

Solution of XOR problem

This classic problem, as shown in Chapter 5, cannot be solved using networks with the input layer directly connected to an output layer. However, with hidden units, a solution can be found as shown in Fig.11.3.

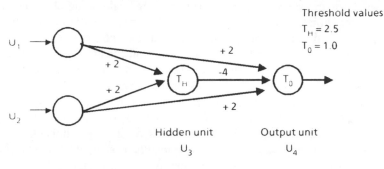

The result will be:

U_1 U_2	U_3	$)T_H$	U_4	$)T_0$	Output
0 0	0	no	0	no	0
0 1	+ 2	no	+ 2	yes	1
1 0	+ 2	no	+ 2	yes	1
1 1	+ 4	yes	0	no	0

Fig.11.3: This network is one of many solutions to the XOR problem using one hidden unit and is explained in detail in the text below. The numbers on the connections are the strengths or weights.

Fig.11.3 shows the responses of the units to the inputs (0,0), (0,1), (1,0) and (1,1). For the first example, (0,0), the input to the hidden unit from U_1 and U_2 does not exceed the threshold for the hidden unit of 2.5 as neither are activated. The hidden unit U_3 is therefore not activated and provides no input to the output unit. T_0 receives no input and therefore is not activated giving an output of 0. For the second example, (0,1), the input to the hidden unit from U_1 and U_2 totals +2 but does not exceed the threshold for the hidden unit of 2.5, so U_3 is not activated. T_0 receives input only from U_2 of +2. This exceeds the threshold of 1.0 and so T_0 is activated giving an output of 1. Working through the other examples we find we have the required output, namely that the output is 1 when one or other of the units, but not both, are firing.

Rumelhart et al. ran the XOR problem many times and with a couple of exceptions the network was always able to solve it in some way. The solution above was determined after 558 sweeps through the network, with a learning rate of 0.5. In this particular example the hidden unit and the output units all have a positive bias which means that they are on unless specifically turned off and the hidden unit turns on if either input is on.

The problem has been solved hundreds of times and in only two cases was a local minimum encountered. They conclude that the frequency of such an occurrence is quite rare and only one other situation in many hundreds of various problems was encountered.

The general result for the number of presentations that needed to be made to the system, or the time to learning, was that the more hidden units there were, the smaller this time became. Be careful not to confuse this with the learning rate. Some results are shown in Figure 11.4.

Hidden units	Learning rate	Number of presentations (time to learning)
2	0.25	245
32	0.25	120
8	0.1	450
8	0.75	68

Fig.11.4: The relationship between the number of hidden units in a network, the learning rate and the time to learning. Note that the inclusion of more hidden units does not necessarily significantly reduce the time to learning rate, the learning rate also plays an important role. If the learning rate was greater than about 0.75 then this was found to lead to unstable behaviour.

Parity

Parity is another classic problem. The output required is 1 if there is an odd number of 1s in the input pattern and 0 otherwise. The XOR problem is in fact an example of this parity problem with input patterns of size two. The basic problem is that similar patterns require different answers, and of course the simple perceptron models are good at mapping input patterns onto similar output patterns.

Rumelhart et al. tried a number of input patterns ranging in size from 2 to 8. In an architecture with hidden units they say you need at least N hidden units to solve a pattern of length N. It was found that the hidden units self-organise in such a way so they can count the number of input units involved in a pattern.

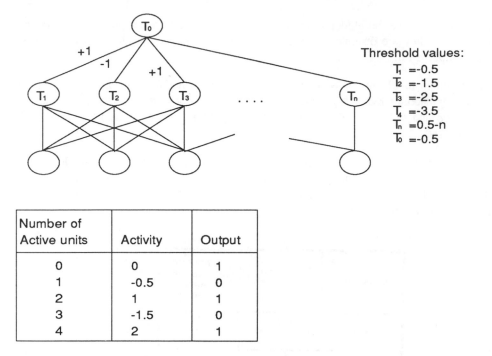

Threshold values:

$T_1 = -0.5$
$T_2 = -1.5$
$T_3 = -2.5$
$T_4 = -3.5$
$T_n = 0.5-n$
$T_0 = -0.5$

Number of Active units	Activity	Output
0	0	1
1	-0.5	0
2	1	1
3	-1.5	0
4	2	1

Fig.11.5: This network provides a solution to the parity problem. The hidden units self organise and "count" the input units involved in a pattern. The output is 1 even when there is an even number of 1's and 0 otherwise.

The hidden units in Fig.11.5 are fully connected, that is, connected to every input unit and every output unit (if there was more than one output unit in the example). The first R hidden units are active when there are R active input units, so a pattern of length R needs R hidden units. In Fig.11.5, the hidden units come on from left to right. The one on the left of the pattern is of length 1 or more, the second from the left of the pattern is of length 2 or more, etc. The hidden units then alternatively connect with positive and negative weights. After 2,825 presentations of the solution, with four hidden units and four input units, the output was as required. That is, 0 for even numbers and 1 for odd numbers.

This is not the sort of internal representation readily discovered by unsupervised learning schemes such as competitive learning because the hidden units do not depend on which units are active, just how many.

It should be noted that although the examples to date have contained only one layer of hidden units, there is no need to place this restriction on models and indeed many have multiple layers of hidden units.

The T C problem

In Chapter 5 we showed how Rosenblatt's model could identify the difference between T and H images. An extension of this is the T C problem, where the network can deal with the images even if they are rotated or moved in a horizontal or vertical direction on the input plane.

Fig.11.6 shows the set of images used to train the network.

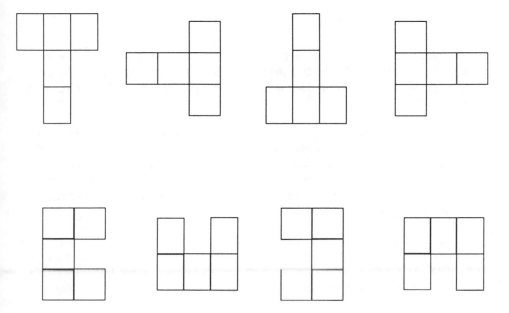

Fig.11.6: This shows the set of training patterns used to train the network to recognise the images T and C even when rotated.

Each pattern is made up of five squares and they differ from each other by just one square. The difference the network needs to look at, as Minsky and Papert pointed out in 1969, is not between pairs of squares because the distances between the pairs do not change however much a figure is rotated, but between groups of three squares.

A different type of network was used for this problem as shown in Fig.11.7.

In the network in Fig.11.7 the input units form a grid on which the T or C pattern can be superimposed. The hidden units are also arranged in a grid pattern and receive input from a 3 by 3 square of input units. All the hidden units output to a single output unit trained to respond with a 1 if the pattern is T and a 0 if the pattern is C. Remember, this is independent of the location or orientation of the figure.

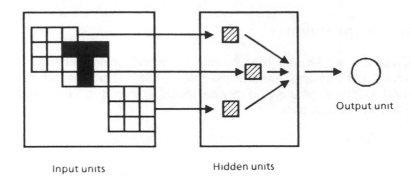

Input units   Hidden units

Fig.11.7: Each hidden unit in this network receives input from a 3x3 grid. The response from all the hidden units is then received by a single output unit which is activated (1) if the input is T and not activated (0) if the input is C. Regardless of the orientation of the input image.

To achieve this independence, all the units were constrained to the same set of weights. This was done by first using the Delta rule to determine the weight changes for all the units, then adding all these results together and changing the weights for all the units by the same amount. This enables the input area to behave as though it were detecting the same feature but in different regions. Learning that occurs in one area will automatically be related across the whole network.

Rumelhart et al. found that the network gave a number of solutions to this problem each of which were arrived at after between 5,000 and 10,000 presentations of the patterns to the network. One of these solutions is shown in Fig.11.8. This is not actually the most frequently occurring arrangement but is by far the easiest to represent.

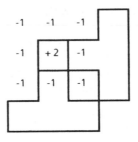

Fig.11.8: This shows the weights developed for one hidden unit by the network to detect the T or C image. In this example two possible orientations of the T are shown, the sum of the weights is +1. It can be seen that there is no way of positioning the C shape to achieve any value larger than 0.

These examples demonstrate some of the representations developed by the hidden units. They learn to respond to certain features which highlight the differences between the T and C input patterns.

It is important to remember that the 3x3 grid of weight values shown in the diagrams represent the weights associated with a single hidden unit and that this will be the same for all the hidden units.

Figure 11.8 is referred to as an *on-centre off-surround* arrangement for obvious reasons and is extremely good for detecting a T shape. Any angle of the T can be placed over the centre weight of +2 and achieve a net input of +1 because it will at most activate only one of the inhibitory weights. The C pattern can at most achieve 0 as it cannot avoid covering two or more inhibitory cells. In this way the network can distinguish between the two. It is important to remember that the learning procedure was set up in such a way that it would be independent of the position of the shape within the grid, thus the same thing is learned wherever the pattern is presented.

There are a number of other interesting problems solved, namely the encoding problem, the problem of detecting symmetry and binary addition which are dealt with in the article by Rumelhart et al.

As pointed out by Rumelhart et al., this work seems to indicate the existence of a powerful enough learning mechanism and should dispel the pessimism shown by Minsky and Papert. Although it cannot guarantee to find a solution every time, for the examples they have used, it has very seldom failed. It also has to be pointed out that this is very much a starting point, these examples are essentially simple and more complex problems need to be considered. It was also noted by Rumelhart et al. that in their experiments they always presented the complete set of patterns to the net. It would be interesting to see whether or not the network could generalise sufficiently in order to define new patterns.

The next example, the family tree problem, is able to generalise.

Family tree

The family tree problem was also solved by Hinton in 1986.

A multi-layer network was used to learn the family trees shown in Fig.11.9 for 24 people from two different families. The relationships were given as groups of three parameters, two people plus their connection, and the network learnt the relations in this way. So for any pair of parameters the network was able to produce the third. For example if the combination of (Fred, has-sister, Mary) existed, to denote that Fred had a sister called Mary, if the network were presented with *Fred* and *Mary* it would complete the pattern and produce something similar to *Fred has a sister Mary*. Similarily, if presented with *Mary* and *has-sister* or *Fred* and *has-sister*.

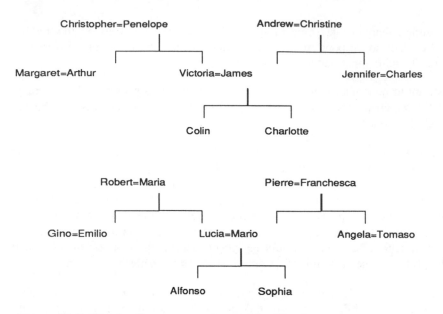

Figure 11.9: The family tree example used by Hinton.

The model used six units in the first hidden layer which forces the model to use a distributed pattern of activity in the layer in order to represent the relationships, rather than having enough units to just memorise the whole pattern.

Training was carried out on 100 of the 104 possible combinations and the network was then tested on the remaining four, which it did generalise correctly. It is most interesting that during the training the network seemed to build up representations in terms of features such as age and to which branch of the family tree they belonged, even though these were not specifically defined in the input patterns. The network was able to extract features and in fact similar people were represented by similar patterns.

Two spiral problem

This problem is similar to the connectedness or parity problem, and again reduces to linear separability. Like the XOR problem using a simple network, a straight line cannot be drawn which will separate the firing and non-firing regions when these are taken to each represent one of the spirals.

Kevin Lang and Michael Witbrock (1988) at Carnegie Mellon University taught a network with hidden layers to solve the problem and analysed the result. The network is defined as having two input units, representing the (x,y) coordinates of a point and one output unit. There are two hidden layers each containing five units. The activation levels of the input can take any value from 0.0 to 1.0. Each unit is fully connected to the units in the layer below with some connections skipping layers in order to provide direct information from the lower layers thus allowing more flexible hidden layer representations. The back-propagation learning algorithm is used to develop the features.

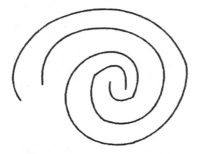

Fig.11.10: The two spiral problem.

When presented as input to the network, one spiral should produce an output of 0, the other 1.

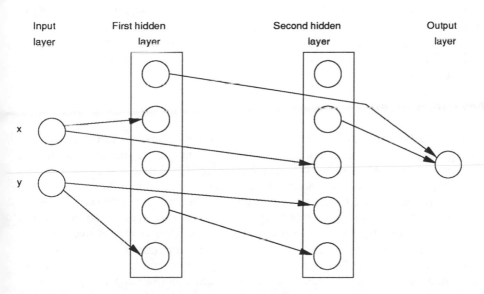

Fig.11.11: Solution to the two spiral problem. There is full connectivity and some connections can skip layers. The input units x and y represent the coordinates of a point in the two spiral image (x,y).

When the network had been trained, the weights were analysed and also the response of the units to patterns of input. The units in the first layer were found to divide the input space into two regions using a variety of angles. The second layer then uses combinations of these first layer features in order to produce curved response patterns. Finally the output unit uses the curved patterns to form the successive turns of the spiral. Fig. 11.12 shows the responses of the two layers of five hidden units and the output unit.

First hidden layer

Second hidden layer

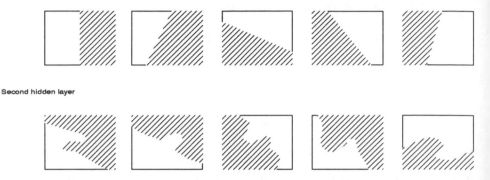

Fig.11.12: Representations in the hidden layers.

Because the network is not told how to respond to the points which do not belong to either of the spirals, it produces a strangely bumpy effect. This underconstrained freedom means that the back-propagation learning algorithm will never produce a perfect solution. This problem can be overcome by providing additional training and constraining the network architecture.

Text to Speech

Language has as many exceptions as it has regularities. Techniques of mapping text to speech using back propagation have proved to be suprisingly successful at dealing with this sort of problem. Sejnowski and Rosenburg (1987) used a network with one hidden layer. The input layer encodes the identity of the letter to be pronounced, a different unit being used for each letter. It also encodes the context consisting of the three previous letters and three following letters in the text, spaces and punctuation being given special treatment. This seven-character window is moved over the text, one letter at a time, sequentially. The output layer comprises a phoneme with 21 vocal features and five features for stress and syllable boundaries. There are 80 hidden units, each receiving input from all input units and sending output to all the output units - 309 units in total (7x29 input, 80 hidden, 26 output) and 18,629 connections.

After a lot of training the model generalises well to new input and therefore has captured the regularities in the set of training patterns. It tends to generalise for new input according to these basic rules it has gathered together.

Deficiencies

Although learning is generally slower using this rule because the process considers ways of using the hidden units, there are many examples using this procedure which show the network generalises in sensible ways. If the network solves a problem, it has found a set of weights which produce the correct output for every input. However, it is not easy to decipher what has been learnt, all that is available is a set of numbers which represent the values of the weights. Methods are being developed to see more clearly what is happening to the hidden units, not only in terms of the value of the individual weights but also in terms of their response to patterns of activation. See ALVINN in Chapter 21.

Aleksander (1990) cites that the model is inadequate in its current form for larger tasks because of the time it takes for the learning process to converge onto a solution. The time can be shown to be of order N^3, where N is the number of weights involved. On a parallel machine with one processor per unit this could be reduced to N^2 but improvements would be made if better use was made of modularity.

There is currently no evidence in the biological sense that neurons use synapses in the reverse direction as this learning algorithm does, and in fact Rumelhart et al. say that the learning procedure in its current form is not a plausible model of learning in brains. They go on to comment that at best it should be considered as something which demonstrates learning which can be done using gradient descent without implying that the brain uses anything similar. The algorithm does, however, provide a solution to many of the problems previously encountered and demonstrates that the hidden units provide a method of internal representation.

Another problem is that the desired output is usually defined in terms of 0 and 1, values which would actually need an infinite potential using the learning equation. In other words, they will never be achieved. Normally this is overcome by accepting values within some limit of 0 and 1, for example 0.1 and 0.9.

Also, these examples have been carried out on networks in which the units send output forward through the net. We need to look at networks which allow feedback.

Example of the Back Propagation Rule

Let us consider the simplest of networks that we could have with just one input, one hidden and one output unit. The units are connected as shown in Fig.11.13 such that the only way the input and output units can communicate is through the hidden unit.

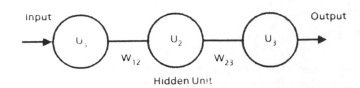

Fig.11.13: A simple network with units U_1 (input), U_2 (hidden) and U_3 (output). The weights are W_{12} between U_1 and U_2, W_{23} between U_2 and U_3.

So we can define:

Unit	U_i	U_1, U_2 and U_3
Activity	a_i	for unit U_i
Output	O_i	for unit U_i
Weight	W_{ij}	between U_j and U_i
Threshold	T_i	for unit U_i
Learning rate	β	
Desired value	t_j	desired value for pattern j
Actual value	O_j	actual output for pattern j
Overall error	E	the overall error for the network taken as the sum of the squares of the errors for each pattern
Pattern error	E_j	the error for pattern j
		$= (t_j - o_j)$

Learning algorithm

ΔW_{ji} the weight change to be made

$$= \beta d_j O_j$$

where: d_j $= (t_j - O_j)O_j(1-O_j)$

$$= E_j O_j(1-O_j)$$

for hidden units d_j $= (\Sigma d_k W_{kj})O_j(1-O_j)$ summed over k

where k is the unit receiving output from the hidden unit.

Note there will be no threshold value for the input unit.

We will give these the following values:

$$W_{21} = -2$$
$$W_{32} = 2$$
$$T_2 = 0.25$$
$$T_3 = -0.25$$
$$\beta = 1$$

Required Response

Let us say that we want the network to produce a 1 if a 0 is input and vice versa.

Find the overall error: E

$$E \quad = E_0{}^2 + E_1{}^2$$

where:

E_0 is the error when the input is 0
E_1 is the error when the input is 1
E_j $= (t_j\text{-}O_j)$

Error when the input is 0:
E_0 $= (t_0\text{-}O_0)$

We know the input is 0 and the desired output (to) is 1, so we need to find the actual output. For this we need to work through the activations for the units when the input is applied to the network.

Hidden unit activation

$$
\begin{aligned}
a_2 \quad &= \quad \Sigma\ W_{2i}O_i + T_2 \\
&= \quad W_{21}O_1 + T_2 \qquad \text{there only being input from } U_1 \\
&= \quad \text{-}2x0 + 0.25 \\
&= \quad 0.25
\end{aligned}
$$

Output for the hidden unit

$$
\begin{aligned}
O_2 \quad &= \quad 1/(1+e^{\text{-}a2}) \\
&= \quad 1/(1+e^{\text{-}0.25}) \\
&= \quad 1/1.7788 \\
&= \quad 0.5621 \qquad \text{this is used to find the input to } U_3
\end{aligned}
$$

Output unit activation

$$
\begin{aligned}
a_3 \quad &= \quad \Sigma W_{3i}O_i + T_3 \\
&= \quad W_{32}O_2 + T_3 \qquad \text{there only being input from } U_2 \\
&= \quad 2x0.5621 + \text{-}0.25 \\
&= \quad 0.8742
\end{aligned}
$$

Output for the output unit

$$O_3 \quad = \quad 1/(1+e^{-a3})$$
$$= \quad 1/(1+e^{-0.8742})$$
$$= \quad 1/1.4175$$
$$= \quad 0.7059 \qquad \text{this is the output for the network}$$

Error for an input of 0

$$E_0 \quad = \quad (t_0-O_0)$$
$$= \quad 1-0.7059$$
$$= \quad 0.2941$$

Error when the input is 1

$$E_1 \quad = \quad (T_1-O_1)$$

We know that the input is 1 and the desired output (T_1) is 0, so we need to find the actual output. For this we need to work through the activations for the units when the input is applied to the network.

Hidden unit activation

$$a_2 \quad = \quad \Sigma W_{2i}O_i + T_2$$
$$= \quad W_{21}O_1 + T_2 \qquad \text{there only being input from } U_1$$
$$= \quad -2x1 + 0.25$$
$$= \quad -1.75$$

Output for the hidden unit

$$O_2 \quad = \quad 1/(1+e^{-a2})$$
$$= \quad 1/(1+e^{-1.75})$$
$$= \quad 1/6.7618$$
$$= \quad 0.1478 \qquad \text{this is used to find the input to } U_3$$

Output unit activation

$$a_3 \quad = \quad \Sigma W_{3i}O_i + T_3$$
$$= \quad W_{32}O_2 + T_3 \qquad \text{there only being input from } U_2$$
$$= \quad 2x0.1478 - 0.25$$
$$= \quad 0.0456$$

Output for the output unit

$$O_3 = 1/(1+e^{-a_3})$$
$$= 1/(1+e^{-0.0456})$$
$$= 1/1.9503$$
$$= 0.5128 \qquad \text{this is the output for the network}$$

Error for an input of 1

$$E_1 = (T_1-O_1)$$
$$= 1-0.5128$$
$$= 0.4872$$

Overall error

$$E = E_0^2 + E_1^2$$
$$= 0.2941^2 + 0.4872^2$$
$$= 0.0865 + 0.2374$$
$$= 0.3239$$

Learning algorithm

$$\Delta W_{ji} = \beta\, d_j O_i \qquad (\beta=1)$$
where:
$$d_j = (t_j-O_j)O_j(1-O_j)$$

For input of 0

Apply the change first to the output unit.
$O_j = O_3$, $W_{ji} = W_{23}$, $O_i = O_2$, $(t_j-O_j) = E_0$
$$d_3 = E_0 \times O_3(1-O_3)$$
$$= 0.2941 \times 0.7059 \times 0.2941$$
$$= 0.061$$

Change in weight

$$\Delta W_{32} = d_3 O_2$$
$$= 0.061 \times 0.5621$$
$$= 0.0343$$

Change in T_3

$$\Delta T_3 = d_j O_i$$
$$d_j = (t_j-O_j)O_j(1-O_j)$$
$$d_j = d_3, O_i = 1 \qquad (O_i = 1 \text{ always for a threshold unit})$$
$$\Delta T_3 = 0.061$$

New Weight value: new W_{32} = old W_{32} + ΔW_{32} = 2+0.0343 = 2.0343

New Threshold value: new T_3 = old T_3 + ΔT_3 = -0.25+0.061 = -0.189

Repeat for W_{21}

$$\Delta W_{21} = \quad \beta d_2 O_1 \ (\beta=1)$$
where:
$$d_2 \quad = \quad (\Sigma \ d_k W_{kj}) O_j (1-O_j) \text{ for a hidden unit where k is the unit}$$
$$\text{receiving output from the hidden unit.}$$
$$K=3$$
$$= \quad d_3 W_{32} x O_2 (1-O_2)$$
and:
$$d_3 \quad = \quad (T_3-O_3) O_3 (1-O_3) \quad \text{for an input of 0}$$
$$= \quad E_o O_3 (1-O_3)$$

Change in weight

$$\Delta W_{21} = \quad E_0 O_3 (1-O_3) W_{32} O_2 (1-O_2) O_1 \qquad O_1=0$$
$$= \quad 0$$

Change in T_2

$$\Delta T_2 \quad = \quad d_2 O_1$$
$$d_2 \quad = \quad E_0 O_3 (1-O_3)$$
$$=$$
$$d_2 = d_3, O_i = 1 \quad (O_i = 1 \text{ always for a threshold unit})$$

$$\Delta T_2 \quad = \quad E_0 O_3 (1-O_3) W_{32} O_2 (1-O_2) x 1$$
$$= \quad 0.2941x0.7059x0.2941x2.1343x0.5621x0.4379x1$$
$$= \quad 0.0306$$

New Weight value: new W_{21} = old W_{21} = -2
New Threshold value: new T_2 = old T_2 + ΔT_2 = 0.25+0.0306 = 0.2806

This completes the first training cycle. The process is repeated until the errors are reduced to an acceptable value. There seems to be very little progress here after a lot of calculations, however we do know that the training algorithm converges in small steps.

Aleksander cited that the example he carried out took 216 cycles to reduce the overall error to 0.0513 with the network giving an output of 0.856 when the input is 0, and 0.175 when the input is 1.

Mathematics for Back Propagation

This algorithm is a generalisation of the Delta rule which works for networks with hidden units. These can be thought of as an area in the network where the data is partially labelled before being dealt with by the output layer.

Desired value	t_j	desired value for pattern j
Actual value	O_j	the actual output for pattern j
Overall error	E	the overall error for the network taken as sum of the squares of the errors for each pattern
Pattern error	E_j	the error for pattern j $= (t_j\text{-}o_j)$
Learning algorithm		
	ΔW_{ji}	The weight change to be made $= \beta \, d_j O_j$
where:	d_j	$= (t_j\text{-}O_j)O_j(1\text{-}O_j)$ $= E_j O_j(1\text{-}O_j)$
	for hidden units d_j	$= (\sum d_k W_{kj})O_j(1\text{-}O_j)$

where k is the unit receiving output from the hidden unit.

The error E for the whole of the network is defined to be:

$$E = \sum E_p{}^2 \qquad \text{where } E_p \text{ is the error for the pth pattern}$$

$$E_p = (t_j\text{-}O_j) \qquad \text{where: } t_j \text{ is the desired output for pattern p}$$
$$O_j \text{ is the actual output for pattern p}$$

Forward Pass

For each input/output pair, the input pattern is applied by setting the states of the input units. A forward route is taken through the network and the total input to a unit is defined as usual to be the total of all the inputs from the other units, after weight adjustment has taken place. That is, the linear function:

$$\text{input} = \sum W_{ji}O_j \qquad O_j\text{=output from unit } U_j, \; W_{ji}\text{=weight}$$

This value is then compared against some threshold value to determine what could be called the potential of the unit. The activity level for a unit is 0 or 1, sometimes -1 and 1 and is calculated using a method similar to the Boltzmann learning function which we looked at in Chapter 10. This is the non-linear function of a unit's total input:

output $= 1/(1+e^{-aj})$ a_j=input from unit U_j

This is carried through all the layers to the output units.

Backward pass

Once the output has been calculated for the network and input patterns, the learning algorithm is applied from the output units back through the network to adjust all the weights and threshold values in turn.

Learning algorithm

The weight adjustments are made as follows:

ΔW_{ji} = $\beta\ d_j O_i$
where:
d_j = $(t_j - O_j)O_j(1 - O_j)$
        = $(\sum d_k W_{kj})O_j(1 - O_j)$ for hidden units
                                    where k is the unit receiving
                                    output from the hidden unit.

NOTE: O_i is always 1 for a threshold unit

The adjustments are added to the old values:

New Weight value: new W_{ji} = old W_{ji} + ΔW_{ji}
New Threshold value: new T_i = old T_i + ΔT_i

It should be stressed at this point that it is not necessary to use these particular functions. Any will do which satisfy certain criteria, namely that the network is able to find values for the weights and converge onto a solution for the particular input/output combinations. There is a mathematical explanation of the criteria which need to be met in order that this holds true which we will not look at here; Rumelhart et al. (1985) give a description for the interested reader.

12

Competitive Learning

Given the limits of a single layer system and the difficulty of developing learning schemes for multi-layer versions, competitive learning was developed as a system which discovers the important features that a multi-layer network can use in order to classify pattern sets which cannot be classified using a single layer network.

Competitive learning is a method of unsupervised learning, that is, the feature detectors can classify the input patterns and develop representations of them without the use of a specific learning guide – a method found to be useful for pattern descriptions. The method has a close relationship with self-supervised back propagation in that a simplified version of competitive learning is a degenerate case.

The basic principle of competitive learning is that groups of hidden units compete with each other to become active. When one of the neurons wins it becomes dominant and inhibits those neurons around it. This idea was initially pioneered by Rosenblatt and studied by Christopher von der Malsburg (1973), Fukishima (1975) (Cognitron, see Chapter 20) and Stephen Grossberg (1976).

There are lots of variations on the basic theme and we will initially look at what could be called the simplest version.

Basic model

Let us look at a model which has two layers plus an input layer as shown in Fig.12.1. Each cell within a layer is connected to all the cells in the previous layer. Within the layers, the cells are split into groups, with M cells in each group. This value for M may well change for each layer. In the example below the first layer has groups of size M=3, in the second layer the groups are of size M=4. These groups are called *inhibitory clusters*. In this example the clusters do not overlap each other and each unit within a cluster has the same input from the previous layer.

Full connectivity

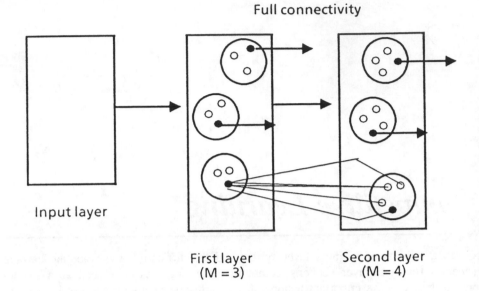

Input layer

First layer
(M = 3)

Second layer
(M = 4)

Fig.12.1: Only one unit in each inhibitory cluster can be active at any time and send output to the next layer. A 'winner-take-all' situation.

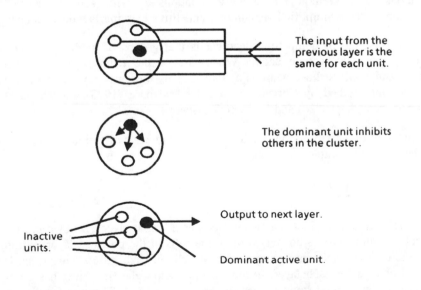

The input from the previous layer is the same for each unit.

The dominant unit inhibits others in the cluster.

Output to next layer.

Inactive units.

Dominant active unit.

Fig.12.1A: The input from the previous layer is the same for each unit. The dominant unit inhibits others in the cluster.

Each unit sums the input which comes to it and the group of units within each cluster will then compete with each other for dominance. This operates under a *winner-take-all* principle in that one will eventually win and that one will then inhibit all the other units in its cluster. The final situation will be that one unit has an activity level of 1, all the other units in the cluster having an activity level of 0. The winner in each cluster has then earned the right to output to the next layer, as only one unit in each cluster may be active at any one time.

Training

Each unit will receive inputs from a number of different units in the previous layers and as in our earlier models for other types of learning, each input line will have a weight associated with it. One of the major objectives is to keep the sum of the weights for a unit the same and we will see why this is necessary later.

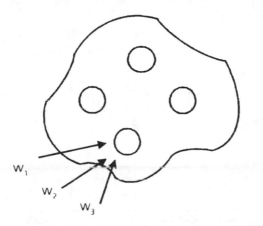

Fig.12.2: An inhibitory cluster, $W_1+W_2+W_3$ (weights) will always be the same for this unit. All units in a cluster receive the same input and the total weights for a unit is always the same.

The sum of the weights will always be some set value for a given unit.

Training is simply a matter of shifting the weights from a unit's inactive input lines onto its active input lines by some given amount. When a unit becomes dominant the appropriate weights on the active input lines will be incremented by a small amount, so a unit will only learn when it dominates. In order that this unit does not then always dominate, the sum of the weights for the unit is kept constant by taking a small amount off the other weights to balance it up as it were. In this way, when a unit becomes more sensitive to one pattern, it becomes less sensitive to others.

Equilibrium in the system can be formally defined (Rumelhart and McClelland 1986) as the state when the average inflow of weight to a particular line is equal to the average outflow. In other words, it has reached a sort of stability. At equilibrium, a unit will respond most strongly to patterns which overlap others to which the unit responds and most weakly to those far removed. A state of equilibrium is achieved when the weights don't change. The probability that a unit will respond becomes stable. The input of stimuli could push the system out of balance and the system could be moved to a different state of equilibrium. Generally if the amount by which a unit responds to a given pattern is very much larger than the response from all the other units this is a highly stable situation.

Now let's look at this using an example.

Example

The example below shows an input pattern made up of four binary digits plus three units A, B and C in an inhibition layer.

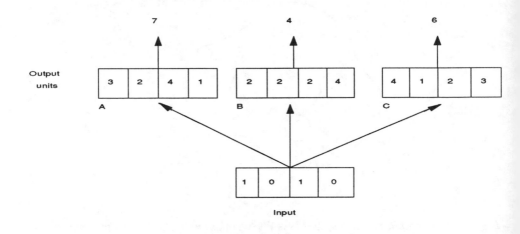

Fig.12.3: All weights add up to 10. Here the winner is A.

Each input unit has the weights which are shown. For example, unit A has the weights 3, 2, 4 and 1. If the pattern 1010 was applied to unit A, this would result in an activity of 7 ($1 \times 3 + 0 \times 2 + 1 \times 4 + 0 \times 1$). When the input patterns are presented to the network, the unit with the most activity wins and supresses the others.

Shown in Fig.12.4 is a table with all the different combinations of input pattern (4 digits, each either 0 or 1), which could be presented to the network and the resulting unit which wins.

Input Pattern	Winner
0000	none
0001	B
0010	A
0011	B
0100	none
0101	B
0110	A
0111	B
1000	C
1001	C
1010	A
1011	C
1100	none
1101	none
1110	A
1111	none

Fig.12.4: The possible input patterns.

To train the network for one particular pattern, say 1010, the active weights for the winning unit are adjusted so that the unit responds more strongly. In this case the winner is unit A. The first and third weights will be active so increase both of these by 1 and decrease the other two weights by 1. The resulting weights for A are 4, 1, 5 and 0. The table for the winners will now be as shown in Fig. 12.5:

No winner	A	B	C
0000	0010	0001	1001
1000	0110	0011	
1011	1010	0100	
1100	1110	0101	
1101		0111	
1111			

Fig.12.5: After training on pattern 1010.

Now. training the network for pattern 1001. The winner for this is C, so increase the first and fourth weights annd decrease the other two weights. The weights for C will now be 5, 0, 1 and 4. The response to the input patterns will be as shown in Fig.12.6:

No winner	A	B	C
0000	0010	0011	1000
0001	0110	0100	1001
1100	1010	0101	1011
1111	1110	0111	1101

Fig.12.6: Response to input pattern 1001.

From this it can be seen that unit A is responding to 1s in the middle of a pattern, unit B to 1s predominantly on the left-hand side, and unit C to the right-hand side.

Interesting features of the Competitive Learning Model

If there are M units in a cluster the patterns can be classified into M groups and each unit will capture about the same number of patterns.

If a pattern has structure the units break it up into its relevent lines and the system will find the clusters if they exist. The problem is then to specify the nature of the structure that the system finds.

If the stimuli are highly structured the classifications will be very stable. Otherwise the clusters may undergo constant changes and shifts in representations.

The starting weights are important and will determine the final groupings, as will the input patterns. If there are a large number of clusters the input can either classify the patterns into a large number of groupings or find a variety of independent features.

Applications

Users of this method say it is an unsupervised method of extracting the features or structure from the input patterns. Problems are that the outcome depends very much on the initial values of the weights and the number of layers and cluster size which is simply a matter of trial and error.

A network is able to carry out the task of word perception well. However, Rumulhart et al (1986) speculate on how this kind of configuration could have evolved within the brain and whether competitive learning is a reasonable expectation at all.

To get around the winner-take-all situation, Rumulhart et al (1986) proposed modifications in the form of a *leaky learning model*. The learning rule postulates that both the win and lose situations cause modifications to the weights of some sort, so losing would then result in learning. Even if the changes in weights were a lot less than the winner's changes, at least it would be an event. This would result in the losing stimuli slowly being moved into the area where the winners are, then competitive learning can occur.

Another solution is the Bienenstock, Cooper and Munro (1982) model of increasing sensitivity. This states that if a unit doesn't receive any inputs it literally becomes more sensitive until it does receive something. If the unit then starts to receive too many inputs its sensitivity is decreased again.

In experiments both these models have exhibited much the same sort of behaviour.

The competitive model of learning has become one of fundamental importance in neural network research as it brings the neural network into a real-time setting, a concept we will look at later in this chapter.

Dipole Experiment

Rumelhart (1986) has carried out a number of experiements on dipole patterns, which have only two active elements. If we see this as being represented in a 4x4 grid with 16 elements in total, there are 24 ways in which a pair of active units can be placed so they are next to each other.

Rumelhart's experiments were generally on a two-layer system which contained one inhibitory cluster of two units. Each unit had 16 input lines which represented one line for each grid position.

The model was set up initially with a random set of weights for the two units and after 400 training patterns the weights were assessed in terms of their relative size. It was found that the units had become associated with a particular part of the grid, perhaps the vertical set-up or maybe the diagonal. In this way the dimensional structure was represented and binary feature detectors had been devised to ascertain which half of the grid contained the pattern. Each unit actually responded to about half the total input patterns.

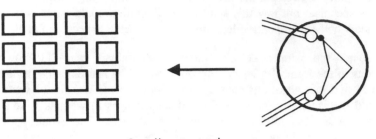

Inhibitory cluster

One line to each
grid position

Fig.12.7: There are 24 possible adjacent dipole patterns in a 4x4 grid. Rumelahart et al. developed a model with a single inhibitory cluster containing 2 units.

When tested for different cluster sizes and in three dimensions, for a cubic arrangement, the results were the same. That is, stimuli which appeared in a certain part of the grid were responded to by one particular unit. The reason for placing the input patterns within a grid is that it restricts the network so that meaningful groupings are forced to be created.

Ordered Maps

Kohonen (1984,1988) has used unsupervised competitive learning to produce networks which learn to respond to different parts of the input pattern. These are referred to as ordered maps.

Here the hidden units are laid out usually in a 2-d space. The weight of the hidden unit receiving the largest input is updated and also the weights for adjacent hidden units. In this way surrounding units also respond to similar input. This can be seen as performing gradient descent. The best way to see how this works is to look at an example. In Fig.12.8 there are eight nodes which each have the weights as shown by the binary representation along the top.

Let us say that we are trying to train the network to respond to the patterns 001 and 100. The response of the network to these patterns is shown in Fig.12.9, where the nodes respond according to how many 0s or 1s they have in common with the pattern.

For the pattern 001, node 1 shows the greatest response. This is the *response focus* for the pattern. We will define the neighbourhood for this node to take in one node on either side, that is, nodes 0 and 2. We will then alter nodes 0 and 2 to respond more strongly to the input pattern by adjusting their weights. This is done by altering either a 0 to a 1 or vice versa. When there is a choice, as in node 2, we can change either. Node 1 will not change as it is already giving a maximum response.

Node	0	1	2	3	4	5	6	7
Weights	000	001	010	011	100	101	110	111

Fig 12.8: The eight nodes have the weights as shown in binary form.

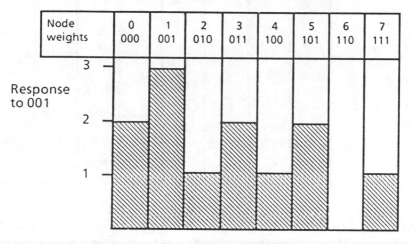

Fig.12.9 & 12.10 : The nodes in Fig.12.8. respond to the pattern 001 according to how many digits in the weight value are the same as those in the input pattern. The response is given as the number of digits in the weights which are the same as the input pattern.

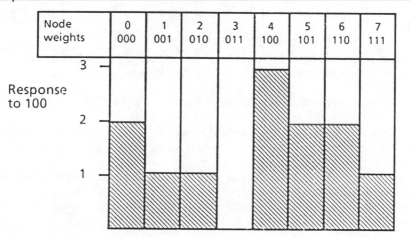

Fig. 12.10: Response of nodes to pattern 100.

Node 0 : change weights from 000 to 001. Response changed from 2 to 3.
Node 2 : change weights from 010 to 011. Response changed from 1 to 2.

The response of the network to this change is shown in Fig.12.11.

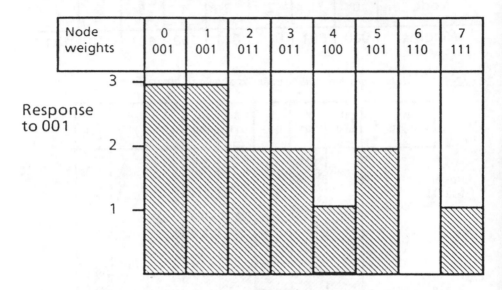

Fig.12.11: New response to 001 after training on pattern 001. The response is accumulating around node 1. Node 1 showed the greatest response to pattern 001 in Fig.12.9. so the weights for nodes 0 and 2 are changed so that the two nodes respond more strongly to 001.

The response to 001 has been centred around neuron 1.

For the pattern 100, node 4 showed the greatest response. So we will then alter nodes 3 and 5.

Node 3 : change weights from 011 to 111. Response changed from 1 to 2.
Node 5 : change weights from 101 to 100. Response changed from 2 to 3.

The response of the network to this change is shown in Fig.12.12.

The response to 100 has been centred around neuron 4. If the response node had been on the edge, for example, node 0, then we would select nodes 1 and 7 to be changed.

In this way the network can be trained to respond to different patterns using different parts of the network.

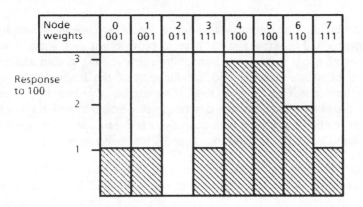

Node weights	0 001	1 001	2 011	3 111	4 100	5 100	6 110	7 111

Fig.12.12: New response to 100 after training on pattern 100. The response is accumulating around node 4. Node 4 showed the greatest response to pattern 100 in Fig.12.10. so the weights for nodes 3 and 5 are changed so that the two nodes respond more strongly to 100.

Grossberg's Models

It is difficult to integrate Grossberg's work into the general structure of this book because his aim has been to develop almost a universal theory for neural networks which has been quite at odds with general trends of research thought. His work is original and inspiring, while at the same time controversial and thought provoking. His theories are rigorously dealt with in a mathematical sense and use a great deal of terminology which is unique to his own field of work. Because of this his ideas are confined to this chapter in order that things do not become too confused.

There are a great number of references at the end of this chapter which explain this work in more detail.

Starting point

Emergent properties in a neural network model are most certainly exciting but in many ways they make it very hard to understand the model. It is unclear how to define the link which must exist between these properties and successful behaviour. If we raise the question: *"When is a model wrong?"* and the model has been defined as *"not necessarily providing a plausible or adequate description of the actual implementation of the brain"*, how can any criticism or assessment be made of such a model?

It could be said that as humans, we have evolved, but that does not mean we have any comprehension of our own mechanisms. What is needed is some kind of abstract language which can be used to analyse the relationships and results which exist.

Grossberg's work has been described as an intersection of psychology, neurophysiology and mathematics and his main aim has been to provide just such a mathematical model. Such a system needs to be defined for a dynamic evolving system and adhere to the limitations of neural anatomy and the function of the brain. In this sense operations must be carried out in *real time*. The classic approach is inadequate because physics provides a language for describing non-adaptive and non-evolving systems – a linear method for dealing with transitions between states. For application to neural network models, Grossberg has developed a non-linear approach.

Grossberg's work started in the 1960s and has been a major influencing factor in neural network research in the competitive network field, and in general research because of the universal nature of his approach. His concern has been the development of real-time networks, able to process inputs as fast as they arrive, with no external control being necessary and no distinction between the model being in either a learning mode or a processing mode.

The success of such networks is measured at the network level rather than at an individual cell level. Grossberg's view was that in a good network model the whole is far greater than the sum of its parts, which is in agreement with the opinion held by von Neumann.

Originally this work was referred to as *embedding fields*. Grossberg started from the point of view that a theory for the activity of the brain would have to involve mathematics, neurology, biophysics, consciousness, psychology, physics and computer science. All these disciplines are involved in some way and therefore there must be a way of unifying them. Problems in integration of different lines of research are notorious and understandable, after all there exists no common language which enables communication to freely occur. It is little wonder that each tends to develop separate theories. Attempts to unify tend to be more disruptive than helpful because of the inability to agree on basic definitions.

Grossberg postulated that because the various areas of the brain are inextricably linked and intertwined, little advantage is gained from separating them. So looking at a process in isolation, analysing it and then trying to relate results back to the original, which is the usual way of dealing with things, is not the correct approach. We have already talked about how the brain is essentially a network of many millions of processing units, the physical side is well understood. Again the problem of a general purpose theory of how those neurons deal with processing and representing information emerges as the serious problem.

Grossberg went back to the experiments carried out by Pavlov and his followers and gathered together the information gleaned with regards automatic responses in animals and man. His approach was not to look at the behaviour of the individual neurons but to study the overall network responses and to develop appropriate theories to describe their behaviour. He concluded that adaptive behaviour can be described as patterns, distributed over a wide area, of short-term and long-term memory traces, not either as individual neuron states or memory traces. His ideas have always been backed up by rigorous mathmatical proofs and his set of neural network laws have predicted the results of future experiments

Research Direction

There are three main aims of the research:

❑ To discover how intelligence or knowledge can be ascribed to the whole of a structure but not to its individual parts.

❑ To find how a system can be stable for stored information and yet adaptive to new learning.

❑ To identify a functional level on which the success of behaviour can be defined.

Overview

The main idea centres around the concept of adaptive resonance. This is the suggestion that perception and cognition can be defined as a state of resonant activity which exists within the system as a whole. Only this resonant state enters consciousness and can then initiate adaptive states. In other words, it is not the activities of individual neurons which are significant, it is the total activity of all the neurons which determines the outcome.

For example, if we look at a sheet of white paper, by definition we are actually seeing all colours. However, we do not perceive in a local manner, we perceive the average input of data from many points. Therefore, what we see is a merging of all these colours which averages out as white.

Once the resonant state enters consciousness a feedback process is activated. This enables stored experiences to be used to adapt the activity into a resultant combination of what we perceive and what we expect.

In his search for mathematical explanations of this, linear theories were rejected because these would simply get larger and larger or smaller and smaller, causing complete overfill or a wiping out of memories. Cooperative/competitive pattern recognition theory was developed, the essence of both memory and processing being patterns of activity with no clear distinction between the two. This method utilises the tendancy for groups of neurons to use an on-centre off-surround topology, that is, if a neuron is excited, the neurons around become inhibited.

Classic conditioning

Grossberg has used the results of many years of classic conditioning (CC) experiments in his work, an area of research which many consider to be hopelessly inadequate for the study of cognition. Grossberg argues that such studies embody one component of complex attention, expectation and the role of feedback is important. So let us look at what is involved in conditioning.

The simplest form of CC is an unconditioned stimulus (UCS), which can be thought of as a shock. The result of such a surprise will be an unconditioned response (UCR), perhaps fear, and associated signs of fear. A conditioned stimulus (CS) such as a bell will not lead to something like fear unless it is associated with an UCS. For example, at the dentist, we are all quite conditioned to the phrase: "Now this won't hurt a bit." The dentist is absolutely correct, his words (the CS) were not painful but his subsequent actions (the UCS) are a different matter. We have already responded to the CS by gripping the chair and feeling quite ill (the UCR).

Conditioning depends on our expectations and will decide which cues we pay attention to as cues are also conditioned. If we find there is an error between what we expect to happen, and what actually happens, then we can only decide which cues were at fault if we were paying attention to them in the first place. When something unexpected happens and we cannot isolate the appropriate cues then we need to amplify all stored cues, now in a supressed state. In this sense feedback is nonspecific. Competition with whatever focused our attention on the wrong set of cues will then occur and help us to reorganise our expectations.

For example, imagine you work on a customer complaints desk, answering the phone all day and receiving a lot of abuse. After work, when you are at home and the phone rings you are going to experience an instant revulsion or aversion to actually answering it. It could take a long time after leaving that job for your expectancies to readapt. Some people never do adapt; my mother shudders whenever she hears an air raid siren on the television. I suppose it must depend to some extent on how often that cue comes into your life and how much reinforcement the retraining is exposed to.

If classic conditioning is just a feedforward process then (Grossberg's example) there would be some confusion if you were eating a turkey dinner with your lover. Looking at the turkey and your lover would surely confuse the issue. Grossberg suggests that a feedforward process may make you want to eat your lover and make love to the turkey! Incompatible responses like this are ruled out by the process of feedback. Mind you, if a turkey dinner was always a preliminary to a night of passion would you become aroused when your lover placed a turkey (CS) on the table?

Experiences which tend to maintain a system are selectively amplified. You will certainly jump enthusiastically out of the way of a bus but probably not someone walking towards you. Such reactions are helped by our feedback expectencies.

Error correction

In Grossberg's definition it is the total resonance of a system which is important. If this is the case, how can a coding error be corrected when no single cell knows it has occurred? Some mistakes will only be obvious in extreme situations. Stalling your car on a level crossing is only a problem when a train is coming. Error correction is of fundamental importance when there is a change in the environment or when our expectations need to be adapted.

It is suggested that the feedback pathways occur in *higher* neural centres and are directed back to the areas that originally excited them. If the feedback indicates the original match was incorrect, this mismatch needs to be supressed. The problem arises when the mismatch is very intense and leads to what is called the *noise saturation dilemma*. If the feedback is too small it will be lost. However, if it is amplified it will saturate the surrounding area and reduce the subsequent sensitivity to input to zero.

To look at how this is solved, we need to look at *on-centre off-surround* formations.

On-centre off-surround

Grossberg's idea was that the brain is modular in formation, being made up of clouds of connected neurons which can deal with a variety of input through self-adjusting mechanisms and communicate with neighbouring clouds. Controlling networks of neurons run through these clouds keeping the clouds within boundaries regardless of how intense the outside stimulus might be.

A mechanism found in neurological research, called on-centre off-surround, seems to act like the control mechanism described, working in such a way that a neuron or group of neurons will turn off its immediate neighbours or groups when it is itself stimulated. This enables a unique unsupervised representation of the environment to be learnt, with no teacher or preset features. Initially all the nodes are the same but a randomly distributed factor is introduced which makes each behave differently. Learning is then a case of allowing the nodes to compete for the right to respond to input, the nodes being classed as feature detectors.

We could think of this as a type of volume control which enables a network to adjust its sensitivity to incoming stimuli. The ear works in this way; we are quite capable of hearing a pin drop, but you generally have to concentrate on listening first. In normal everyday life our ears are not tuned to such fine sounds, it would be too much to cope with. But you can alter the sensitivity of your ears by deliberately turning up the volume.

So competive interactions between the cells automatically retune the sensitivity to input. These are called *shunting interactions*, and are carried by the off-centre on-surround formations. The retuning is due to *automatic gain control* by off-surround signals being inhibited. In this way a pattern of input can be inhibited no matter how intense it is. This is what is needed.

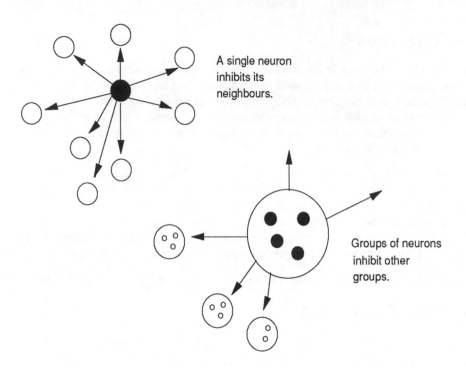

Fig.12.13: On-centre, off-surround topology.

Shunting

In a shunting network, excitatory inputs drive activity towards a finite maximum and inhibitory inputs drive activity towards a finite minimum. This displays the same principles as the classic neural model of single nerve cell dynamics for which Hodgkin and Huxley won a Nobel prize in 1963.

Noise supression has some natural properties. One is spatial frequency detection, that is, enabling particular cells to respond to particular regions. The other is that it can carry out pattern matching.

Another problem is that of determining which pattern it was that originally caused the mismatch, in order that it can be inhibited. This is a bit like sending 10 nearly identical portrait photos in separate envelopes all at once to a friend. You know in which order they were taken; the friend then says he likes the third one he looked at. Neither of you can identify which is which.

The solution to this is a *quenching threshold*.

Quenching mechanism and attention filter

Our senses are bombarded by a plethora of stimuli at every moment of our lives, both when awake and asleep. Not every one of these experiences is vital to us. If we are walking down a road we do not need to remember every tree, cloud, car that we pass but we may well need to remember the route we take. How then does the brain separate experiences which need to be retained and those which can fleet in and out of our memories just as quickly? We can, of course, force ourselves to remember things by concentration and repetition. Most number plates can be forgotten, but if the need arises to remember one you are able to shift your attention and commit it to memory. Grossberg described this in terms of an *attention filter*, which enables patterns to be selected for retention by adjusting the current response of the neurons – a quenching threshold which can adjust in level to determine which images go into memory and which just fleet through.

The mechanism is achieved by a function referred to as a *sigmoid* function, so called because of its shape (see Fig.12.14). This is well known and widely used in electronic circuitry. Basically the function causes a slow start to response to stimuli which picks up speed very rapidly as the input increases.

By increasing or decreasing the slope of the sigmoid, it can be used to determine the response of the neurons to stimuli, making them more or less sensitive. Input which is above the quenching threshold can be sent on to memory, being enhanced and detailed on the way, whereas that below is literally thrown out before it has a chance to be stored.

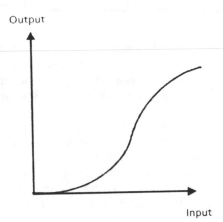

Fig.12.14: The sigmoid function starts off slowly, increases rapidly and then levels out.

By lowering the slope of the function, high sensitivity to experiences can be achieved.

The quenching threshold determines which activities are supressed and what is stored in STM. This is used to define noise in a recurrent net and can be tuned to suit current requirements.

Antagonistic rebound, on-cells and off-cells

An event which inhibits one response can cause another to be initiated. The response to you hearing your car start when you turn the key in the ignition will be for you to stop turning the key. If the engine starting was simply a signal that it had started there would not be any subsequent action. You would not be stimulated into releasing the handbrake etc. So the starting of the engine must also selectively initiate subsequent actions. The cells that are inhibited by the response are called the *on-cells*, and represent the turning of the key. Those turned on by the engine starting are called *off-cells* (a response mechanism). The activations being caused are called the *antagonistic rebound*.

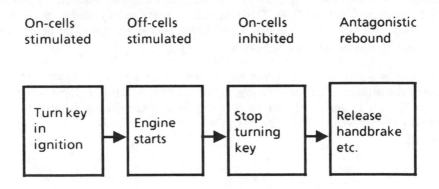

Fig.12.15: This diagram illustrates the relationship between groups of on-cells and the resultant antagonistic rebound. The on-cells stimulate the turning of the key, when the engine starts the off-cells are stimulated which in turn supress the on-cells. The antagonistic rebound comprises the actions carried out when the engine has started.

The size of this antagonistic rebound can be thought of as matching the amount of on-cell activation that has to be inhibited – the turning of the key is inhibited when the engine starts. In the event of a fright which turns out to be a mistake, the antagonist rebound may be quite large in order to supress fear and initiate a sense of relief. If such a mismatch is large enough to trigger a large arousal, all the necessary amendments to the stimulus will be made in order that the same mistake is avoided in the future.

A group of cells can be defined as being a field of *on-cell off-cell dipoles* such that the on-centre off-surround anatomy and the off-cells also interact with a recurrent on-centre off-surround anatomy. Using a dipole (see earlier) as a major field element has been a new insight into resetting errors and searching for new code. Another new idea is the way in which the arousal fluctuations interact with slowly varying, competing transmitter gates to cause either a rebound or a shift in the adaption level.

The way in which shunting interactions define the quenching threshold, normalises field activity and regulates contrast enhancement.

There is a difference between recurrent inhibition within a subfield and dipole inhibition between on-cells and their off-cells. The first creates a balance between mutually exclusive categories or features; the second normalises and tunes the subfield giving a one or the other, but not both, situation.

Continuous changes within subfields and complementary changes when dipole rebound causes a flip between the subfields has certain properties. *Dipole-on-cell* inhibits off-cell. This can disinhibit other off-cells which inhibits its own on-cell which responds by rebounding outwards, producing a negative after-effect to certain stimuli. This could be thought of as having circular symmetry if a cell excites other nearby cells and inhibits cells which are far away.

Nonspecific arousal is triggered by unexpected selectivity and will enduringly inhibit an activity. There will also exist broadly distributed waves triggered by unexpected events.

Adaptive Resonance

If an approximate match occurs mutual reinforcement will take place, with activities being amplified and locked into STM. Feedback expectancies enable sampling to take place and subsequent storage of a response in LTM. This is referred to as *adaptive resonance*. A global interpretation is provided with the cells reacting randomly until resonant feedback enables convergence to take place. No coding takes place in LTM until the resonance has occurred (in this respect this is a bit like the idea of chaos, see Chapter 16). The resonant state gives a context dependent code, the pattern being deformed before it is further reorganised by competition. In this way, adaptive resonance can be thought of as the functional units of cognitive coding. The central problem seems to be the classification of resonances that occur, the process involving whole fields of cells and not just individuals.

Feedback is essential for stabilising a developing code. Types of feedback used can be compared to previously derived attention mechanisms.

Stability Problem

One problem with all network models is that of stability, termed the *plasticity-stability dilemma*. This is the problem of finding how a model can be adaptive to new experiences, the plasicity part, and yet at the same time, not lose past experiences, the stability part. Researchers tend to get around this problem by either restricting the input patterns so the model is only presented with a certain type of environment. The problem is then changed to one concerning model capacity. Rumelhart and Zipser (1985) looked at simple environments whose probabilistic rules don't change with time, and Kohonen (1982) stabilised learning by physically intervening and shutting off plasticity before the previous learning is wiped out when a new environment is presented. These methods not only generate problems themselves but the general instability problem is still looming large.

Grossberg (1976) proved that if there were a restricted number of input patterns and the patterns did not form too many clusters, learning the recognition code eventually stabilises. He also showed that a competitive learning model could not learn a temporally stable learning code in response to arbitrary input, a situation which could easily occur in many applications. This is because of the net's adaptability which allows previous learning to be washed away by more recent learning, a problem which is common to most of the models now being developed. Grossberg developed the *Adaptive Resonance Theory* (ART) to deal with the problem.

Before we look at a class of models developed by Grossberg which use Adaptive Resonance Theory, the ART models, we will define the outstar and instar configurations.

Outstar

Developed by Grossberg in the 1960s, the outstar relates directly to the idea that sensory organs such as eyes and ears actually do a bit of processing themselves on the raw data prior to sending off to the brain what they have discovered.

The idea is that the eye has contact with a cloud of neurons called an outstar which grabs the raw pattern from the 50 or so types of feature extractor retinal cells and carries out a process of feedback and reinforcement to continuously refine the data. The input reaches the retina as a raw image, a pattern of dots if you like, because that is just about how meaningful the pattern is at that point. The outstar then responds to the pattern and sends the information to the brain which then combines the image with past experiences, expectations etc. in order to make more sense of it.

This resonating outstar cloud of neurons which grabs at perceptions can also be applied to grabbing on past experiences from long-term memory. The outstar is often used in spatial pattern learning.

Outstar (fan-out)

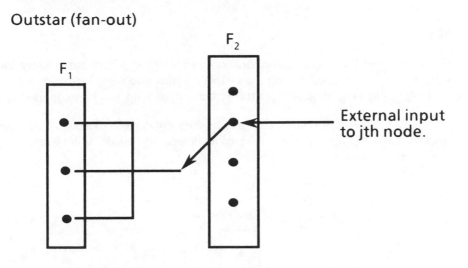

Fig.12.16: When applied to the existing pattern across F_1, F_2 can recreate the pattern at F_1 because the signal will be proportional to the original pattern.

A weight pattern from the jth node in F_2 is applied to the existing pattern across F_1. When the jth node is subsequently activated, a signal will be transmitted to F_1 which will be directly proportional to the original pattern at F_1, even though it is no longer there. So F_2 can recreate the required pattern at F_1.

In 1969 Grossberg developed an *avalanche* model which is in essence a series of outstars, a model capable of learning and performing an arbitrary space time pattern.

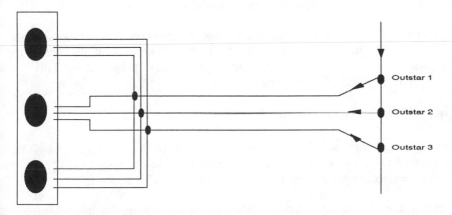

Fig.12.17: Avalanche model – a series of outstars. The pattern of activity at time t is a(t) and the outstar active at time t will learn the pattern of activity a(t).

Instar

This is an idea which explains how experiences can be incorporated into memory and how memory can be updated and yet the system remains stable, old memories are not washed away. The theorem guarantees that features in patterns will be recognised.

The instar often appears in systems designed to carry out content addressable memory or adaptive coding (Kohonen 1980). The basic competitive model is an instar filter and a competitive neural network.

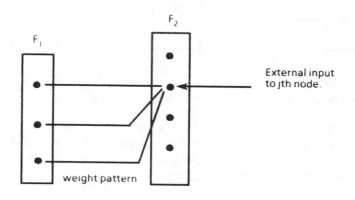

Fig.12.18: The pattern of activity created by the weight pattern from F_2. The jth node at F_2 has the most activity whenever the pattern is at F_1.

This is the reverse of the outstar configuration. The weights coming from the jth node at F_2 will cause the pattern at F_1 to be created. The outstar enables the jth node at F_2 to be maximally activated whenever that particular pattern is present at F_1. This can be thought of as the effect of past learning.

Competitive learning model

The basic learning properties of competitive models can be described in terms of the definitions we have made. Fig.12.19 shows two layers of units, F_1 and F_2. These are connected by an instar filter and there is a competitive neural network at F_2.

The network at F_2 can receive external input. In the absence of this, the total input will be from the instar. The pattern from the instar will cause the appropriate node in F_2 to be activated. With an external input to F_2, the signal will then be a combination of present and past. As this involves competitive learning the present signal may well dominate and overrule past experience. There will also be the opportunity to enhance the input and make it more meaningful by encorporating past learning into the process.

Outstar (fan-out)

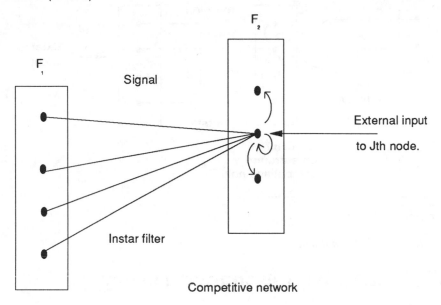

Pattern of activity.

Fig.12.19: Layers F_1 and F_2 are connected by an instar filter. Layer F_2 contains a competitive network. Input from the instar filter and from an external source to F_2 provides a combination of past and current experiences.

Computational maps

Systems designed to learn computational maps were a development which arose from the embedding of competitive learning systems into other neural networks, basically creating an instar outstar system (Grossberg 1972). These systems allow very different input and output patterns to be associated and for different input patterns to map onto the same output pattern.

In this general model in Fig.12.20 the instar unit is between layers F_1 and F_2, the competitive net is at F_2. These together form the basic competitive model. Joined to this is a layer F_3, with an outstar joining F_3 to F_2 enabling pattern learning of the result from F_1 and F_2 to take place.

Outstar (fan-out)

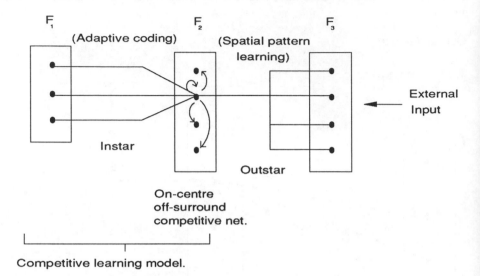

Fig.12.20: A computational map.

ART – Adaptive Resonance Theory

This model was developed by Stephen Grossberg in 1976 as a method of overcoming the plasticity-stability dilemma.

Simplifying or restricting the patterns to be input to a model means that one has been developed which is highly restricted in what it can and cannot deal with. This may well be adequate for sensory input models, for example, reading vision deals only with characters, ears deal only with sounds. Models such as this can have no general application and will still have severe limitations. The method of physically shutting off parts of the process is tricky because of the problem of knowing when to halt the model – too soon and learning will not take place, too late and previous memories may be erased. For a general purpose cognitive model, it is critical that it can deal with new environments. People do this every day. We are not told that we are driving along a road that we have never encountered before, nevertheless we can still negotiate the next junction and find our way home. We learn without the aid of a teacher; this is self-organisation.

Adaptive resonance theory (ART) is a model which can switch itself between its stable and plastic modes. This enables the model to remain sensitive to new events, yet at the same time remain stable in response to what Grossberg calls *irrelevant events* – his *blooming buzzing confusion* representation of everyday life. The model can, without a teacher, distinguish between familiar and unfamiliar events as well as between the expected and unexpected by the self-organisation of a sequence of input patterns into various recognition categories.

Now this sounds like quite an amazing achievement and certainly merits closer scrutiny. Grossberg defines four properties which are basic to the workings of his model and points out that essentially all other learning models leave out at least one of them.

Four vital properties

Self-scaling units

The system has to decide when a pattern is just noise and when it is to be treated seriously. For example, consider the diagrams in Fig.12.21.

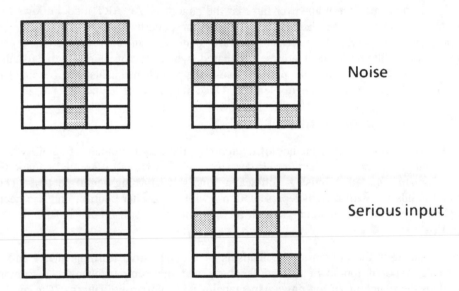

Noise

Serious input

Fig.12.21: The top pair must be treated by the system as the same pattern, the extra features being noise. The bottom pair of patterns must be seen by the system as being different even though they differ by the same features as the top pair.

The bottom pair shows two patterns which must be treated by the system as being different. In the top pair, the same mismatch occurs and the two patterns differ by the same feature, but in this one it has to be treated as noise and ignored.

This introduces the idea of a *critical feature*. When is a critical feature not a critical feature? When is it just noise? This is where the idea of scaling comes in because the gist of it seems to be that in the first example pair there were only three features so each must be important, whereas in the second pair there were a lot more so the extra is judged on a scale not to be important.

Self-adjusting memory search

As the knowledge structure changes through learning, the search mechanism that was efficient may well become inefficient. The ART system uses a parallel memory search which automatically changes to best suit the current conditions. It should be stressed that this is not programmed but is part of the network's self-stabilising mechanism, adding a bit of randomness to the initial memory recognition codes which enables the search to continue until it becomes stable.

Direct access to learned codes

People can recognise familiar objects very quickly. Models in general will need to carry out the same search however familiar the pattern is. An ART model allows the search mechanism to be disabled and a familiar pattern to directly activate the appropriate category. These critical feature patterns can also be activated by non-familiar patterns if the features are shared, which acts as a prototype for the whole class. Totally unfamiliar patterns cause the search mechanism to be enabled and a suitable recognition category learned. Once the pattern is learned it is disabled.

The General ART model

ART was put forward as a method of overcoming the major problem of stability and of explaining memory and learning. It describes, using a set of differential equations, a self-organising, self-stabilising, self-scaling and self-adjusting neural network. The model builds its own internal representations, with no teacher control, and has been applied to eye models, learning, speech recognition and has also been independently verified.

The model uses the bottom-up mechanisms of a competitive learning model and a particular type of top-down learned feedback and matching mechanism. Learning involves the matching of top-down expectancies with bottom-up patterns. The model uses previously discovered mechanisms, which Grossberg formally shows enables code learning to self stabilise for an essentially arbitrary input environment (Grossberg 1976).

A model of vision developed by Grossberg is able to recognise partially obscured geometric figures. Continuously shaded elements of a scheme being organised into perceptual groupings by sensory objects. It has been shown that a feedback loop between the cooperative and competitive levels (like the eye) in a network of analog processors could cancel noise. This has also been independently verified.

Different environments may demand either fine or coarse recognition between the same set of objects. For example, if you are splitting a list of numbers into those above a certain value and those below, you need to pay less attention than you would if you were asked to put them into numerical order. The ART system is able to also become more vigilant to detail and more sensitive to mismatches. There are currently three ART models: the first one we will look at has two layers and is the simplest.

Architecture

Grossberg's description of how his model deals with input at each stage of the processing has a large number of pattern definitions. Basically the input pattern is turned into different states depending on whether it is then expressed as a pattern of activity across some units, or as a pattern which has undergone some process and changed. Grossberg's terminology has been used if you wish to refer to his papers (Grossberg 1990). The basic architecture for the model is shown in Fig.12.22.

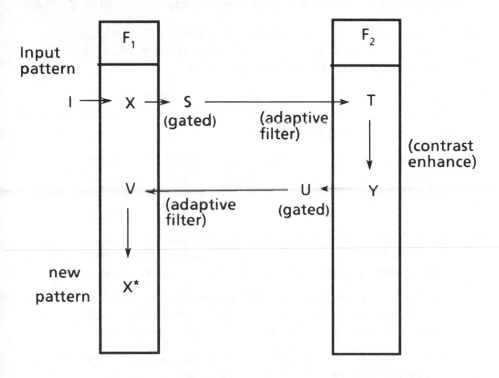

Fig.12.22: This diagram shows the patterns as they progress through layers F_1 and F_2 in the ART model.

The model is the same as the computational map except that it folds back onto itself. The top layer F_3, can thus identify with the bottom layer F_1. So this uses a bottom-up competitive learning system together with a top-down outstar pattern learning system. We will look at exactly how this network responds to input.

ART Network reaction to input

Before we look at what happens to the input pattern, it should just be noted that the pattern may be preprocessed, for example in the case of speech or vision, into the input pattern form we are now going to look at.

In   The input pattern, when it hits the model, becomes a pattern of activity across the set of feature detectors, referred to in their entirety as F_1 in the diagram. F_1 can be thought of as short-term memory (STM).

S   Nodes within F_1 will each have a state of activity, which as usual will be compared with some kind of threshold value to decide whether or not their activity is large enough to warrant them firing and passing output to the next stage, a group of units called F_2. The output signal pattern from F_1 is called S.

Gate   While the pattern S is on the way to F_2 it is gated by the path's long-term memory (LTM) trace. This gating mechanism acts rather like a weight and multiplies the individual outputs by some value.

T   The nodes in F_2 add up their total input from the gated values of pattern S and the pattern of activity thus formed over F_2 is called T. The transformation from S to T is called an *adaptive filter*

Y   The F_2 nodes then *contrast-enhance* the pattern T to give a new pattern Y which is stored in STM by F_2. It is worth noting at this point that this process also occurs in a CL model. Y is a category representation for S, the activity at F_1.

U   Pattern Y in F_2 will cause STM activities and those large enough to be taken into account create a new pattern of activity called U. This travels back down from F_2 towards F_1, referred to as a *top-down excitatory* signal pattern.

V   The U signals are also gated by LTM traces on the way back down and when the pattern U hits F_1, the F_1 nodes sum their input. This produces a pattern of activity across the F_1 units called V which is the output pattern.

        So the transformation from U to V is also an adaptive filter and pattern V is called a *top-down template* or *learned expectation*.

X*   The units which make up F_1 now have two patterns, I and V, to contend with which together give rise to a new pattern called X*. This will almost undoubtedly be different from the original X. If the two patterns I and V are not sufficiently similar according to a vigilance parameter, the representation is supressed and the process repeats itself to try to find a better category representation. The search continues until something close enough is found or a new category is established. The setting of this vigilance parameter is important because it will determine how much of a mismatch can be allowed to occur. Johnson (1989) likens a low vigilance to daydreaming where many strange situations can be tolerated.

So the patterns are:

I   Input pattern

bottom-up

X   pattern across F_1 of I
S   output from F_1 – depends on activity levels
T   input pattern to F_2 of S through adaptive filter
Y   pattern across F_2 of T – contrast enhanced, stored in STM

top-down

U   output from F_2 – depends on activity levels
V   input pattern to F_1 of U through adaptive filter
X*   resulting pattern at F_1 from combination of V and X

The adaptive filtering is carried out very quickly, too quickly for the LTM traces to change at all but prior learning will influence the resulting Y and X* patterns.

This enables past learning to be blended with the original input signal so that the resulting activity pattern is a combination of past and present rather than current input alone. Even with rapid learning this has been shown to lead to stability.

Conclusion

The adaptive filter is general enough to allow modules to be developed for associative memory, category learning and pattern recognition. Many systems developed over the last few years are variations on this modular theme. The aim is that this may be the start of a core vocabulary able to be used for further analysis.

The Cognitron and Neocognitron are examples of competitive learning models for character recognition and are desribed in Chapter 20.

13

Reinforcement Learning Procedure

The achievements made by back propagation and the Botzmann machine are quite simple (Arbib 1990) and are examples of gradient descent methods which yield comparable solutions. To this end a neurally realistic algorithm needs to be developed. Terence Sejnowski is of the opinion that perhaps the reinforcement learning procedure is the right direction.

This learning method views patterns created by the neurons as memory pathways maintained by the walker's traffic, with unused ones gradually disappearing and others being reinforced by continued use.

Some aspects of the learning procedure consider the activity of neurons in terms of automata and associated actions. Other areas make the comparison with genetic constraints in evolutionary terms as a method of improving responses to input.

Reinforced Learning

The central idea behind the procedure in most models of this kind is that a credibility is assigned to a decision made at a local level by measuring the effect it has on a *global reinforcement signal* (GRS). This is done by making slight changes to the signals (weights or states) and then looking to see how much the GRS has changed.

If enough samples are taken each local variable can average out the noise which may in effect be from other variable changes and leave just its own effect. The network then carries out a gradient descent procedure on the *expected reinforcement* (ER) by changing the probability distribution of the local variable to increase the ER.

This method is easier than back-propagation which calculates the effect of local variable changes, because there is no need for computations. The model can be used in a complex system but it does become inefficient if too many variable are involved. The reason for this is that you have a situation where a total is available but no information about the individual contributions. Larger systems could be divided up into smaller modules.

There is a local minima problem associated with the model. As the network gets more and more information about the results of combinations of units which give the highest ER value, there is less information available about the other combinations.

Delayed Reinforcement

In many models there is a temporary time delay between an action and resulting reinforcement. This means the information being worked with could literally be either out of date or very relevant. Do you assess something on its current achievement or continued performance over time?

This is solved in back-propagation by calculating the effect of each activity on the total. In reinforcement learning the procedure is to learn to associate *secondary* reinforcement values with the states between action and reinforcement, with the view to pushing the inbetween state reinforcement value towards a weighted average of past values. Eventually the reinforcement value will be equal to that of the previous one and ultimately to the final reinforcement value. The idea behind this is that it is more effective to do this calculation for the next state than for the final result (Sutton 1987).

A_{r-p}

When mapping automata theory onto a neural network each unit can be treated as an automata. The states of the units can be thought of as its actions. This is the idea behind *associative reward penalty* (A_{r-p}) (Barto and Anandan 1985), a system which uses stochastic units like those used by the Boltzmann machine.

If the input vectors are linearily independent and the network has only one unit (one automaton with many actions), the optimal weight values can be found using A_{r-p}. If extended to a network with hidden units these are found to develop useful internal representations of the patterns.

Global Optimality

This is a method where the connections are treated as automata and the weights as actions. During each network trial, the connection selects the weight value, the choice being reinforced if the input vector maps successfully onto the output vector.

Thatachar and Sastry (1985) have developed a learning procedure for updating the probabilities of particular weight values being selected. If the changes for these probabilities are slow enough it has been found that the network is guaranteed to converge onto a globally optimal combination of weights for a given pattern even if hidden units are involved.

The drawback of this is that a table of weight values has to be maintained, containing one entry for every combination of weights. With 10 units this value will be 10! (10 factorial) which is 10x9x8x...x3x2x1 = 3,628,800 assuming full connectivity and non-symmetric weights.

Relative Payoff

If we are quite happy with a local as opposed to a global maximum being achieved a simple learning rule can be used to map automata onto the neural network.

Minsky (1954) defined a stochastic switch with an associated probability of being closed. If the switch was found to be open it sends a 0 to the post-synaptic unit (no connection), if closed it sends input. Real synapses can be modelled using such a set of switches operating in parallel. Each circuit computes a fixed number of inputs and learning is the process of changing the probabilities of the switches being closed (able to send input) to maximise the ER signal.

This can be applied to reinforcement learning as a very simple process which guarantees only a local minimum. This is done as follows:

Set the switch configuration using the current probabilities which are determined independently for each switch.

Run the network under that configuration. There are no constraints on the connectivity (there can be loops) and any unit can receive external input.

Find the reinforcement signal.

Update the switch probabilities according to the following rule:

For each switch closed during the test run, add the following small amount to its probability:

$eR(1-p)$ where: R: the reinforcement found during the test
                     p: the probability for the switch
                     e: some small amount

If the amount e is small enough this will correspond to the idea of taking small steps and will cause the result to converge towards a solution – i.e. gradient descent.

If a number of trials are carried out before the update to the probabilities are made this is called *relative payoff*. This procedure involves changing the probabilities so that they are equal to the fraction of the total reinforcement received when the switch was closed. This will always (given enough trials are observed) either increase the expected reinforcement or leave it unchanged.

Genetic algorithms

Holland (1975) and Davis et al., (1987) have studied this type of learning, *genetic algorithms*, so called because they are inspired by evolution, as is all the terminology involved.

The algorithm aims to change a population such that a better adapted population energes. The simplest version of this is where each member of the populus is assigned a number of values likened to genes. The idea of learning is to produce *fitter* members of the population. This is done by choosing pairs of existing members of the population as *parents* and choosing a combination of the *best* genes from each to form a fitter offspring.

Holland has shown that for a large class this provides a good method of discovering the fittest individuals.

Genetic algorithms and Relative Payoff

When all the offspring are updated simultaneously the process is similar to the relative payoff method of applying many trials before the update takes place.

In a simple example of the genetic rule, we can consider an offspring as having several parents and to have selected the best genes from all of them. The way the genes are chosen seems initially to be quite absurd because the components are copied at random from the parents. However, once a new set of offspring have been established in this way they are then assessed for fitness and the worst are rejected. It could be viewed as assigning a reinforcement of 1 to those that are retained, 0 to those that are not.

The probability at this point that the ith component has a particular value is equal to the fraction of successful candidates with that value. This is exactly the relative payoff rule.

Unfortunately, having randomly chosen the parents, information about any correlations between them and their offspring will not be retained. This can be avoided by choosing just two specific parents from which to propagate.

Iterative Hill-Climbing

Genetic learning can be combined with gradient descent to form the learning procedure *iterative hill-climbing* (IHC) which seems to work more effectively than either rule in isolation (Brady 1985, Ackley 1987).

It is described as a *multiple-start hill-climbing* process and can be viewed in two different ways. On the one hand, gradient descent is achieved by mating together local minima to produce the starting points. Alternatively it can be seen as genetic learning because each new individual has a chance to prove fitness or otherwise prior to being judged for addition to the population.

Ackley shows that a stochastic variation of IHC can be implemented using a neural network required to learn which combination of values produces a high enough payoff to satisfy certain external conditions.

14

Recurrent Networks

So far we have looked only at feedforward networks, that is, networks in which a layer can only send input to the layer above it, the one closer to the output layer.

Networks with feedback are called *recurrent networks* and allow connections to go in either direction from all the layers and have been defined by Michael Jordan as:

> *"If a network has one or more cycles, that is, if it is possible to follow a path from a unit back to itself, then the network is referred to as recurrent".*
> M.Jordan, 1989

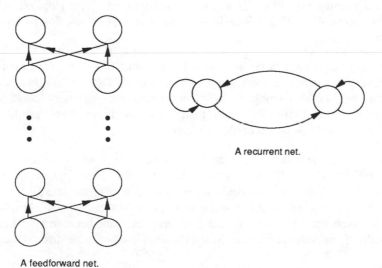

A recurrent net.

A feedforward net.

Fig.14.1: A recurrent network allows feedback.

Thus the output of the network not only depends on the input but also on the state of the network at the previous time step.

The reason for using recurrent networks is that they possess important features which feedforward networks do not have, namely that events from the past can be retained and used in current computations. They also allow the network to produce complex, time-varying outputs in response to simple static input which is important when generating complex behaviour. They also enable constraint satisfaction.

Stability

It has been found that recurrent networks are unstable only very infrequently and when no measures have been taken to ensure stability (Sejnowski 1989). One method of assuring stability is symmetric connectivity first introduced by Hopfield (1982) and later used in the Boltzmann machine. This does not seem to impair the performance of the network at all (Almeida 1989). Another method (Grossberg 1983) is lateral shunting inhibition. Perhaps the easiest way of avoiding instability is by not having feedback at all.

Application to Hopfield's network and the Boltzmann machine (Almeida 1989)

Back-propagation can be viewed as moving stable states towards desired positions. If the network has weight symmetry, the feedback weights are set to 0 and there are no hidden units, this is the same as the Hopfield net. In this way back-propagation could be seen as a training algorithm for a graded Hopfield net. (The Hopfield net uses binary values normally.) This is put forward as a natural choice for patterns with analog value features.

Because back-propagation can be used with hidden units this particular drawback of the Hopfield net would be eliminated. There would also be no necessity for symmetrical weights, this being a sufficient though not necessary condition for stability. However, stability could not then be ensured but there would be no limitations on the patterns which could be stored.

A Boltzmann machine can be defined by having a network with feedback and symmetric weights, the feedback weights being set to 0 and an appropriate function amendment. So back-propagation could be used to minimise the energy function at some desired location. This could be faster than the Boltzmann machine but does not guarantee the existence of global minima at desired locations because all minima are treated equally. However, the minima do tend to be moved towards desired locations.

Back Propagation and Training

There have been many approaches to this. Rumelhart, Hinton and Wiliams (1985) suggested a general framework in terms of a multi-layer feedforward network which was the unfolded version of the recurrent network and grows by one layer every time step. Algorithms based on this architecture are referred to as *back–propagation through time*. These work well when enough is known about the time structure of the problem in order to limit the number of layers to a reasonable value.

Many problems unfortunately are not of this type. If a net with a limited set of carefully chosen recurrent connections is used this can learn some of the tasks but limitations do not allow complete generality. Another method is to have units with connections back onto themselves and none with other units (Mozer 1988), a very simple method which allows learning.

Another approach is to allow the network to settle at the end of each teaching cycle into a stable state using the actual and desired values.

Without going into great detail here, Williams and Zipser (1988) have derived a learning procedure for a network with the following architecture. Any unit can be connected to any other unit and all can receive external input. The networks run continuously, sampling inputs on every update cycle and any unit can receive training signals on every cycle. Storage and computation is independent of time, and no previous knowledge of the temporal or complete nature of the task is required. No relaxation or anything similar is needed, and the algorithm is non-local as each unit needs to have knowledge of all the weights and errors for the whole network.

The learning algorithm is basically the same as the method of back-propagation and can be loosely defined as follows:

Given   N units
          M input units

Then

     $y(t)$ a list of the N outputs at time t
     $x(t)$ a list of the M inputs at time t
     $z(t)$ some combination of y(t) and x(t) such that:
                $z_k = y_k(t)$ k in U   output   (k is in a set U)
                $z_k = x_k(t)$ k in I   input   (k is in a set I)
     w_{ij} the weight from the jth unit to the ith unit

A bias can be incorporated into the model.

The units are assumed to be semilinear although the definition can be applied to non linear units.

$$S_k(t) = \sum W_{ki}y_{i\ (i\ in\ U)} + \sum W_{ki}x_{i\ (i\ in\ I)}$$

$$\sum W_{ki}z_i(t) \qquad\qquad \text{where i is in U or I, k is in U}$$

Discrete time intervals are used although it is easily extended for the continuous version.

$$y(t+1) = f_k(S_k(t)) \qquad \text{the next time step}$$

where f_k is an undefined squashing function.

Note that the input at time t does not affect the output from any unit until time t+1

Like the method of back-propagation the weights are adapted and the process is as follows:

measure the performance of the network
compute the gradient in the weight space
minimise the error

$$e_k(t) = \quad d_k(t) - y_k(t) \qquad \text{k in T(t)}$$
$$ 0 \qquad\qquad\qquad \text{otherwise}$$

where $d_k(t)$ is the desired output

$$J(t) = \quad 1/2 \sum [e_k(t)]^2 \qquad \text{(summed over k in U)}$$

the network error at time t

This total error is minimised for the network's complete run time from t_0 to t_1.

The weights are accumulated and the weight change made at the end of this run time.

Improvements to Feedforward models

Real time

The process of accumulating the weights and updating them at the end of the network's run time is equivalent to the procedure in a feedforward net of presenting all the patterns, then making the weight changes, rather than changing the weights at the end of each pattern presentation.

Because of this it was more useful to make the weight changes while the network was actually running. This will bring the model into real-time and allow on-line training to occur. This is referred to as *real-time back–propagation* and the weight changes are made at the end of each time step.

One problem with doing this is that the path taken by the network may well depend upon the weight changes and can be viewed as *another source of negative feedback in the system*. To avoid this the learning rate needs to be kept very small.

An advantage of updating the weights in this way is that the path of the network will obviously reflect the changes much more accurately and there will be no need to define time boundaries during training. The algorithm can be run continuously.

Teacher Forcing

Teacher forcing is the procedure whereby the activity of the network in the future is based on some predefined value rather than just allowing it to free run. The dynamics are altered during the training of the network which implies an amendment to the learning algorithm. The algorithm is basically the same except that the procedure is as follows:

❑ compute free running state of the network at time t based on the teacher forced state at time t-1

❑ compute the values of the weights

❑ compute the weight updates for time t

❑ set to zero all the weights for which teacher forcing is to be imposed

❑ set the teacher forced state of the network in preparation for the next step

This process has turned out to be essential for training networks to oscillate (see Chapter 20, Chaos theory) and appears in the work of Pineda 1987, Widrow and Stearns (1985).

Simulations

One of the main goals was to see how efficient the algorithm was at solving problems with the minimum of previously presented knowledge. The model used was one with all units fully connected and each able to receive input. A subset was used to give the output and this was the only one contributing to the error value. Initially the weights were randomly set. The version without teacher forcing was used except for the examples with oscillations.

Examples are given to show that recurrent networks can do things that networks with tapped delay lines are unable to, that is networks that require the preservation of state. The simplest example needs only a flip-flop (see Chapter 17), and the most complex is a network that learns to emulate a Turing machine carrying out a parenthesis balancing problem. Also included are examples of networks doing feedforward computations with unknown delays, a task which needs the original recurrent network to organise itself into a multi-layer feedforward net with the right number of layers. Examples of networks learning to oscillate in a number of ways are also given.

They conclude that the algorithm is powerful and general enough to train completely recurrent, continually updated networks to learn temporal tasks, no previous information being given to the network concerning the temporal nature of the task.

Brain State in a Box

This model defines a basic linear *autoassociator* with error correction and a simple non-linearity. The model is associative because it associates a vector with itself and autoassociative because the output is fed back into the network as input.

In 3-d the model has three input values which could be thought of as the vertices of a cube.

When the input is fed into the model, the error between the actual and desired output values is found and an associative learning algorithm is generally used to adjust the weights to reduce the error.

The space within the box is divided into areas of attraction and if we were to follow the path of the activity we would find that it heads for an edge and then follows it to a corner. The input is then classified by the corners of the box. This has been shown to be the same as minimising an energy function (Hopfield 1982).

The stability problem is avoided by bounding the model within a box and after many iterations, the model becomes stable in one of the corners and does not change. It tries to push out of the corner but cannot because of the boundaries. The fact that it cannot escape from the corner does present problems because the network is unable to respond to new input.

Anderson (1981) relates this model to a measure of human performance with the stabilisation time representing the response.

Learning has been carried out using two different learning rules. The simplest is put forward by Anderson and Mozer (1981) who allow the system to settle and then use Hebbian learning. The Delta error correction rule has also been used (Anderson et al.,1990) where the input provides the teaching as well as being a source of activation, forcing the system to give more accurate associations.

15

The Organisation of the Brain

"Human action, memory, learning and percption are far richer than those of any machine yet built or likely to be built in the near future". Arbib 1985.

By attempting to understand the brain through developing models and observing the results a better understanding should be achieved.

There is a great deal of research going on to try and discover how the brain works. Progress is made tricky by the fact that there are many ways in which cells respond. Neurons are not typical, some have an axon as long as a leg, others have no axon at all. Some even go bang, as biologists put it, and then just stay on. There are not many of this last type but they are very good at creating single nerve pulses perhaps to detonate an event. One thing that seems to be apparent is that the brain can be split into different regions and cooperative computation exists between the different structures.

Understanding the brain

Although research is making a lot of headway with understanding the mysteries of the brain, there is currently no strong theory, because not much is known about how the sense organs process incoming perceptions, and how the brain deals with the information sent to it. Physiologists can look inside the brain, and theorists can notice the sense organs performing cognitive functions. There is a need for pure neurology to be integrated with mathematics, psychology, physiology and computer science before a full picture will be available.

There are ways in which the brain's cells, pulses and chemicals combine in order to produce what we could term intelligent thought. It is necessary to use the philosophy of integrating neuron knowledge, mathematics about the brain and the computer technology in order to implement and model the whole process with success.

Computer models which *look like* a pattern of connected neurons can, and have been developed, but how the seemingly simple interactions between the neurons actually represent knowledge and thought is a completely different problem.

Simulations of such models have also been developed using traditional serial processing systems, but there is quite a difference between a simulation and a model. A model can give new insight into actual events. A simulation, however, can only tell you what you already know (see Chapter 4) – nothing new can be learnt. Technology at this point does not allow us to build accurate models of the brain, the sheer physical problem of attaching 10,000 or more connections to 100 billion processors is infeasible. Because of this, and the fact that the brain does comprise interacting modules, studies and research tend to focus on particular parts of the brain. For example visual and audial perceptions, speech recognition, areas which are also of great practical application in the real world.

Animals or machines?

Because *humans are animals* we can look at animal brains to try and find information. On the other hand, if *humans are machines* the similarities and differences between our capabilities and those of artificial intelligence machines can be studied.

By viewing humans as a distributed computer enables us to understand how machines can give insights into the brain, This was the aim of cybernetics which is defined as the *"study of control and communication in man and machine"*, a discipline which has been referred to more recently as cognitive science.

There are many different approaches used – studies involving linguistics, sentence structure, the response time and eye movement involved in sentence comprehension and the effect of brain damage. All these are very different and tend to deal with specific applications. The first two look in at the brain from the outside, the last looks at its structure.

Artificial Intelligence

AI aims to discover how existing computer systems can be programmed to display intelligent behaviour. No connection is intended to be made between such a program and the brain. The premise is that suprising complex behaviour can be broken down into conditional structures of simple units.

Brain Theory

Brain theory uses mathematics and simulation in an attempt to discover the organisation principles behind the construction of a representation of the environment, and how interactions of the components of the brain can yield perception, memory and motion control. Ideas and theories are put to the test by computer program, simulation or using a theory of mathematics. The results are then compared with data from experiments.

This line of work has developed into:

Computational neuroscience   the development of better computational models

Neural engineering   a new branch of AI which deals with the design of machines based on the brain but not very faithful to it.

Cognitive Science

Cognitive science is the middle man, bringing together research on AI, brain theory and cognitive psychology descended from cybernetics (Arbib 1989). The requirement of a cognitive model is to explain psychological data, and units in such a model not necessarily having to correspond to brain structures. The emphasis in the past has been mostly on symbol manipulation and the structure of the brain has been ignored. More recently, increased attention has been paid to structure because it has been found that neural networks exhibit properties which are useful to the researchers. (Rumelhart and McClelland,1986).

Levels of research

There are also many different levels of brain study; Top-down, starting with observed overall behaviour and ending with a functional analysis of that behaviour in terms of agents called schemas, through to bottom-up deduced from the properties of the neurons. Schema theory (see Chapter 18) provides a link between a functional description of the brain and neural networks.

Brain Damage

A great deal of information about the brain is gleaned from observations of people who have suffered brain damage, or undergone surgery. For example, using a study of people suffering from gunshot wounds, Fritsch and Hitzig found that a part of the brain related directly to the eyes, and that there were well defined parts of the brain relating to muscle control. Observing the effects of damage to the brain is a seemingly straightforward yet interestingly complex method of research. As Dr. David Touretzky (Personal communication) points out, this kind of research is similar to shooting a bullet through a computer and then studying what the effects are.

A great deal of useful work has been done in this direction but when the brain is a collective and cooperative entity, it is tricky to isolate parts. The whole system is so very complex and our methods for research are still very limited. Some actions like breathing, fight or flight responses, are built in as automatic functions, the result of structures in the brain. Others are initiated by a *conscious* effort, and most are carried out without us even having to *think* about them. We are as Jerre Levy (1990) points out: *"trying to understand the most complex piece of matter in the known universe"*.

Parts of the brain

There has been a popular belief for some time that the left side of the brain relates to logical thought, the right side is the centre of creativity. It has been said that if you are talking on the telephone, and the call is one which requires rational thought you should put the phone to your left ear. When you are talking to a friend, or need to be understanding and helpful, put the phone to your right ear.

Jerre Levy is a researcher at the University of Chicago who has been trying to dispel the rigidity of this idea. She says that: *"No complex function-music, art or whatever can be assigned to one hemisphere or the other. Any high-level thinking in a normal person involves constant communication between the two sides of the brain"*.

The origins are in science: Roger Sperry carried out a number of experiments, for which he won the Nobel Prize, on the minds of people who had undergone surgery to sever the *corpus callosum* (the link between the two sides of the brain) which is a treatment for intractable epilepsy. It was found that if an object was put into the left hand of such a patient who was blindfolded, they would deny its existence. But if asked to search a group of objects for something similar to the one they were told was in their left hand, they would choose the right one, even though they said it was a guess. Sperry had found that the two sides of the brain had different specialisations. However the resulting speculation made by others was an exaggeration of the facts.

Sperry certainly found that the left side was better at logical deductions such as those found in mathematics, and the right side was better at everday logic, drawing conclusions and integrating information. Almost all activities are a combination of the two and because of this there is constant communication between the two halves. In language, for example, the left side is better at understanding syntax and grammar, while the right is better at understanding the tone of a phrase and interpreting emotion. This can be applied to everything – music, art – they all involve both sides of the brain. The idea of the left side relating to the logical and the right side to the artistic side of a person is perhaps not an unreasonable assumption given the results of the experiment above, but the real solution is not so clear cut. The brain is far more complex and such observations can actually be very misleading (Dejerine 1982).

There is also the popular belief that only 10% of the brain is actually used. This grew out of a misunderstanding derived from statements that the brain suffers little or no effect from cell damage. Basically it is another case of not really knowing what the neurons do. So what do we know about the structure of the brain?

Central Nervous System

We do know that the central nervous system (CNS) enables a continuous stream of information to be collected from the millions of receptors in the sense organs which constantly monitor changes in our external and internal environment. These travel via the CNS, of which the brain is the headward part, and sent to the midbrain for analysis and processing. The route taken is via a channel of nerves between the vertebrae of the spinal chord. The total CNS is usually taken to be the brain and the spinal chord.

When these signals reach the brain, they interact with billions of signals, and are modified by existing memories. In this way current action depends on both current stimuli and past experience. Effectors in the brain then cause effects on our bodies and subsequently the outside world.

Body Control

Muscles are made up of thousands of fibres and are controlled by motor neurons in the spinal chord. The axons along which these messages travel may be very long, for example, from the spinal chord to your big toe, or they may be very tiny. The smallest functional unit on the motor side is the motor unit, a *motor neuron cell*, made up of an axon plus the group of muscle fibres over which it has an influence. Like any neuron, the motor unit receives input. The response, however, to this input is that the muscle fibres contract and so control bodily movement. A similar process operates for cells which control sweat glands, tears or the release of chemicals into the blood although the response will take a different form. When the input to a motor unit controlling a muscle stops, the muscle fibre relaxes and another pair of muscles returns the limb to normal.

Evolution

If we think of the brain as something that has evolved over time, it can be viewed as layers, beginning with the brain stem. This controls bodily functions and is made up of a number of parts, including the surrounding cerebellum. It is the oldest, evolutionary-wise, part of the brain structure, other parts having been built on top as the brain grew and developed. Initially the brain was required to deal with daily functioning of the body – movement, heart rate, breathing etc. Later there developed the need for structures with the ability to deal with things such as current perceptions, short-term memory, emotions, and more highly coordinated bodily functions such as riding a bike or playing tennis. The old and new exist and function together, giving a person a combination of primordial impulses, reasoning and emotions to consider. From reflex actions to delayed emotional shock, and logical reasoning, all exist side by side and have carefully evolved over time, to deal with developing needs.

Brain structure

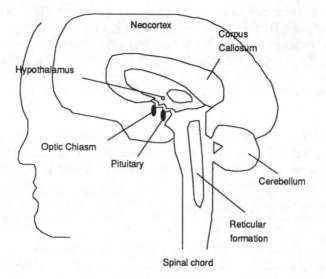

Fig.15.1: A cross section of the brain showing the central structure.

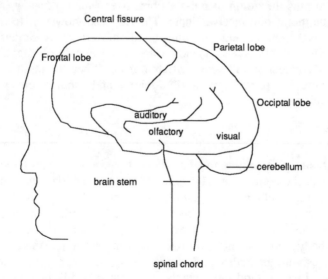

Fig.15.2: The brain viewed as a whole showing the external lobes.

White and Grey matter

The brain is generally referred to as being made up of two types of matter, white and grey. The white matter comprises neural tissue, mainly axons, the grey matter is rich in cell bodies and dendrites

Cerebral cortex

The cerebral cortex is a sheet 1/8th inch thick, about 50 to 100 neurons in depth. This is folded to form the image of the brain as a grey wrinkly mass which appears to be in two joined halves. In fact, this contains many billions of neurons in its folds. Humans have a new cortex or neocortex, which dominates the brain.

Cerebrum

The Cerebrum is the area made up of four lobes called the frontal, temporal, parietal and occipital. It is made up of two parts which are joined by the corpus callosum, an underlying white matter connected to the cerebral cortex, the grey matter.

Hippocampus

The hippocampus is a large and intricate structure situated between the midbrain and the cortex layer, spiralling around the thalamus and ending in the hypothalamus.

There are many other named regions of the brain but these are the major definitions that we need to know.

Brain functions

The brain enables a person to create an image of their environment from outside stimulus. From years of experimentation and observations of both animals and people, it seems that each part of the brain deals with a different aspect of the environment. For example, it appears that the back of the head relates to visual sensations, the information about which is fed forward to the temporal area, which deals with integrating and changing experiences. Then on to the parietal lobe, which could be thought of as assembling a world view. In this way the subject is able to gather current information and also to draw on past experience in order to create a total picture of the environment. The cortex or grey matter, is thoroughly connected to the rest of the deep brain from beneath by fibrous white matter. This information highway handles the chain of activities which starts with conscious thought and ends in action.

Two bands run across the top of the brain receiving perceptions from the body's surface, with one fold under the temporal lobe relating to hearing. The frontal lobe seems to deal with long range plans and high-level cognition, which has been deduced from the fact that people who have had lobotomies are found to be incapable of, and unmotivated towards, achieving complex future goals.

Cortex

The cortex is thought to contain functions which allow perceptions to be stored in short-term memory, and thus is the key to learning.

Outer cortex

It seems now that the outer cortex of the brain deals with most of the pattern recognition functions. There has been found to be six distinct layers, the outer layer relating to primordial sensation, which seems to feed down along the slabs to more abstract forms of pattern recognition. For example, a slab may be one part of the visual field, and deeper within the slabs are features, detectors and object information. For the most part these look like flat sheets with no cross over connections.

Cerebellum

The cerebellum is thought to be involved in learning the control of movement and contains five major types of nerve cell. Two types of input are needed, through what are called the mossy fibres and the climbing fibres. The mossy fibres contact a particular class of output cells indirectly via other cells, whereas the climbing fibres contact them directly. Theories have been developed by Marr (1969) and Albus (1971) which define the climbing fibres as those which relay direct instructions to other cells in order to control elemental movements, and the mossy fibres relay the context in which the movement is carried out. There is continuous communication between the different parts of the brain in order to enable a person to perceive and react to their surrounding environment.

Cerebrum

The cerebrum is thought to be the newest area of the brain that has evolved, and represents intelligence. This has always been thought to be true; people with large foreheads tend to be percieved as being more intelligent, this common belief being reflected in certain researchers of electrical appliances shown in television adverts.

Midbrain

The middle of the brain is believed to deal with cognition, with the thalamus as the central control. Raw data is received from the senses and is combined with memories stored in the long-term memory. The thalamus, surrounded by the limbic system and connected to the cerebral cortex via the white matter, seems to relate the new information to the correct part of the cerebral cortex in order that it can be integrated into experience.

Hippocampus

The hippocampus seems to play an important role in certain types of learning and memory (Zipser, 1986). It has been shown that spatial learning, the problem associated with how animals find their way around, is severely impaired by hippocampal damage. There seems to be cells within the hippocampus which respond to particular areas of a familiar environment (Dr.John O'Keefe). It could be that the hippocampus forms an internal representation, like a spatial map, with different cells representing different places, or that the hippocampus learns distances and directions of certain important objects with respect to each other. Hippocampal research has become an important issue. For example, Dr. R. G. M. Morris and Dr. D. J. Wilshaw have been awarded a Programme Grant to study the hippocampus. Part of their research will focus on the development of a computer model of spatial learning.

Schmajuk (1988) suggested that the brain is separated into modules capable of storing limited amounts of different information eg. sensory, spatial, motor etc. Gazzaniga (1984) had previously proposed it was the hippocampus that relates the storage of new information into the memory modules. It has been said that attentional mechanisms in the brain determine the level of processing assigned to each stimulus, with an intensity proportional to the novelty of the stimulus; also that the brain constructs a neural model of external events and a response is given when new input to the brain is not recognised in which case new aspects are stored. If the input is recognised a response may occur without changing the existing neural model.

Once a neural model has been obtained, it is suggested that the hippocampus reduces attention assigned to those stimuli associated with non-reinforcement, or that it acts as a filter preventing the process of information storage when the system is stable. Monkeys with hippocampal and amygdalar lesions have a reduced capacity for getting new information from the world but not in the ability to acquire new perceptual-motor skills. These are interesting insights but do not describe all features, although the approach is a powerful tool for comparing theoretical results with actual events.

Chaos

"Nonlinear dynamics and theories of chaos have given new insight into the functions of the cerebral cortex".

The idea of chaos is not new and is discussed in more detail in Chapter 16. Here we will look briefly at the work of Freeman who has carried out many years of experiments using rabbits and smell association in order to reach some very exciting conclusions.

Basically his experiments have attempted to discover how the brain can almost immediately transform sensory stimuli into perceptions. He did this by measuring the electrical activity of the brain.

He concludes that when a sensory input is received by the brain, a mass of neurons in the cerebral cortex have a sudden burst of activity which could be likened to an explosion. In the process a pattern is created that replaces the stimulus. This explosion is chaotic behaviour thought to be essential for the normal functioning of the brain.

Consciousness

Chapter 23 is dedicated to the question of consciousness. It is generally viewed as a seemingly random array of neural activity from the sense organs to the neurons of the brain. The mind functions through complex system coordination with raw senses being received by the sensory organs in the form of sight, sound, touch etc. These pass through many levels of processing, sifted on the way, before being received as clear and distinguishable perceptions upon which the brain can act. The whole lot is then dumped into short-term memory together with any associated experiences and memories from the long-term memory that may be relevant. Perceptions then are a summary of current experience plus past memories and emotions.

It is becoming apparent that different parts of the brain play major roles in different functions, from basic physical needs and maintenance of the body, to abstract thought processes, and that there is a great deal of coordination and communiaction between the different modules of the brain. There seems to be a lot of importance in how the areas communicate and also, how the groups of neurons are arranged or connected.

Connection and structure

Computer simulations of neural networks are usually an array of fully connected neuron-like processing units arranged in small groups or layers. In the brain, the nerves are not completely interconnected and in fact, the patterns of connectivity vary between the regions.

There have been found to be levels of organisation within the groups of neurons from local circuits, columns, and laminae, to topographic maps. The reasons for these specialised organisational features are not clear as yet, but some headway towards understanding the processes involved is beginning to be made. It has also been found that properties apparent in the lower levels can emerge from the organisation and interaction of these groups at a higher level. For example, the rhythmic pattern generation which exists in some neural circuits is a property of the circuit, and not one of the isolated pacemaker neurons (Getting). It may be true that the perception and analysis of a particular subject depends upon some temporary combination of a set of functional units distributed throughout several different maps and nuclei (Goldman).

Setting up such models in order to emulate this kind of modular approach will require the use of distributed processing techniques. Much research has been carried out using the PDP approach which has brought many interesting features to light. (Rumelhart and McClell 1986).

A model of the Cortex

It is known that within the cortex, the number of connections that exist is far greater than the number necessary for handling the input from the sensory organs, and output to the motor structures. It would seem that the cortex actually spends most of the time talking to itself.

The synaptic connections within the cortex are interesting because there are essentially two different types: long range ones, of which there are relatively few, and a very large number of short range connections. All the connections are excitatory, the only inhibitory effects being those which locally limit the number of cells which can be active at one time.

The incoming signal to any neuron will delay with time and so the timing of arrivals could be critical if a group of stimuli are to reinforce each other. After a time the signal is inhibited which means that only the first few stimuli which arrive will be taken note of.

A model which attempts to adhere to this complex physical behaviour of the cortex has been developed by R. Cotterill (1986). The model reflects in particular the different types of connections present in the cortex – both long and short, the different types of cells and the fact that the cells appear to be arranged in columns, normal to the surface of the cortex. The model itself is described by Cotterill as being *"desperately small"* – a square array of 625 processing units which represents a square of neurons of side length 25. Each unit is connected with all other units within a 5x5 square as shown in Fig. 15.3.

So one unit will have short connections to 120 other local units, unless it is near the edge of the model. In addition to this each unit has one long range connector as described below. The complete array is divided into 25 regions as shown in Fig. 15.4.

It is important that these regions are not viewed as compartments; there are no boundaries as such, local connections being made freely across the dividing lines. The reason for these regions is that each unit has one long range connector to a randomly selected unit in each of the other 24 regions of the array. So each region contains 25 of the processing units, and both long and short connectors.

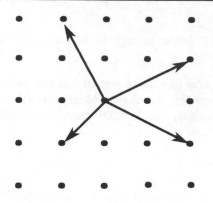

Fig.15.3: Short range connections. Each unit can be viewed as being in the centre of a 5x5 square of neurons (unless it lies at the edge of the model) and is connected to each other unit in the square.

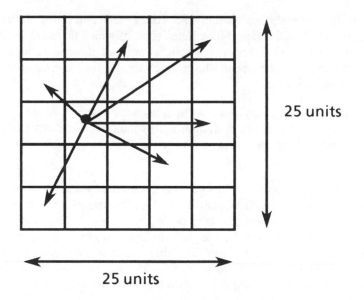

25 units

25 units

Fig.15.4: Long range connections. Every unit is connected to one other random unit in each of the other 24 regions.

All the connections are excitatory; it is the regions themselves which represent the inhibitory effect. At each step the region is checked and the number of cells in a firing state is calculated. As more cells fire within the region, the inhibitory effect for that region is increased.

At each stage or iteration of the process, the net voltage is calculated for each unit, and if this is above a certain threshold value the unit will be activated. In this way, the activity across the array can be followed.

Cotterill describes this arrangement as being *"nicely complicated"*, the effects of the long range connections adding an element of the unknown into the proceedings.

To deal with the potential problems which may be encountered by the edge units which will only have one half the usual number of local connections, the system has a normalising factor which is a function of the total synaptic input to all cells.

The input to the network, representing the sensory organ, was selected to be the top right 25 cell region and also the top left 25 cell region – two sensory inputs which could be located anywhere within the design.

Initially a pattern was presented to only one of the input units. It was found that this spread out across the whole network in a wave-like form, but more quickly than would occur with no long-range connections, and in a more fragmented fashion, with small areas breaking out. Eventually the network entered a cyclic state where the same series of patterns was repeatedly attained. The same thing happened when both sensory inputs were activated.

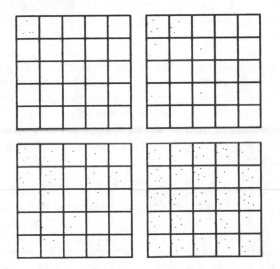

Fig.15.5: Because of the long range connections, activity breaks out across the network.

It was noticed that there was a marked effect at the edges of the array, although this is also true of the cortex, so perhaps this is the start of an accurate representation.

Vision and sound

Much work has been carried out to understand the visual and auditory processes of the brain, perhaps because this sort of sensory input is precisely the kind of problem that neural networks are highly adapted to and conventional systems find very difficult.

McCullock and Pitts (1959) showed that the higher levels of the brain only give us part of the story about cognition. Neural networks which exist in the organs themselves seem to carry out their own *thinking*. This view has been pursued by a number of researchers who look at intelligence in the sense organs themselves.

Using a simple analog chip to map visual signals from moving objects onto sounds, Mead (1989) has designed and developed a model to help the blind to get an idea of their environment. He has also developed a silicon retina and electronic cochlea. See Chapter 17.

The eye

Lettvin et al.(1959) at MIT showed that a frog's eyes saw and perceived a bug and then sent a *bug* message to the brain. It would seem that neurons in the body are not much different from those in the brain. There are over 50 different types of receptor cells in the human eye and neurons are beginning to be perceived as being at least as smart as a pocket calculator.

Nature carries out motion processing before the information is sent to the brain, the reason being that it would be too costly in terms of time to reconstruct the image afterwards. Movement gives information concerning the speed, direction etc. of an image which is frozen by the eye and passed on to the brain. This can be done because if an image is there in front of you all the time, there is no need to remember each frame. It is only if something in the environemt changes that there will be a necessity for more information.

The retina itself is a 2-d thin sheet, as are many neural areas, and this is replicated in the visual cortex and several auditory areas. All cells in the retina are connected to a great many others.

The process starts with the visual scene passing through the lens onto the retina. Light is sensed by a 2-d array of photoreceptors which register rate of change. They each generate an anolog potential proportional to the amount of light. The photoreceptors correspond to a specific area – a *receptive field*– and the location of the light on the retina will give the direction of the source. The information is sent to other layers of neurons for feature extraction.

Further layers make use of inhibitory feedback to improve motion detection, and register light intensity changes when movement is detected. Their function being to add a spatial analysis to the time dimensional analysis of the first layer. Processing proceeds and representation becomes more complex.

From there the information is sent on to higher cognitive centres in the brain, the receptive fields of adjacent neurons corresponding to adjacent regions of the visual field. The information is constantly being modified through changes in the world around us. In the fly this takes up most of the processing or neural activity in the eye because there is no need for the information to be recorded, the important details are simply extracted. Mead refers to this process as the *"neural iceberg beneath the cognitive tip of conscious thought"*. In other words, we do it but we are not aware of it.

The visual centre in the brain constructs a 3-d model based on the patterns received. Motion signals play an important role. The visual depth information is gleaned from these and the movements of the body itself. We use binocular stereopsis for close-range assessment of distances and move our heads for things which are far away. This is *motion parallax*, a function which is not dependent on binocular interaction, objects which are furthest away moving the least.

Time varying signals

Events are a function of time and a lot of information is a result of body movement. The retina carries out time-domain processing. The eye has no precise representation of shape, it is overwhelmingly obssessed with motion. This makes sense in terms of evolution because one of the most important aspects of survival is to see a preditor coming towards you and to be able to judge how far away it is. Cats know this; they will sit absolutely still for hours knowing that they probably won't be noticed. Depth and distances can be judged by moving your body or your head and noticing which objects move the most. The ones furthest away appear to be static, ones closer will move in relation to those far away. This is not a conscious action or thought. When we use our *attention system* and focus on something, the shape determining mechanism then comes into play. The only part of the eye which actually really sees anything is a tiny highly accurate bit in the middle. This part is used for reading and close scrutiny of objects. When we look at a tree, the only part of it we see is the tiny bit in the centre – all else is periphery.

The ear

The ear evolved before speech and understanding how humans use acoustic clues for location has helped in the development of models. The ear is engineered to localise and identify the source of a sound which is done using horizontal and vertical planes enabling the direction of a sound to be isolated. This does not work in a completely unique sense in some cases. If you close your eyes and get someone to hold a ticking clock, it is very difficult to distinguish between it being in front of you or behind you. However, the localisation is pretty accurate in other senses.

Biologically speaking, the cochlea is a 3-d, fluid-filled dynamic system. Sound is heard through the analysis of information from the cochlea combined with the auditory centres of the brain. In order to maintain a representation of the environment, the brain is able to distinguish between complex combinations of sounds. Some will be background noise and can be ignored, while others should stimulate a response. These need to be separated somehow.

The electronic version of the cochlea (see Chapter 17) had remarkable similarities to the actual cochlea but Mead is of the opinion in general that *"it will take ten years to map out the information steps between sensor and cortex"*, let alone build an accurate model.

Mathematics of the brain

Many models are inspired by the mechanisms of the brain and use computer simulations to describe their characteristics. There is a definite need for some kind of unifying theory to be developed, taking the form of mathematical theories together with mathematical models of analysis. In this way the intrinsic neural mechanisms common to many models may be deduced and the limitations and capabilities of neural mechanisms can be understood.

Amari (1988) suggests that the cortical map is a localised neural representation of the signals in the outer world, early development being guided by genetic information and refined using self-organisation.

There are a number of details that a mathematical theory needs to clarify about such maps:

❑ Resolution (size of the receptive field or range of signal space which excites the same cortical neuron)

❑ Amplification property (signals appearing most frequently are projected onto a larger portion of the cortical field with finer resolution)

❑ Dynamic stability of a continuous map.

Since Babbage, computation has been seen as an important brain function which can be mechanised. Modern needs have pushed this opinion. Digital computer developments have provided a very fast processing speed which has been seen as the way to solve all computational problems. It was not that people were not aware of the differences between the brain and the digital computer, it was simply that digital systems were cheap and easy to construct.

Von Neumann found the difference between the processing carried out by digital systems and that of the brain was as enormous as it was profound, most of all because the mathematical language of computers was well established, while that of the brain was unknown.

"The outward forms of our mathematics are not absolutely relevant from the point of view of evaluating what is the mathematical or logical language truly used by the central nervous system". (von Neumann 1958)

Because no mathematical description exists for the nervous system, parallel expressions are carried empirically to *patterns* by computer simulation (Farley and Clark 1954). We can create computer simulations of processes without understanding or being able to define what is happening. If every time an aeroplane was built and the only specification available was that it should be able to travel through the air, it would be rather like reinventing the wheel every time one was built – trial and error.

Other methods of studying the mechanisms of the brain, such as Piaget's (1980) concept of *schemas* (Chapter 18) also does not involve the use of mathematics.

The best mathematical explanation to date for massive parallelism is *vector formalisation* (Wiener 1948). This gives an expression in quantative terms which is classical and most intuitive, but largely comprising qualitative concepts. The best application of this is the mathematics of the association concept which has led to learning rules, eg. Hebbian, Delta, back-propagation etc. to produce a class of modified Hopfield-type models.

Tensor network theory (TNT) was introduced as an improvement on current brain theory, a language of the brain emulated by neurocomputers (Pellionisz and Llinas 1985). The objective is to provide a general mathematical language of the functioning of the brain and the neurocomputers that implement it. The theory is based on a mono-reductionist view that expresses itself not in terms of technology but in terms of being part of nature and evolution. The brain is not seen as being just for computation and control but also as providing a geometric representation of the world from the interactions of neurons.

It is interesting to note Hopfield's (1986) comments on the illogical behaviour of a neural network when solving the travelling salesman problem, which it does very successfully. The problem is to decide which cities should be visited and in which order, so there are constraints which mutually exclude each other. On watching the network Hopfield noticed that before settling into a stable state (a solution) there would be many of these constraints activated simultaneously. This suggests that the network is considering the salesman visiting two or more cities at the same time. Hopfield also says that:

"the ability to use the non-logical interior of the space seems to be an important part of the power of these collective "neuronal" networks". (P.310).

He also questioned whether or not it is sensible to try to understand the brain by *"giving up simple logic and moving towards analog, analytic, and collective behaviour".* Von Neumann had already considered this and decided that neural networks had very little to do with logic.

Many hypotheses have been put forward, but none can be either verified or disproved, for the operating principles of even the simplest neural system. Connections are vast and intertwined, one function unable to be separated from another; traditional reductionism fails completely. Even very simple systems in the brain are buried by the sands of time. Evolution has given us highly efficient, highly integrated and impossibly opaque systems.

16

Chaos

Towards Chaos

Centuries ago, the concept of the mind was that there existed, inside our heads, a little man called a *homunculus,* busy giving orders to the brain and following some kind of universally defined schema. Recently this idea was replaced with an automaton - a mindless brain within our bodies which simply functioned like a computer, carrying out instructions and following some sort of predetermined path. After all, our efforts to mimic the human brain have resulted in supercomputers, processing faster than a speeding bullet but with less free will and creativity than our ever popular slug.

The idea of reductionism has led to the brain being taken apart bit by bit. About 60 neurotransmitters have been identified, our main wiring schemes have been fully documented and the electrical impulses of single neurons recorded, but we still know nothing about emotions, feelings, or the very basics of what comprises consciousness.

As we saw in Chapter 10, Hinton and Sejnowski deliberately use the idea of randomness in neural nets in order to encourage the network to settle into a stable state which represents a good solution to the problem. The ball rolling across a bumpy surface would, under normal circumstances, simply roll to the nearest low point, which most probably would not be the best one. However, give it a bit of a juggle around and it then has a lot more hollows to take into consideration.

John Hopfield uses this random search system to *"free-associate"* memories, mixing amd mingling them into new combinations. A system can be trained to learn, and to mimic the actions of a real neural network, for example to avoid toxic food in the same way that the slug Limax does. A practical application has been to minimise the number of channels used by a telephone system, a task which, if tackled by a supercomputer requiring an exact solution, would take days to complete. This alternative system finds a good solution, which may not necessarily be the optimal one, but it is better to have a good solution instantly, than the best in a few days.

The idea of disorder is not a new one. Although an avid follower of Newtonian mathematics, Pierre Simon de Laplace was one of the first scientists to study disorder. He showed, using a theory of probability, how large numbers of events could behave in a typical way even though the individual events are unpredictable. This seemed to be incompatible with deterministic theories which also described changing systems but in such a way that the future can be determined from past events. Quantum theory was perhaps the first real challenge to determinism using probabilities to describe the behaviour of electrons. The second challenge has come from something initially observed by Henri Poincare a century ago when he proved that the motion of three bodies under gravity can be extremely complicated. This technique developed from the 1960s onwards into something called *topology theory*, dealing with strange shapes and interacting dimensions. This is now known as *Chaos theory*, the ability of simple models with inbuilt random features to generate highly irregular behaviour.

This notion of adding a bit of randomness into a process was referred to by Heinz Pagels in his book *"The Dreams of Reason"*. He pointed out that problems are rarely solved using a rationally deductive process.

> *"Instead I value a free association of ideas, a jumble of three or four ideas bouncing around in my mind. As the urge for resolution increases, the bouncing around stops and I settle on just one idea or strategy".*

Random behaviour which enables the brain to come to some sort of decision is one which rather flies in the face of classical physics in which particles are orderly, their behaviour predictable and able to be analysed. All that is needed are some initial conditions such as direction and velocity, which then never again affect the path of a particle. The only things to be taken into consideration may be for example, in the case of a bullet, air resistance and gravity. However, when we consider the behaviour of water flowing around stones and through crevices, cloud formations and weather forecasts, all of this sort of behaviour can only be defined as being inherently unpredictable. There may be distinct trends but long-range forecasts are impossible to certify. We depend upon programs to run systems in a strict and predetermined fashion (maybe for control) to enable us to predict how something evolves over time. However, there does in fact seem to be some sort of hidden structure to all this seemingly chaotic behaviour which is now starting to create a great deal of interest, particularly after the success of random elements having been introduced into neural network systems.

In the mid-70s, a paper was put forward by Edward Lorenz of MIT, documenting an astounding result that he had discovered during his wrestle with a number of equations depicting climatic patterns. Lorenz had failed to make any sense of the equations and had fed them into a computer and displayed them graphically. The result was not a jumble of meaningless squiggles and loops but amazingly enough, the three dimensional image generated had a distinct form which looked like a black mask with two eye holes, but twisted so that the left and right sides seemed to be bent in different directions. From within the chaos had emerged a hidden structure. Strangely enough (or maybe not, if one remembers that digital systems were being developed with some fury at the time) very little notice was taken of Lorenz's discovery. However, some 20 years later, this theory of chaos is now becoming a subject for serious and excited research.

Paul Rapp, of the Medical College of Pennsylvania, studies the rhythms of the functioning of the brain, which are hidden in the brain's electroencephalogram (EEG). Brain traces are very difficult to decipher and on one occasion Rapp decided to run the signal that he had through a computer, and transform it into a geometrical image. The result was not the expected mess, but was like a *"tulip with multi-coloured edges, and with each rotation another petal unfolded"*. The resultant *"No shit!"* response from his collegues to this unexpected and beautiful image should really be thought of as an updated *"Eureka!"*. Rapp had discovered order within the chaotic functioning of the brain. Patterns such as those generated by brain scans have been named strange attractors. As Ian Stewart (1989) says: *"that does not mean that they are in any way unusual: indeed the only thing unusual about them is that they are unusually common. It means that nobody understands them very well"*.

It has been found that the more complex the problem that the subject is contemplating, the richer the strange attractor. A difficult mathematical problem results in what Rapp has likened to the starship Enterprise, whereas an easy problem gives a flat shape, rather like a frisbee. It would seem that the greater the mental challenge the more chaotic the activity of the brain becomes. Rapp says the reasoning behind this is: *"You want to be able to scan as wide a range of solutions as possible and avoid locking on to a suboptimal solution early on"*. What is needed is: *"a certain amount of disorderliness or turbulence in your search"*.

Chaotic systems involve nonlinear dynamics. The paths do not continuously and simply feed forward, but there are backward loops, the output of initial effects being fed back into the system. The brain functions in this manner, receiving a kick back from neurons which causes other activity and responses. Of course, the problem with such systems is that they are widly unpredicatable. Rapp says that a strange attractor can be thought of as an: *"idealised state towards which an unpredictable - that is strange - system is attracted"*. The system oscillates widly within a given range or norm with a complex structure at any level. It appears that the surface of an attractor is smooth, but looking closely reveals infinitely many layers. Although this motion on the surface is totally unrestricted, there are boundaries, and very distinct ones.

Current Research

Christine Skarda and Walter Freeman (1987), of the University of California at Berkeley have been carrying out research involving the documentation of electrode recordings from the olfactory bulbs of rabbits which have been taught to differentiate between a variety of odours. Results suggest that the initial work done by the rabbit's brain when presented with an odour it has been trained to recognise is definitely chaotic, involving many patterns of neurons. When the odour is recognised, the neurons converge onto a solution, which can be represented as a strange attractor. If a new odour is presented to the rabbit the initial activity is far more chaotic, and only after several exposures does it then converge to a new attractor. This evidence from EEG research suggests that the brain may indeed use compuational methods like those found in connectionist type models.

Skarda proposes that the brain relies on chaotic activity as opposed to steady or random activity. Chaotic activity forms the basis of collective neural activity for all perceptual processes and functions. It acts like a controlled source of noise and is a method of ensuring that the brain has access to previously learned patterns, and to also learn new ones. Freeman has said that chaos is a wonderful state of readiness for an animal as it ensures continual access to all learned sensory patterns at any given instant.

The model developed by Freeman and Skarda is not described as pattern completion although they say it may well do that. The system, they say, does not know a pattern or how it is activated and, of course, neither do they. A *nerve cell assembly* (NCA) is activated wholly by input to one member. The output is not really a pattern but the entire bulb governed by an attractor.

Pattern completion generally depends on presenting the solution with an optimal or best form of the pattern during training and then encouraging the network to produce the required response. The neural system is different: there is never an optimal pattern it can be absolutely sure about and can use as a comparison against future patterns. Chaos is the rule and the *"patterned activity to which the system converges is never the same twice"*. So in this respect *"patterns have no meaning"*.

Destabilization is a better description of the process. The *"input destabilizes the system, leads to further destabilization and a bifurcation to a new form of pattern activity"*. Convergence to one pattern destabilizes the others. So behaviour can at best be modelled as a sequence of ordered, stable states in an evolutionary trajectory. The input causes the system to be constantly destabilizing and then forcing itself to converge into to a new state.

Medical Research

Chaos theory is beginning to reveal variations in the rhythms of vast collections of neurons - unsuspected patterns triggered by problem solving, moods, memories and neurological conditions ranging from Parkinson's disease to schizophrenia.

Studies into schizophrenia have shown that chaotic behaviour in the brain may sometimes be harmful because this disease seems to be a result of too much chaos. However, research is also showing that the brain functions normally, even optimally, when it is in a highly chaotic state. It seems that when we are healthy and alert, the interval between the electrical waves is never rigidly fixed but always vacillates around a certain frequency range. Moreover, when we are mentally challenged, the interval between the electrical waves becomes even more variable or chaotic. Chaos may actually be highly beneficial during problem solving.

It seems that many mental illnesses can actually be attributed to too much order in the brain. Rapp has noticed that prior to an epileptic have a fit, the brain patterns become extraordinarily smooth and regular. In fact heart research has shown that the normal rhythm of the heart is slightly erratic, and its natural beat may be more regular in people who are more likely to suffer heart attacks. As cardiologist Ary Goldberger of Harvard Medical School says: *"the healthy heart dances while the dying heart can merely march"*. Maybe we could liken this to soldiers breaking rank when crossing a bridge otherwise the regularity of the vibrations could cause the structure to collapse. Arnold Mandell, at the University of California at San Diego, has a T-shirt with the words *bounded chaotic mixing produces strange stability* printed on it. In other words, if a person is flexible yet controlled, that person is well balanced.

Creative thought

Perhaps chaos theory will provide the answer to questions about creativity and free will. Working widly and unpredictably as the brain does, chaos theory has revealed that we are still bounded and structured although able to be of free will, within limits, and creative. James Crutchfield, at the University of California at Berkeley, has put forward an idea that creative thought may start with a tiny fluctuation in the functioning of the brain which oscillates widly around and is then blown up into a new global pattern, thus providing a seed for the creation of new ideas within the mind. This certainly seems a possibility - a bit like a whirlwind.

Chaos and Neural Networks

Neural network models can be modified to produce chaotic and oscillatory behaviour, a feature which is not currently included and in fact is most definitely avoided as it leads to instability. Not only are we currently lacking the mathematical tools but the whole situation is viewed as being undesirable and unstable.

Freeman raised an interesting point about neural network models such as that proposed by Hopfield and Tank (1986). The model captures the position of a system after a certain amount of activity, the input then causes it to converge into a well which is a stable energy minimum. Freeman likens this to death for the system because it cannot then escape from the well and has to be reset. Real-time neural network models (Chapter 12) seem to provide a method of avoiding this.

Higher Order

Chaos theory is currently being viewed as some higher form of order, used by astronomers to model the early Universe, the motions of the stars, satellites, comets and planets in the galaxies. It is also used to study the motion of particles trapped by the earth's gravitational pull, and how the movement of the atmosphere generates our weather patterns. Biologists use chaos theory to study the changing populations of insects and birds, in the spreading of epidemics and the propagation of impulses along our nerves. Engineers are also involved as chaos can lead to the loss of particles from a particle accelerator, or to the capsize of a boat in rough seas. Chaos theory cannot be applied to every chaotic situation we do not understand. Some things are simply chaotic in the normal sense of the word and not in the scientific sense. However there is a multitude of disciplines to which this does have relevance.

Responses to Chaos Theory

The response to Freeman and Skarda's work has been received with mixed feelings. The research is very exciting and intriguing but the implications of what they are suggesting does seem to tip over a few apple carts. One point is that the brain does not produce the same pattern of activity for the same input.

Here are some extracts from reviews of their work: (Skarda and Freeman 1987)

> *"The computational metaphor, although not immune to attack, cannot seriously be threatened by this kind of attack"*. Robert Brown (Dept.of Psychology,Uni.of Exeter)

> *"technical virtuosity, physical intuition and intellectual courage"*, Stephen Grossberg (Adaptive systems,Boston Uni.)

> *"Fad or insight?"* ...."*an attractive biological flavour of predictions"*, Donald Perkel (Theoretical neurobiology,Uni.of Texas at Arlington)

> *"Only time will tell whether chaos is in fact the route to making sense of the world"*. Boynton (Dept.of Physchology,Uni.of Calif.at San Diego)

Plato said many centuries ago that: *"Geometry will show the soul towards truth"*. Chaos theory strongly supports current research on neural networks, and vice versa, from all the wild jumble of seemingly meaningless patterns of activity observed within the brain there does seem to be some kind of order. We obviously still know very little about what goes on between the defined limits exposed by a strange attractor. Paul Rapp says: *"If there is a Holy Grail to Neural functioning, chaos theory will help us find it"*.

17

Hardware like the Brain

The von Neumann Principle

Von Neumann is probably most closely associated with the development of the serial computer principle. However, he had in fact recognised the brain to be logically shallow, with few transformations taking place, but on a massively parallel scale. It was simply the technology of the time which did not enable his ideas to be realised. This has been a critical factor in deciding the path that research into computer systems will take, and indeed that is the case today. The only difference is that we are becoming more and more aware of what is needed from technology to solve the problem, rather than having the technolgy and trying to sort out how it can be used to solve the problem.

The language of today's computers is based upon an idea proposed in 1854 by George Boole in his book *An Investigation of the Laws of Thought*. He argued that all logical expressions can be computed using algebraic expressions, so that everyday problems could be solved by automatic procedures, and indeed showed this to be the case. He called his proposals the *laws of thought*. Boole was under the impression he was dealing with the mysteries of the mind and that he had found a connection between language and algebra which was part of some higher order of logic law.

It was Charles Babbage who first put this notion into practise in the early 1900s with the development of a loom, controlled by punched cards. In the 1930s, the Massachusetts Institute of Technology (MIT) built mechanical machines using gear ratios to perform mathematical functions.

This mechanical process of expressing truths in terms of logical expressions supported the reductionist principle, and the *Turing machine*, a model put forward in 1936 by Alan Turing, was deemed an ideal computing machine that could manipulate meaningless symbols in a formal system. The model was intended to be general purpose and precise, and to include all known forms of computation. Turing laid down the principles for defining what is and is not computable, his idea being that any computation consisted of a series of clearly defined processes, and a machine should be able to recognise the symbols used and manipulate them according to a few simple rules. Boolean logic, using the codes 0 and 1, together with Turing's definition, has provided the basis for all digital computers to date. Even the most sophisticated parallel processor, with many hundreds of processors working simultaneously, is based on this priciple.

Von Neumann then applied the principle to electronic circuitry developing what has become known as the *von Neumann Principle*.

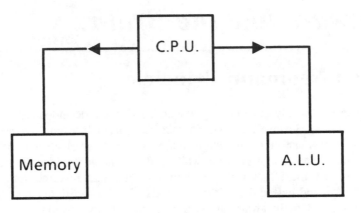

Fig.17.1: The von-Neumann principle. This is a serial process, one step at a time: 1) CPU retrieves data or instruction from memory; 2) CPU instructs ALU to carry out operations on the data; 3) CPU stores results in memory.

The system includes memory to store both instructions and data. The central processing unit controls the process of retrieving data from memory, instructing the arithmetic/logic unit to carry out data manipulation, the results being then stored in memory. The whole process is carried out one step at a time – a serial procedure.

Von Neumann and Turing were both perfectly aware that this was not an accurate model of the brain and von Neumann's idea of serial processing was a compromise of his real beliefs. He had concluded that the circuitry required to develop a network of neuron-like units was too complex for the current technology. Von Neumann did not find a satisfactory solution to his idea of how the brain computes but concluded of digital computers that a process should be used which:

> *"...will lead to theories (of computation) which are much less rigidly of an all-or-none nature...than formal logic. They will be of a much less combinatorial, and much more analytical, character".* von Neumann 1948.

Turing knew that the brain carried out computations in a manner which did not depend on algorithms, or stored instructions, and he described the activities of a neural network in 1936. Turing was interested in devloping a computing machine and saw that a completely different approach was required than that used by the brain. However von Neumann wanted to model the brain and proposed machines which accurately mimicked nerve impulse. These were far too cumbersome to actually build and his pulse density principle was considered at the time to be highly radical, numbers being represented by a frequency of pulses over time. In addition, the hardware was far too complex for consideration. Other researchers found that his ideas of neurons were very interesting but could not see the relevance to the work being carried out on computer systems.

All digital computers are now based on this principle of a common memory for instructions and numbers. Von Neumann himself, pointed out that nature had devised automatic machines, saying this should be the example on which systems are based, but his discussions of neurons and biological computations were not pursued.

The Digital Chip

The digital chip was found to be ideal for application to Boolean logic, Turing logic and von Neumann principles. The transistor is small and uses little power which was a great advance on valves. A drawback was their unreliability. However, if these digital systems were only to use 0 or 1 to code the data and instructions, this was a fairly obvious difference which was easy to detect, as opposed to analog computing which, although using the same program type, needed precise voltage levels and therefore accurate components. This was the downfall of analog systems; the technology at the time made it far more cost effective to go towards digital systems whose accuracy was increased simply by adding more components – from 4-bit to 32-bit micros by increasing the capacity of the chip.

There were originally worries about cost, size, power supply and ease of use but it was soon commercially viable to solve these problems and others such as peripherals eg. printers and tape drives, as systems became larger and faster. Microchips were used to control peripherals and this idea was quickly used to develop a small system with limited features – the microprocessor.

Digital Limitations

Despite all these advances, modern technology seems to have reached its limits in terms of speed, with supercomputers producing processing speeds in excess of billions of processing steps per second. Many chips with different functions have to be very densely connected together to form the complete system, and if the connections are too long there is a time delay involved. The heat generated in such a system can cause a melt down and a significant amount of the high cost of such systems can be attributed to the necessary cooling systems.

It is only now that we are beginning to have real difficulties with the problems inherent in such designs. The number of processing steps that such a system achieves is far greater than that achieved by the brain, but there is a very real bottleneck problem between the memory and the processor as higher performance levels are required. Memory only looks at one location at any one time and data cannot be accessed fast enough – the physical limitations on speed have become a real issue. In addition to this, each system is run by a program, a sequence of instructions which are rigidly followed by the computer. As systems become more complex so do these programs. Thus there is more chance of error, and less chance of anyone actually understanding the complete program, as in the case of the Star Wars program which is reported to have millions of lines of code.

New designs are being developed which attempt to overcome these physical limitations in the form of parallel processing designs. The Connection Machine, from Thinking Machines, uses 64,000 small microprocessors networked together and operating simultaneously. This is an idea that mimics the brain with respect to the physical configuration, but the system still requires a set of instructions – a program – in order to function. The problems of coordinating the activity of so many elements is a tremendous task which has proved extremely difficult. The sheer physical problem of wiring together so many units has also shown that to consider carrying out an undertaking for a structure such as the brain with 100 billion processors, would be totally impractical given our current technology. A number of methods of overcoming these difficulties are being researched, such as the use of light as a means of communication between the elements. Specialist chips are being developed. One example is the Transputer, the processor on a chip developed by Inmos. Another is the analog chip, a neural network in silicon. Also being used are neural nodes fashioned from conventional digital random access memory, RAM. We will look at all these examples later in the chapter.

It has been said that it would take millions of today's computers to operate like the brain, and also it would take millions of brains to operate like a computer. The two processes are so diverse. When a computer leaves the path of a plan, the result becomes incomprehensible. But when people make mistakes they still have a good view of the problem and are also aware of those mistakes and probably the methods of correcting them in the future.

It is interesting to note that things we can explain, such as arithmetic or the analysis of moves in a chess game, digital systems perform very well and in general we do very badly. Things which we cannot explain, such as recognition, intuition, finding a solution with the barest of facts, the things which are computationallly most intensive, digital systems are very poor in carrying out. These are the things we do very well and which are applicable to neural networks.

Networks of Electronic Devices

In 1948 von Neumann supported the work being carried out by McCulloch and Pitts on neural networks. They were quite unique in this line of research at the time. In the early 1940s they had tried to model neurons using electronic components which mimic the neuron properties, using input patterns which produced an all or nothing output. In this way they were able to derive the general properties of networks of such devices and gave the first clues to the mystery. An electronic neural network such as this has been devised by Hopfield and Tank using an array of electronic components called a *flip-flop*.

Flip-flop

This is the simplest circuit used in the electronics industry.

The circuit has two stable states, and it makes a decision by selecting one state in preference to the other. It is built from a pair of saturable amplifiers, that is, an amplifier in which the output voltage has a maximum and minimum level beyond which it does not change. The amplifiers mutually inhibit each other, so as one increases, the other is forced down. So the device has two states. It is strange but no matter what the initial values are, the flip-flop goes quickly into a stable state (Hopfield and Tank, 1985). This can be thought of as decision making, and if you connect n such amplifiers, each connected to all others with inhibitory connections, there would be n stable states. More complex systems along the same lines can be developed where configurations of amplifiers represent solutions, which is a more economical way of using a set of n units. The simple version, one unit to one solution, has been used by Tank and Hopfield to find the largest of a set of numbers. In 1985 they found that this sort of development could rapidly compute good solutions to optimisation problems. eg. task assignment problems.

A problem may have a large number of solutions if the number of permuations is high. For example, the number of ways of arranging five cards in a row is 5x4x3x2x1=120; the number of ways of arranging 10 cards would be 10x9x8x7... etc. A problem where the mutual dependencies should be considered at the same time, is carried out quickly and efficiently. The particular example which they give is that there are six people working in a library and each person is capable of putting books onto shelves in different sections of the library eg. geology, physics etc. at different rates. Each amplifier is fed an input current proportional to a particular person's shelving rate for a section. The valley corresponding to each solution then becomes deeper by an amount proportional to the sum of the corresponding shelving rates. The circuit follows a path and usually settles into the deepest valley, as it were – that is, the optimal solution. They showed that this circuit will almost always find the best solution, a more complex circuit will always find it. Perceptual problems can often be thought of in terms of this kind of optimisation problem, all the information our sensors gather and our interpretation is adjusted by what we already know from experience. This can be represented by a set of constraints, similar to task assignment. Several important problems in computer vision have also been shown to be optimisation problems, and can be solved by such a circuit which has been given knowledge as a set of constraints. Partial information of a 3-d object could be taken and the missing parts reconstructed, such as finding the edges which may be hidden.

Another application for the circuit is associative memory, a form of optimisation.

Associative memory

Hopfield (1985) likens the valleys to particular memories. A pattern of voltages input would go to the amplifiers and the valleys would be configured, the circuit then following a path to the deepest. The memories need not have a particular association between each other so the valleys will be randomly scattered, with irregular connections. Connections between the amplifiers need to be found such that the required memories are simultaneously represented by the network's stable states.

This simple associative memory of six interconnected amplifiers shows how the information can be stored.

		Node					
		1	2	3	4	5	6
	A	+1	+1	+1	-1	-1	-1
Memory	B	+1	-1	+1	+1	-1	+1
	C	+1	+1	-1	+1	-1	-1

Fig.17.2: Six interconnected units form an associative memory. See text for details.

Each memory state is represented by six bits, each corresponding to a state of each amplifier. For example, memory A would be represented by (+1,+1,+1,-1,-1,-1). To ensure stability, each node with a value of +1 must have an excitatory connection to every other amplifier with the same value for the given memory, otherwise an inhibitory connection. All inputs to each amplifier are added to give a value. Many other memories can be overlaid on the same circuit as the patterns are distributed across it, although problems occur if the patterns are too similar or there are too many.

Networks of Analog Chips

Analog Computation

Digital computations have taught us much about how neural computation is not done, and relatively little about how it is done. Part of the reason for this failure is that neural computation is carried out in an analog rather than digital fashion (Mead 1989). One rewarding aspect of the analog method is that the basic computations are a direct consequence of the fundamental laws of physics, a feature which has an analogy with real neural systems that evolved without the benefit of mathematical or engineering analysis – simply using the laws of physical phenomena.

Digital systems use boolean logic, characters, numbers etc. In analog computations, current and voltage are used. Mead has shown that these can be used to perform addition and subtraction, multiplications, exponentials and logarithms using the laws of physics. Also, in digital systems the signals are combined using gates or logic elements with the decision being made on input. The nervous system uses a large number of inputs brought together or *aggregated* in an analog manner. The simplest neuron sums the inputs and compares the result to a threshold value. In silicon, as in the brain, wiring fills nearly the whole space: a system that seems to be so inefficient.

There are two main stumbling blocks to the development of neurons using a silicon medium. The connectivity involved is simply too large and we do not know enough about the organisation of such a system. Research into the organisation has been, and in many ways still is, reductionist. We think that if we know the details of molecules then we know the system. We know the parts that make up a computer, yet it is often impossible to provide a proof that even a program we have written will give an answer or even terminate. This is with a traditional *controllable* digital system.

The complexity in a neural network arises from the interactions, not from its constituent parts. Knowing about the channels will not help us know about the system, it is the organisation which provides the secrets. Neural computation is an emergent property which is only vaguely evident in the components of a neural network.

> *"...our ability to realise simple neural functions is strictly limited by our understanding of the organising principles, and not by difficulties in implementation. If we "really" understand a system, we will be able to build it".* (Mead,1990)

Much progress has been made in terms of determining the organisation of neural architectures but there is still no global view. Breakthroughs have been made most significantly in the areas of visual and auditory research and it is towards these applications that research tends to focus attention. This is partly because of the knowledge now available and partly because perception is an application to which neural networks are highly suited. Like all models, the starting point is at the beginning with *"simple and stupid"* systems. Even so, these will be smarter than the first evolutionary animals.

The Role of Silicon

A great number of research projects tend to be directed towards image processing, speech recognition or synthesis and as such are highly computationally intensive. To be useful in the world of neural networks, silicon circuits need to have hundreds or thousands of neuron-like units, be densely interconnected, and have a simple method for modifying the interconnection strengths.

Very large-scale integration (VLSI) gives a medium in which tens of millions of transistors can be interconnected on a single wafer. A silicon chip about 1cm square can hold about 1 million transistors. The densest configurations currently use metal-oxide-silicon (MOS) transistors, originally conceived as a digital device for microprocessors, memory etc. These are noisy devices, not suited to analog procedures because of the low level of precision they can provide. However, neural networks are robust under the failure of individual components, so it seems reasonable to expect a very robust and reliable system to be the result of such a configuration.

The constraints on developing analog chips are the same as those for implementing neural networks: wiring, power, robustness and reliability. Mead pays a lot of attention to the guidelines set down by neural systems saying that: *"the effectiveness of our approach will be in direct proportion to the attention we pay to the guiding biological metaphor"*. They can't be copied, any more than we can build a bird, but a glider is a good metaphor.

Implementing models of neurons in silicon will give a synthetic element to computational neuroscience, allowing hypotheses concerning neural organisation to be tested. Also an engineeering discipline will be developed by which collective systems can be designed for specific computations.

> *"The success will create a bridge between neurobiology and the information sciences and will bring us a much deeper view of computation as a physical process. It will also bring us an entirely new view of information processing, and of the awesome power of collective systems to solve problems that are totally intractable by traditional computer techniques"*. (Mead 1990).

Even with VLSI, it is currently impossible to build a complete replica of the brain out of anything; it is simply too complex and too massive. The current method is to take some of the broadest and simplest strategies in the brain and adapt them for use in silicon devices. Taking advantage of the speed of calculation in silicon can be used to make up for lack of processing units and connectivity (Mackie 1989). So let us now look at some of the subsystems used in these developments:

Electronic Subsystems

MOS transistors

These provide a source of both positive and negative current – the *most ideal active devices* in which the current levels can be controlled. They can be used to develop complete neural subsystems for vision and hearing, as we shall see further on in the chapter.

Electronic neurons

The *differential transconductance amplifier* is a simple circuit, a device that generates as its output a current that is a function of the differenece (the differential input) between two input voltages. An ordinary conductance will turn this voltage difference into a current through the same two terminals, a transconductance turns it into a current somewhere else. In a transconductance amplifier, a voltage difference at two inputs is turned into a current at the output.

Transistors are not created equal but these mismatches can be tolerated. By self-compensating for voltage offsets, the system can tune itself up. This is a useful feature because circuits age over time. In vision and hearing the systems *must* be self adjusting as the input will be unknown prior to it being received. For practical reasons, the assumption is made that all input is from another circuit, and all outputs are sent to another circuit. If we think of the ear, the input will be from two audio input channels.

There is no reason to think that any ideas that may exist concerning elementary functions are reliable but it will be possible to build systems out of any reasonable set of primitives. The course chosen was to follow evolution and use those which are most efficient.

Because neurons are not quite to be trusted, some rules need to be defined about their effect. Statisticians have a notion of reasonable behaviour: if a result is way out of line then its global effect is reduced. In experiments it can often be assumed that the output will be some smooth function of the input, if the input is not changed too much too quickly then the output won't suddenly change. A range can be determined beyond which the output is not expected to stray, a *region of smoothness*. Unexpected data points can easily be identified as being of great interest or simply wrong.

Wiring

Neurons share the signal paths in an effort to keep the wiring to a minimum. Every location can put signals into the network, read voltages off the network and use the network to sense a weighted sum over its neighbours, including itself.

Segmentation

The physics of simple nonlinear systems enable complex problems of region boundaries to be dealt with using *segmentation*. Discontinuities such as boundaries carry the most information about an image. A natural result of the circuitry is that there will be a big drop across the resistor at the boundary, so the region can be identified and segmented.

Smoothing Over Time

In real time, neurons are continuously receiving input from other neurons. Most models tend to introduce a time step and adjust the weights according to that step. A *follower-integrator circuit* enables a temporal smoothing to be carried out such that the output at any time is made up of the input for all previous times, with inputs in the past fading into insignificance with time. Thus you get a sort of moving average. This is for small signals. Large input signals present problems in that the model changes from being a linear system into a highly nonlinear one. This is because doubling the input does not double the output. As the input tends towards a maximum value the associated output slows down significantly and behaves like a small signal response. See Fig.17.3.

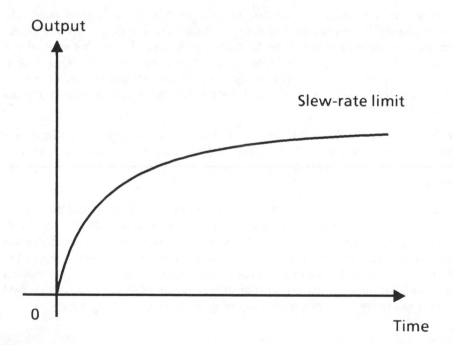

Fig.17.3: As the input increases with time, the output slows down and approaches the slew-rate limit. This describes a model with large input signals, showing the change from a linear to a non-linear system.

This limit is the *slew-rate limit*. When it is reached the model can't accelerate beyond it, so the model is not linear even within the required voltage range. Mind you, as this is VLSI, if one goes wrong the amount of *damage* it can do is limited.

Stability

Introducing feedback into the model will introduce potential problems with oscillation. Neural systems naturally generate *large-signal limit-cycle* behaviour like a heart beat. In fact, how they manage to be stable at all is a mystery. Shepherd (1979) gives a hint about this.

> *"broad curtain of inhibition..through which excitation pierces, carrying specific information about the stimulating molecules."*

Inhibition is concerned simply with magnitude of activity, not whether it is positive or negative. The auditory system also has problems in distinguishing a negative pressure pulse from a positive one. The nonlinearity of negative feedback may be the key to analog systems, together with a great deal of gain and time delay, to keep the *"entire mess"* stable.

> *"We know we will understand these matters only when we can build such a system – and can keep it stable"*. (Mead 1990).

Designing Chips

The key problem is in the selection and arrangement of the specific subsystems which combine to provide the complete function (Mead 1989). Each of Mead's examples is built out of the previously described subsystems.

Silicon retina

A chip was modelled on the distal part of the retina. This device generates, in real time, outputs which correspond directly to the signals seen in its biological equivalent. Principles of signal aggregation are used with a natural tolerance for imperfections. The structure of the model was similar to the neurobiological version with the same constraints that we have mentioned before, namely wiring and organisation. Modelling using an analog microchip demands highly connected wiring, and a solution is to create a hexagonal array which provides the maximum number of inter-cell connections in two dimensions. The way in which this model parallels a real eye is described in Chapter 15.

A resistive network is used in the model of the retina and can be built from transistors with the resistance set electronically. It is used as the simplest element to build an electronic analog of a neuron's dendritic tree.

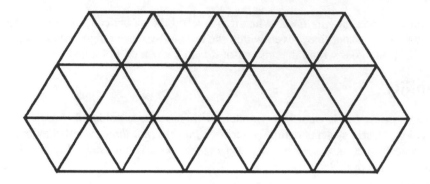

Fig.17.4: This hexagonal wiring arrangement between the nodes gives the maximum number of connections posssible in two dimensions. This is used to model the retina.

Like the vertebrate eye, the lens in the model maps onto a 2-d array of pixels, photosensor and associated local processing. The light falling on a pixel from some direction in space. The location of a pixel corresponds to the image location in the visual scene. The intensity and time information is taken and computation is locally done on the chip. Directional information is retained.

There are many explanations of retina operation, all of which seem to pick up different aspects of the functioning but there seems to be one underlying structure. This is that in the retina a highly evolved mechanism can serve many functions at once. The results achieved by the silicon model are remarkably similar. The model is sensitive to input changes, regardless of viewing conditions and is able to compute contrast ratio and enhance any edges. The model maintains operation over a large range of both intensity and contrast.

Electronic cochlea

It is not understood how hearing is carried out in terms of how the brain deals with word recognition and understanding, taking into account context, inflection etc. When this process has been sorted out we may be able to build a model for the hearing mechanism. Research is motivated by the fact that simple electronic systems can be built which can hear in simple ways.

An analog electronic cochlea uses a lot of the current knowledge about the function and physical aspects of the ear. Biologically speaking, this is a 3-d fluid-filled dynamic system. Sound is heard through the analysis of information from the cochlea combined with the auditory centres of the brain. It is the vibrations of sound waves on the eardrum which are heard as sounds. Remember the question: If a tree falls in the desert and there is no one there to hear it, does it make a sound?. The answer is of course no, it does not make a sound because it is our ear mechanisms which change those waves into a noise.

In order to maintain a representation of the environment, the brain is able to distinguish between complex combinations of sounds. Some will be background noise and can be ignored, others should stimulate a response. These need to be separated somehow.

The time-domain information is converted into spatially encoded information by spreading signals through space according to a timescale. This is the procedure carried out by the model in silicon which, like the retina model, bears an uncanny resemblance to the real thing.

SeeHear

Mead (1989) specifically designed and developed this model to help the blind to get an idea of their environment. It is a simple analog chip onto which an image is projected by a lens. This serves to map visual signals from moving objects onto sounds which can be heard through earphones.

The model has three stages:

❑ encode the intensity and position of a light source in a 2-d projection

❑ process electrical signals representing intensity to emphasise changes

❑ generate a sound to indicate the source and position

The model uses continuous sound-synthesis methods that preserve the analog nature of the pixel signals, taking advantage of spatial information in the retinoptic visual array.

The device is small enough to be worn on the head. It uses biologically inspired representations of visual and auditory functions to derive the inner processing of the chip. The optical processing is carried out using intensity information based on signal processing in the vertebrate retina which emphasises motion. The auditory stage emphasises transient events, a facility known to provide optimal information for spatial localisation.

The location of each visual thing needs to be encoded to provide the necessary acoustic information. Events occurring simultaneously have to be put into a 2-input channel such that the depth information is preserved.

A number of listening tests were carried out and the model was found to give an astoundingly realistic sense of horizontal location. A mildly convincing vertical sense was given that could easily be learnt by the listener. SeeHear is capable of generating three principle auditory localisation clues in response to visual signals anywhere in the retinal field.

The mapping of sensory input to the appropriate internal representation is seen as the key to compact and efficient implementation of these devices. The natural mapping of space and time in analog VLSI systems is the same as the processing carried out by the brain, in that the properties of physical devices are used as computational primitives. The system is limited by interconnections and not by computations.

The subsystems used in the design of the silicon retina, electronic cochlea and SeeHear were defined by Mead. We will now look at some other approaches to the design of neural-type chips.

Transputer

VLSI allows identical devices to be manufactured cheaply so it is cost effective to have a network of homogeneous units where each can be programmed. The *Transputer* is such a component, designed to execute the parallel language Occam (May 1989).

The Transputer is a single VLSI device with memory, processor and four communications links for direct connection to other transputers. This resides on a single chip. These devices can be used as the building blocks from which concurrent systems can be created. There are a number of advantages to the Transputer.

Communication between devices is very much slower than communication within a device. Conventional serial systems access memory on a regular basis, the process tending to cause a bottleneck. As the Transputer has its memory and processor on the same chip, this problem does not arise. Connections tend to take up a lot of physical space in a system, the Transputer uses point-to-point serial communications links for direct communication with other transputers, giving maximum speed with a minimum of wiring.

The language Occam enables a series of concurrent *processes* to be defined. These communicate with each other and the peripherals through *channels*, in a synchronised manner. This means that if one process requires input from another the first will wait for that information to be available before continuing. This is like having lots of programs running in parallel and being able to pass information between them.

Many applications decompose fairly naturally into a large number of quite simple processes and the Transputer has been used in applications with much success.

The Computing Surface, commercially produced by Meiko, uses several thousand connected Transputers which can be used by someone who needs the processing power of a Cray supercomputer (Brierly and Kidd, 1986). It was used in an impressive highly computationally extensive example which generated a 3-d colour replicate of the Computing Surface itself. Using an array of 16 Transputers, a configuration developed by CAP was able to reduce the conventional system process of fingerprint recognition from 50 seconds to find a match, to three seconds (Carling 1988).

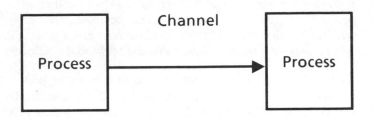

Fig.17.5: The two processes communicate through a channel. The processes receiving input will wait for that input from the sending process.

The Connection Machine

This configuration is considered to be feasible as a general-purpose neural computer (Recce 1989).

One of the fastest machines ever constructed, the Connection Machine was developed by W.Daniel Hillis (1987) and is made up of 65,536 identical *intelligent memory cells*. These are connected in such a way that the processors are able to exchange information to best suit the current problem – the key to the flexibility of the system. About a dozen of these machines were in commercial use in 1987 used for image processing, computer graphics, and problems requiring commonsense reasoning.

Each of the cells is less powerful than a personal computer and each contains a copy of the same program. A *rule table* determines the next state together with the input and output functions for a node.

A cell reacts to an incoming message according to its current state and the type of message received. The cell will then perform the appropriate steps which could be arithmetic computations, storage of a value, sending a message, changing state etc.

The system is designed to carry out concurrent operations on a knowledge base represented as a semantic network. This is a directed graph where the vertices represent objects and the arcs represent the binary relations between them, for example, set membership. A concept is assigned to a node and then connections are established between the nodes in order to represent relationships. When something needs to be retrieved a parallel search is carried out on all the nodes.

Like the Transputer, this is not faithful to a neural network because the system is programmed. It is a highly parallel machine operating using serial digital principles based on an AI symbolic method of data manipulation.

Programmable systolic chip (PSC)

This chip is currently being used at University College London as a primitive processing element for building a parallel neural computer. An array of these elements is used, each with communications, local memory and a processor. Each has the same simple program and messages can be passed between the elements.

The chips can be assembled into a number of topologies to support a family of systolic algorithms. Once connected, they are configured for a particular array by having identical code loaded onto them. The system then operates as a synchronous pipeline with the data being pumped between chips. A PSC processor is defined as being five functional units operating in parallel and communicating simultaneously using three buses.

The limitations of this arrangement are that it is Single Instruction stream Multiple Data stream (SIMD) in that different data is processed by each element but under the same instructions, the elements not being independent of this central control.

The problem with all these systems is that versatility has to be balanced against hardware complexity and computational power.

In the next section we are going to look at a novel approach developed by Professor Aleksander which uses conventional RAM devices as neural nodes.

Using RAM

"An unorthodox approach in the world of neural computing". (Psaltis 1990)

RAM Neurons

Random-access memory (RAM) together with the silicon chip, are responsible for the success of the microcomputer, providing a cheap and reliable method of storing data. The RAM uses an address to store data and then to subsequently retrieve that data from memory. The address is simply a location finder. Conventional RAM memory can be used as a neuron unit in a model because it is able to learn and re-learn, a property which has been recognised for some time.

RAM works by having a group of memory registers which are able to store information. The location of each is defined using a binary address, that is, a pattern of 0s and 1s. When a binary pattern is input to the RAM the line to the appropriate location becomes active. The data in the location can then be retrieved and output from the RAM.

The number of 0s and 1s in a pattern is called the number of bits (digits), so an N-bit pattern will have N digits (0s or 1s). If a RAM device can deal with the input of an

N-bit pattern it can access a maximum of 2^N memory locations, that is, the number of different combinations of N 0s and 1s that can be defined. Let us say that the pattern stored in memory has M bits, as shown in Fig.17.6.

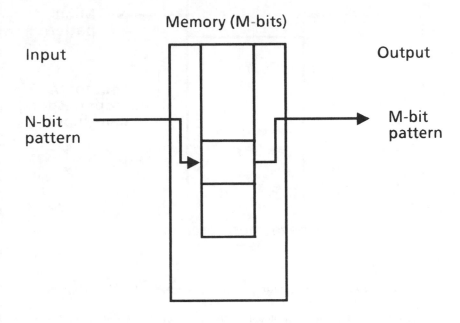

Fig.17.6: RAM neuron. The memory stores M-bit patterns. The input is in the form of an N-bit pattern. So an N-bit input will cause an M-bit pattern to be retrieved from memory.

The basic type of RAM used for *logical neural nets* receives N binary inputs (memory locations) and produces one binary output (memory contents). The unit is trained by being presented with the input and associated output patterns. A writing mechanism is energised which allows updates to be made to the information stored within the RAM node. There have to be well defined learning phases using this method because when the network is running, the writing mechanism must not be energised. Previous learning enables computations to be carried out when the network is free running.

To relate the RAM to a neuron we have to think of a RAM which stores M bits per memory register or *word*. So the pattern stored in the memory is M bits long. We can think of this as being a number M of RAM neurons each with only one bit in their memory registers and each connected to the same N bit input pattern. The M outputs will each be able to learn a different response to the same pattern, as shown in Fig. 17.7.

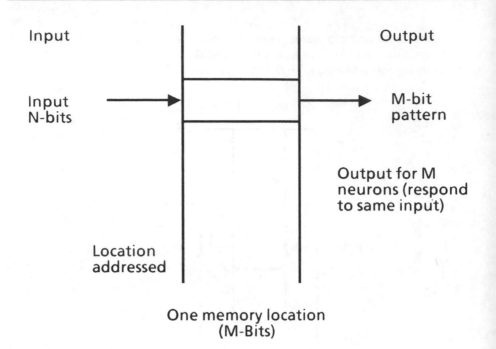

Fig.17.7: The M outputs will each learn a different response to the same pattern.

An *N-connected canonical net* (canonical in the sense of being standard) is R nodes with N inputs per node. The minimum value for R is N+1, as a unit can connect to all others except to itself – it is generally accepted that this may cause the node to get stuck in a loop. The network will be fully connected if R=N+1.

Aleksander (1990) has shown that a network of RAM nodes retains the central characteristics of Hopfield nets, the Boltzmann machine and error back-propogation. Also it is more direct and faster than back-propagation.

An advantage of these systems is the directness of implementation using digital techniques. The system can make use of probabilistic output and be either synchronous or asynchronous, the latter being fundamentally stable, the former needing some method of noise reduction in training to ensure stability.

The system does not need a sophisticated training algorithm, the training is carried out as simply as described above. Although there is no generalisation in the RAM node itself, it has been shown that networks of such devices generalise in a way comparable to the properties of a neural network.

RAM devices have been used by Aleksander to develop the Wizard model described below.

Wizard

The WIlkie, Stonham and Aleksander's Recognition Device (Wizard) is an adaptive pattern recognition system. The prototype was completed in 1981 at Brunel University in London and became commercially available in 1984.

It uses conventional RAM, looked at in the preceding section, as a neural node. These nodes are arranged into single layers, called *discriminators* each of which acts like a single layer perceptron. The trend is to use 2^N RAM nodes in each discriminator, 2^N being the amount of memory contained in each RAM. In one application Wizard is used for the recognition of hand printed characters. One discriminator is used for each letter, so there will be 26 in total.

There is a thorough and detailed chapter in Aleksander's (1990) book, and these RAM nodes have been used in models which are commercially viable, for example, character recognition, monitoring of premises for intruders and quality control tasks.

The advantages of a system like this is that it uses simple analysis and is easily implemented with conventional hardware techniques. Aleksander describes some further applications for the RAM device.

Logical Memory Neurons

Logical memory neurons (LMN) generate weightless systems. Imagine that the state of a neural node can be described using a truth table. Changes to the node will be reflected in the table changes, so by simply changing the table the weights can be ignored. This procedure can be directly implemented as networks of RAM nodes. PLNs (see below) are a typical example of such devices, being RAMs that store the probability of the node firing – a counterpart to back-propagation.

Probabilistic Logic Node

Aleksander (1989, 1990) describes the Probabilistic Logic Node (PLN) as providing a basis for understanding the functioning of a network. This is because the device operates as a look-up table as described above for the LMN.

The PLN differs from a RAM neuron in that it deals with q-bit numbers rather than a single bit stored at an addressed location in RAM, this value being the probability of the node firing. Such a *logic-probabilistic* system has been shown to be of two orders magnitude faster than back-propagation techniques currently in use.

This work is seen as bringing the advantages of connectionism closer to implementation, giving the engineer a predictive theory for informed design and lending an insight into a broad class of systems.

Optics and Holography

Why Use Light?

What is one of the fundamental problems behind most computer systems? The reason why we are unable to build systems which have the processing capabilities of the brain. We may not know how the brain functions, which is hardly a trivial problem, but even more basic to that is the problem we have with actually building something which looks anything like the brain.

Billions of neurons are each connected to at least 10,000 others. It is this physical problem af actually wiring up the connections which presents quite a stumbling block. On a silicon chip, the processing units can be there but so are the connections and there comes a time when it is just totally infeasible to try to cram any more in. Somehow the brain manages to deal with this problem and perhaps one of the most impressive sources is within the eye.

The eye's lens receives light from millions of points and redistributes it to millions of sensors in the retina. The beams cross one another and do so without interfering with each other – they stay separate.

As light beams can interact in this way and yet not change at all, this is the thinking behind using light, the primary advantage being its ability to provide the massive communications required by systems. Get rid of the wires as a form of connection and replace them with light beams.

What is a hologram?

We must all be familiar with holograms. They even come free with packets of breakfast cereal, one of the ultimate signs that something has become cheap and cheerful. So what is a hologram? There are basically two types: one is the flat sort that stares at you from your credit card (a planar hologram); the other is referred to as a volume hologram embedded into a photorefractive crystal – a 3-d version.

Planar holograms are found on a thin medium or film and can direct any light beam which hits one side to any source on the other side, provided the total number of light beams is not greater than the number of spots on the film. A single one inch square can receive as many as 100 million light inputs. A volume hologram uses a photorefractive crystal which has certain special features. If the crystal is exposed to light with a particular photon energy, electric currents are generated within it which cause the refractive nature of the crystal to change according to the intensities of the light. The local density of the charge will determine the local refractive density, a holographic image being recorded onto a crystal in terms of this varying refractiveness (a measure of how fast the light travels through the crystal). The image can then be retrieved by illuminating the crystal with a light beam. The crystal acts as a holographic grating which gives the required output given the associated input.

Holograms redirect light in a predetermined manner, in other words, they can send a beam of light in a specific direction according to the instructions stored in them. In this way they can be used to form the pattern of connectivity for the neurons in a network. Holograms are fabricated so that the information they hold is distributed throughout the holographic medium rather than in any localised way. If part of the hologram is destroyed the information remains completely intact except for some slight loss of detail – a property in common with our idea of human memory. But perhaps the most amazing quality of a hologram is that it is able to reconstruct the light belonging to one object, out of the light of another.

Holograms can also be programmed to represent the required connections in a neural network. It would be useful if some kind of dynamic hologram could be found which would allow continuous modifications of the strengths of these connections to allow learning to take place.

A General Model

Psaltis's (1990) model uses the basic idea that given a set of optical units corresponding to neurons, which can receive and transmit light, holograms can be used to form the connections between those units.

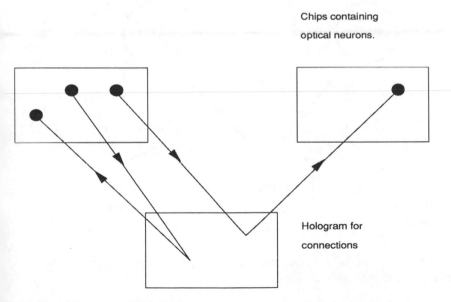

Fig.17.8: The hologram is used to act as the connections between the neurons which are contained on the chips. The light from one neuron is defracted off the hologram in a direction which is programmed into the hologram.

A holographic grating placed in front of the unit's output can diffract the incident light in a direction determined by the grating. The strength of those connections can also be adjusted by altering the modulation strength of the grating.

So in terms of neurons we can think of the hologram as representing a synapse point, the optical paths being the dendrites.

One hologram image is needed for each connection and it has been found that a single crystal can hold many superimposed images. There are disadvantages to having more than one connection configuration sharing the same medium, namely that changing one synapse may cause a change in the others. The advantages are the high storage density that can be achieved and the ease of fabrication. Basically there can be about 10^{12} (1 trillion) synapses per cubic centimetre, representing the connections between about a million neurons.

Holograms can be used for the synapses but optoelectronics need to be used for the computations and to provide the optical energy necessary for these devices to be incorporated into a large network. Because light beams do not interact in space, something needs to be present at the location of the optical neuron which detects light and can change its electronic state. In this way the optical properties can be modified and a beam travelling through this matter can influence another beam.

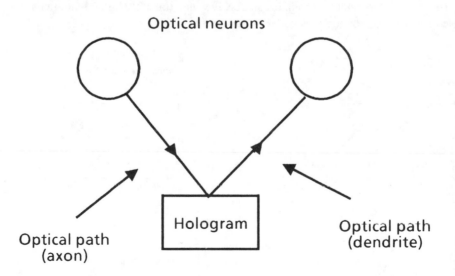

Optical neurons

Optical path
(axon)

Hologram

Optical path
(dendrite)

Fig.17.9: The hologram has the same role as a synapse. The optical path can be thought of as a dendrite of an axon.

Such elements can be made from an optical material which has nonlinear properties, that is, the transmittance features will change as the brightness of the light changes. One such material is gallium arsenide. The elements are made by sandwiching a layer of gallium arsenide between two partially reflecting mirrors. Such an arrangement can abruptly change its transmission properties depending upon the intensity of the input light beam.Two-dimensional switching arrays have been made using this method. In such an arrangement, the brightness of one beam controls the transmission of another.

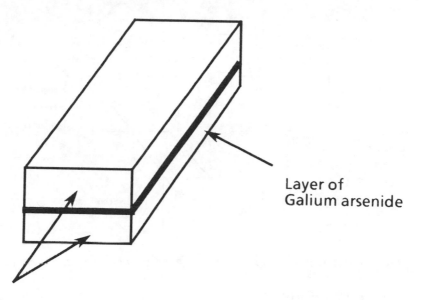

Layer of
Galium arsenide

Mirrors

Fig.17.10: This is used to detect the strength of the light within a layer and between layers.

The method of fabrication for these units creates a 2-dimensional array, a layer of neurons with the holographic connections between the layers separately defined on another plane. Reflective holograms are used for connections within the layers. The fact that the arrangement is planar is not really a problem because most neural networks tend to be configured into layers. A simplified version of the complete set-up is shown in Fig.17.11.

The advantage of this arrangement is in the electronics. Wiring limits the number of transistors which can be put onto a chip but here the planes only have to contain the neurons as the connections are separate. Well over 100 times the number of units can be put onto a layer like this.

One specific example (Psaltis 1989) defines each neuron as having a phototransistor to detect input. A second bipolar transistor is used to generate the current to drive the light emitting diode (LED) used for communications with other neurons. The threshold level of a neuron is controlled by an external current source. In this way electronics and optics are combined with optics for the connections, electronics for the processing.

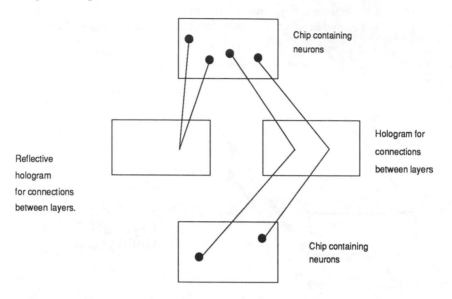

Fig.17.11: The holograms here have connections within a layer and between layers.

Associative memory

When holograms are used for associative memory the connections between the neurons are contained within the hologram itself. In principle the holographic associative memory has the storage capacity for a number of associations between pairs of images which is equal to the number of neurons in the plane. Some 111 associations have been stored on a single crystal (Psaltis 89).

To store information in the memory a laser light is used to illuminate the object. This lighted image is passed through the hologram, then redirected using mirrors and passed through the hologram again. The original image and the redirected one form an inference pattern which is recorded by the hologram. See Figure 17.12.

When the original image impinges onto the hologram the stored pattern of interference is able to reconstrust the original image. This is the same as recording a hologram of an image using its associated pattern as a reference beam and in this way the reference and object are associated. This creates a simple associative memory. Dana Anderson gives the following example (Anderson,D. 1986, 1987):

When a laser beam is applied to the ring, any one of the stored images or object light beams, will begin to oscillate. They compete for the energy and are all *"greedy"*.

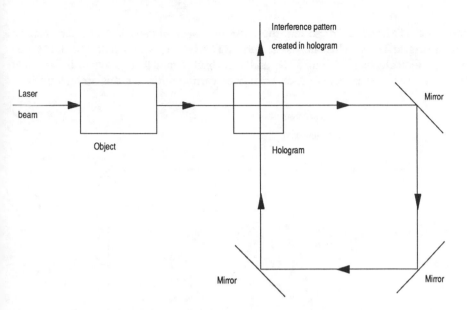

Fig.17.12: The illuminated image passes through the hologram and is then directed using mirrors to pass through the hologram again. The resulting inference pattern is stored in the hologram. The original image can then be reconstructed.

Presenting partial information into the ring will cause the closest stored image to oscillate the most and so win over the other images. This partial input will cause the complete pattern to be retrieved. If no information is injected into the ring any of the stored images may win and in fact they take turns in winning. Anderson likens this *mode fluctuation* to daydreaming.

One problem with holograms is that they are dynamic and do change. As an image oscillates, it starts to erase the effect that the other stored images have and will eventually cause the system to forget them completely. Alternatively, the image may erase its own trace which actually may be a useful function in associative memory as other images could then have an advantage. The strength of the memories equalises.

Holograms and Learning

Learning can use a process similar to Hebb's rules with the connections between input and output neurons being reinforced simultaneously and in parallel. Photoreactive crystals are used to record the holograms, there being no limit to the number of times the hologram can be changed. However, for multiple associations the crystal has to store each with equal strength and the practical limit seems to be around 500 because of the reduction in efficiency that occurs (Psaltis 1990).

The number of training cycles needed for a learning process such as back-propagation is not known in advance and can easily be more than 1,000, which presents a problem. Psaltis et al. are now looking at the potential of using two crystals, representing STM and LTM, so that the exposures accumulated in STM can then be copied across to LTM. This means that the STM is not overloaded. The LTM can also be periodically copied into STM and then back again to rejuvenate it. We will now look at some experiments which have been carried out using this architecture.

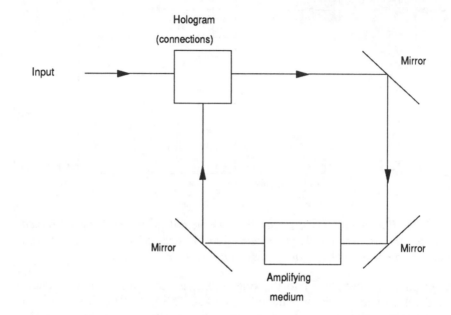

Fig.17.13: Simple associative memory. Images can be stored in the hologram. To recall an image, partial information can be generated into the ring as a light beam which will cause the complete image to be recalled from the hologram.

Image Recognition

At Caltech (Mostafa 1987) experiments were carried out using a 2-d array of more than 10,000 neurons. These were simulated by a threshold device with 10,000 tiny elements each switching the front beam when the intensity of the beam at the back reaches a certain threshold limit. In this way the units act as neurons.

The model uses a pair of planar holograms, a system of lens, mirrors and pinholes to specify how the light gets through and how much each element receives. The image is projected onto the system by reflecting it in front of the threshold device. The lens and pinholes then enable the reflected image to interact with the image stored in the two holograms (both have the same image). The best match to the input pattern is the brightest image emitted from the second hologram. This is directed to the back of the threshold device which responds so that the image of the best match is reflected off the front for a second pass around the loop. Successive passes reinforce the image until one pattern dominates which is the output image. This works even if only part of the initial image is input.

Optical Futures

The main comment about these optical architectures is that they bear a remarkable resemblence to the basic properties of general neural network models. As such, it seems there must be a place for their inclusion in current research because of the practical problems for which they can provide solutions.

A major disadvantage is that we are looking at the early stages of the technology and as such many questions remain unanswered. There are specifically no really appropriate devices for the simulation of neural planes. A weakness is this provision of complex nonlinear processing units. However, it could be said that most neural networks only need simple processing units. Anderson (1988) points out that what is needed is a slowly evolving holographic medium and a relatively fast non-linear decision making element that can implement competition and recall. These systems are also vulnerable to errors but as the networks are inherently fault tolerant, as are neural networks in general, this is a problem that is well established. There will be no problems with speed because the holographic memory will be processing at the speed of light.

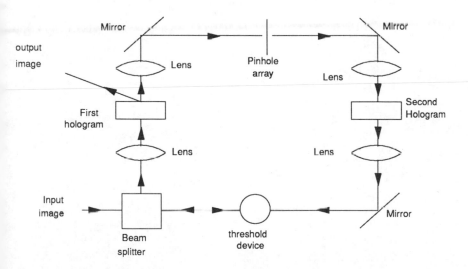

Fig.17.14: The same four images are stored within the two holograms. This system finds the best match between an input image and the stored images.

Conclusion

Von Neumann's ideas of studying the brain and the activity of neurons has been realised by many to be the key to future work, but it has only been in the last couple of decades that the technology has been available to break away from the idea of serial processing and develop machines with parallel processing capabilities: like the brain, a large number of highly connected, simple processing units. However, representing the physical configuration is one thing; enabling the system to function like a brain is another thing entirely and as yet no theory has been put forward to explain how or what the neurons actually communicate. Although the structure of the operation remains a mystery, it is clear that this is the scale of power needed. Although when one considers that one square centimetre of the cortex (the outer layer of the brain) has over one million neurons and more than one billion interconnections configured in three dimensions, the mere act of attempting to duplicate such power becomes a seemingly insurmountable task. We do not possess the technology to currently mimic such a network. Even if we were able to build a system with 100 billion processing units, each connected to 10 thousand others, and it is not unlikely that one day this will be possible, this is a bit like building a car with no engine. It looks like one, but we have no idea how it is driven.

Slugs, Frogs and Schemas

"Frogs don't play chess - but there are plenty of things we don't understand about frogs". (Sejnowski).

Much research these days is concerned with the study of invertebrate animals, sea slugs or starfish for example, to try and understand the nervous system in terms of thought, memory and instinct work. These creatures have comparatively few neurons and are quite easy to study in detail.

A type of worm currently being studied by NEC has, for example, only 955 neurons. 302 are assigned to what could be called its brain functioning with 653 to control motor functions. The method of study used is to focus laser beams on particular cells or neurons and the eggs that these organisms generate in an attempt to discover something about inherited characteristics.

The behaviour of an animal can be broken down into units called schemas. We will look at how these are created and defined and how particular models have utilised this notion.

Looking at simple animals enables some kind of study to be made of the organisms' principles, not just at a cellular level but also the functional, structural and computational strategy involved. This is to allow some understanding of the relationship between detailed neural circuitry and more schematic models. This decomposition of complex tasks into schemas, is an important part of the study of neural networks.

Developing Schemas

Schemas have been around at least since Kant in 1787 and the concept was introduced into neurology by Head and Holmes in 1911 in the form of body schemas.

By observing people who had lost limbs and yet could still feel them, they deduced that the brain may construct reality as it still perceives it.

Even so, the idea of schemas has been rejected throughout history by experimental psychologists as being too vague. In the mid 1970s the system gained credibility by trying to offer a clear view in terms of specified computer models or formal implementations.

> *"It seems...the ingredients of most theories both in AI and psychology have been on the whole too minute, local and unstructured to account – either practically or phenomenologically – for the effectiveness of common sense thought. The "chunks" of reasoning, language, memory and "perception" ought to be larger and more structured, and their factual and procedural contents must be more intimately connected in order to explain the apparent power and speed of mental activities".* (Minsky 1975).

Minsky and others said that a new, higher-level conceptual structure was necessary for the representation of complex relations which are integral in a knowledge base. This basically defines a schema, which is a data structure for representing models of the outside world.

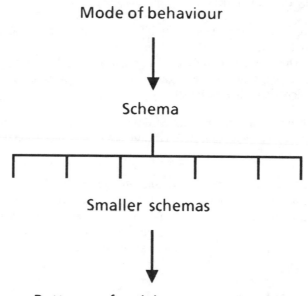

Fig.18.1: A model of behaviour can be described as a schema. This in turn can be described as a set of other, smaller schemas. This process can be continued down to a level which represents patterns of activity across the neurons.

The problem is generally approached in a top-down fashion starting with a structural analysis of some mode of behaviour and attempting to define it in terms of functions of behaviour units called schemas. There is then a further reduction from the schema to the individual neurons.

The structure needs to be flexible because the information has come from observation of behaviour and not from a knowledge of what actually occurs.

Piaget (1980) has been most influencial with respect to schemas. He defines the schema of an action as the *"generalisable characteristics of this action, that is, those which allow the repetition of the same action or its application to a new context"*. A child builds up schemas, starting with the basics, for example walking, through a physical interaction with the world. This development continues until shemas for abstract thought become defined which are not dependent on physical actions. New input and internal processes update the associations which exist between the schemas. The internal state is also updated by the knowledge of the state of execution of current plans. In this way two sorts of schemas are defined: *perceptual schemas* which define processes for perception and *motor schemas* which define processes for action.

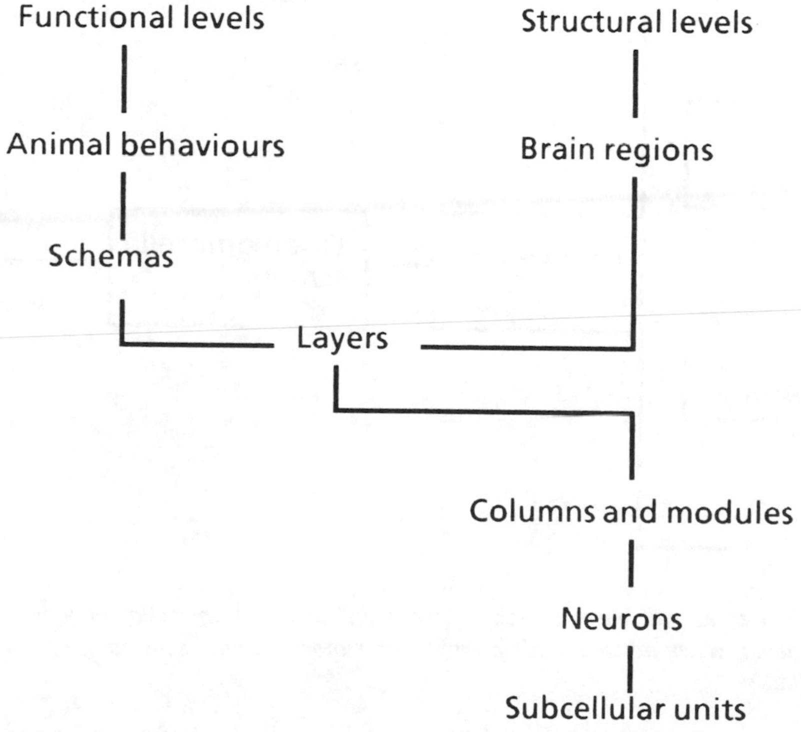

Fig.18.2: *The gap between functional and structural levels is bridged using layers of schemas.*

A group of schemas create the organisms' internal model of the world and have been used in the context of robotic search and planning, rats in a maze and the detour behaviour of toads. The intention is to bridge the gap between the functional and the structural. This relationship is shown in Fig.18.2.

Schemas can be defined as being made up of a group of *smaller* schemas, several being able to combine to form new ones. In particular one schema may occur several times in a larger ones.

For example, think about the processes that are involved in opening your umbrella when it is raining. Initially you will notice it is raining, which is a perceptual schema stimulation deduced from perhaps seeing other people putting up their umbrellas or the feeling of rain on your face. This will then stimulate the motor response schema of physically opening your unbrella which is in turn controlled by various *umbrella opening* schemas.

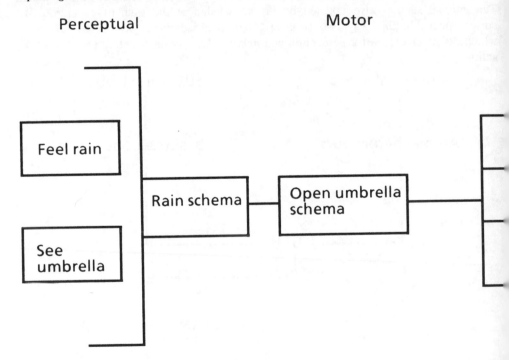

Fig.18.3: Perceptual schemas such as "feel rain" and "see umbrella" may make up a rain schema. When activated this prompts the motor response schema of opening an umbrella.

A perceptual schema determines whether or not a particular interaction occurs which will depend upon the credibility of the event. You would not, for example, open your umbrella if it was raining but you were sat on a bus at the time.

Ambiguous pictures can give some clues about schemas, for example the Necker cube shown in Fig.18.4 which can be viewed as projecting forwards or projecting backwards, depending on your point of view. There is also the infamous candlestick or two people image. It is interesting that when you stare at these you will never see the two images simultaneously, you have to make a little mental jolt to alternate between the two. The images must use separate schemas which are probably mutually inhibitory. This is not the case if two images are side by side; it is not difficult to comprehend a picture with more than one cube in it. This has led to the notion that at a lower level perhaps only one schema is activated but that schemas can be replicated.

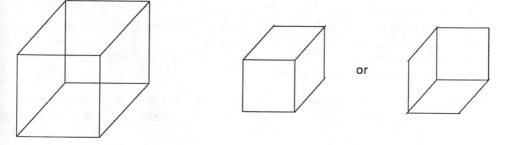

Fig.18.4: The Necker cube can be viewed from two perspectives as shown in the diagram below. In addition, the picture below is the classic "two faces" or a "candlestick" image. The images use separate schemas.

Memory and Schemas

Memory could be viewed as being made up of schemas – an assemblage of schemas giving us short-term memory (STM) which combines with an estimation of the environmental state to give a representation of current goals and needs. Long-term memory (LTM) can be thought of as a collection of stored schemas from which STM is built. STM keeps schemas active, both perceptual and motor, even if the current context is weak. STM and attention are integrated with attention only being focused on changes in the environment and subsequent updating of current schemas.

A general rule is that new schemas are reflected off existing schemas and old ones can be reconstructed and modified through experience as well as incorporating and creating new ones. This idea, that existing schemas can be enriched, is an important one. Very important, otherwise we would always repeat the same mistakes and never be able to rid ourselves of old habits.

Which Schema?

The initial problem is to correctly identify the reason for the behaviour. For example, a frog may jump in a particular direction not to escape from a preditor, but to jump towards potential prey. Both actions may appear the same but are stimulated by different circumstances. A difficulty with all the theory and definitions is to decide which actions belong to which schema.

Consider the difficulties involved in word perception. When dealing with individual letters there will be a struggle for dominance and eventually one will win. This is quite a straightforward process. When those letters are combined to form words and sentences a word is viewed as a picture, no longer are the letters taken in isolation otherwise the word would be meaningless. Modifications are then made to the word picture depending on context and other associations including past experiences. Recognition is beyond simple character recognition.

It should also be remembered that we only extract relevant information from the world around us – a great deal is thrown away. The way in which things are perceived also depends upon the way we have to respond towards them. For example, do we use our savings to pay our excessive telephone bill, or do we spend it on a holiday? Expert chess players have been found to look at the board for less time than novices, because they only pick out important points. They also have a better recollection of the positions of the pieces unless they are randomly arranged. When the whole image fits into their schemas it is more meaningful and easier to remember.

Summary of Schemas

We can define schemas as follows:

❑ At the very least they represent perceptual structures and programs for distributed motor control.

❑ They may be instantiated. For example, we may have one schema for the generic knowledge of a chair, and many schemas for the perception of a chair (wooden or leather, high or low, nice or nasty etc.).

❑ Schemas may operate concurrently. Many may be initiated simultaneously for different objects and for the planning and control of different activities.

It has to always be remembered that behaviour is very real but schemas are theoretical, an approximation to reality. They seem to be too neatly separated and appear to be more credible if they are expressed in terms of assemblies of finer schemas.

Now we will look one particular schematic development devised for a model of a frog's detour behaviour.

Frog

The computational frog was developed by Didday (1970) as a model of the neural circuitry underlying visuomotor control. That is, how the frog responds in a pysical sense, to what it sees. This has been further developed by Collett and Udin (1983), Arbib (1988).

Pattern recognition

Retinal *feature detectors* in the frog cause an image to be registered. The response may either be a snapping action at small moving objects, or a jump away from large threatening objects, with no response if the objects are stationary.

So here defined are two behavioural schemas: *prey catching* and *predator evasion.*

The shape of the input was seen to be important with respect to the response that was initiated. For example, a frog may try to eat a worm, but only if it sees something that looks like a worm, in terms of size, shape and movement, and is not too far away.

Prey selection

Didday used *foodness* to refer to how much a stimulus could cause a snapping response in the frog. How much of this an image has depends on where it is in a spatial sense. The frog has a foodness threshold, that is, how much stimulus is needed before the frog will snap at the image. Didday wanted to define the model so that activity in one area of vision will cause the frog to snap. Spatially the regions compete, only the most active will exceed the threshold and cause input to the snapping motor circuitry. If there is more activity in one region the frog will snap at the correct space. However, if there are two regions both with similar activity levels they may both dominate and the frog ends up snapping in the middle. Alternatively, the activities may cancel each other out and be ignored.

Too much build of inhibition will prevent the frog from responding to new stimuli. For example, for the two areas of equal activity, if one suddenly becomes more active, the frog should snap at it but this response was not evident in this model. So

Didday defined a monitor cell associated with each cell and if there is a reasonable increase in activity from one region then the inhibition is overridden and the frog responds correctly.

Depth and Detours

If the frog is presented with an obstacle between it and the food, it either goes over the barrier or around it. Even if it loses sight of the prey it keeps going although the action of snapping is not completed. The behaviour depends on how far it is from the prey, the depth. Separate retinal maps are needed for the prey and the obstacle such that the prey attracts and the barrier repulses. If the frog gets close enough to the prey it will approach, and snap. Specific motor controls were introduced for sidestep, turn, snap, hop, etc. Some of these having a blocking effect on others.

There are other examples in the book which make use of schemas particularly the example of word perception, Chapter 19.

19

Words and Speech

"Virtually nothing is known about how language is represented in real brains so we have to make things up as we go along". (Dr.David Touretzky, Personal communication).

Speech recognition is one of those tasks which people seem to carry out with relative ease, given the complexities involved, and is something which computer systems have great trouble with. We seem to be presented here with the same old problem: how can we develop a system to carry out a process when we do not know ourselves how we achieve that task? Research has indeed identified the parts of the brain used for language but it is the representation of language within those areas which presents problems.

There are major problems with trying to develop a system which maps words onto speech, not least of these being the irregularities that occur in the English language. A neural network aims initially to extract generalities from groups of patterns and to then build up specific associations. Within the English language there are so very many exceptions to general rules, and unique circumstances, and so the issue becomes greatly complicated.

In this chapter, we will look at some of the issues which are central to the development of this type of model, and some of the models which have been developed over the past few years. The objectives of these models are really of prime interest to the researcher because by highlighting certain aspects of speech recognition, and developing a model specifically to look at those properties, one can maybe use the results to shed a little light on the way the brain deals with language.

At this stage it should be said that this chapter is not intended to be an expert approach to the subject. It is a description of the neural network models which have been defined to cope with language. Many people have learnt to speak, yet could not tell the difference between a past simple and past participle in verb usage. One could argue that one does not need to be an expert in linguistics in order to make use of language, so is it necessary to expose a neural network to such expertise or should it be taught in the same way as the majority of the populace? It depends on whether or not you are trying to develop a neural linguist! We certainly need such expertise when we are analysing and trying to understand the results of our efforts.

General models

There are in general two types of model used for producing speech. One has arisen out of speech engineering and artificial intelligence, examples of this being the HEARSAY model (Erman et al.,1980), and DECtalk. The other type has developed from experimental psychology attempting to account for aspects of psychological data on the perception of speech, for example NETTALK (Sejnowski & Rosenburg 1987) and TRACE (McClelland et al.,1986).

Machine models tend to be judged by their actual performance in terms of producing speech. Psychological models are judged on their ability to account for details of human performance, these are referred to as the *computational* and *psychological* measures. Here, we will be looking at the latter, the psychological aspect, simply because these models have taken advantage of the connectionist aspect of neural networking.

After looking at the issues involved we will consider specific models. The first uses the Delta rule to study ambiguities in terms of word frequency and context. One uses the Perceptron convergence rule to look at role processing in sentences. Then there is an interactive activation model called TRACE and two models which use back-propagation, one of these being NETTALK. Finally there is a word perception model which looks at how the brain deals with ambiguities in word recognition.

Issues

There are a great number of issues in language processing. It is one thing to develop a model, another entirely to decide how the words/sounds/meanings of a word are to be represented, also, how the model is going to deal with such things as context and ambiguity.

There are several important features of speech which have played a significant role in the development of models. These are cited by McClelland et al. as being the most important in the development of the TRACE model of speech perception which we will look at later in the text. These are described here as they are all central issues when developing models.

Input of language to the model

It is obvious that the model has to receive the words and sentences in some way in order to then produce that input as speech. The input may be in the form of audible sounds, written text or perhaps keyboard or electronic input. Whatever the method used, the language needs to be coded in a way that the system will be able to deal with it, which, of course, depends entirely on how the model has been set up in the first place. In addition to this, like a child learning to speak, the model has to be communicated with at a level that is in line with its current ability. Not all the following problems of language are applicable to every method of input but they are all valid considerations. These are things which we have all learnt to carry out and therefore must aim for a model to achieve.

Temporal nature

Speech is a continuous flow of sounds and stresses and it is often difficult to actually distinguish one word from another.

Within this stream is a collection of words which as far as a model is concerned, have to be separated and interpreted. This recognition process will depend heavily on the context because there is hardly a situation when a word is processed independently of the words which surround it.

She looked out of the window at the boy with the binoculars.

This sentence takes on a whole new meaning if we know that the girl was a bird watcher. It is also worth remembering that text both before and after a word will have an effect on that word's meaning and pronunciation. This implies that the record of a word or sound that has already been recognised must be open to future amendments.

Lack of boundaries and temporal overlap

Unlike the printed word, speech is not made up of neat packages of separate sounds or units. McClelland et al. see it as unproductive to actually try to divide speech up into separate sounds or phonemes prior to identifying the unit to which they belong. They work along the principle of allowing the speech stream to be examined for general characteristics.

This sort of parallelism occurring in speech such that words overlap into other words is referred to as *coarticulation*. Jordan (1989) puts forward a solution to this phenomena. It is a problem, but less so than that presented for the overlapping of phonemes. Although there are certain clues for word boundaries these are not reliable enough and many errors displayed by models can be put down to word segmentation.

Context-sensitivity of cues

The cues for a particular unit depend greatly upon the context in which they occur, for example, speed of speech, position of a letter in a word, stress and the person who is speaking. Everyone has a unique voice pattern so it is not possible to generalise in a complete way about anything that is said.

Context plays a vital role (Dascal, 1989) in resolving ambiguities when processing language, whether it is a human or a machine. There are a number of approaches to this particular debate.

If one believes that language is an autonomous process, certainly all meanings for a word will be activated and the contextually appropriate one then selected. If, however, language is taken to be an interactive process only the contextually appropriate meaning should be activated. Models have been developed to demostrate both these principles (Kawamoto, 1988).

The frequency in terms of how often one hears a word in association with a particular meaning may also have some bearing on the activation level for the interpretation of an ambiguous word. Kawamoto has said that a word may be activated initially according to its frequency rather than its context, the context then coming into play as a sort of check facility.

A combination of these approaches has also been suggested, that more than one meaning for a word is initially activated, the degree or amount of that activation depending upon both frequency and context.

Noise and indeterminacy in the speech signal

We cannot always have the situation where someone is in a quiet room, speaking very slowly and clearly. People are extremely adept at recognising what someone is saying above loud background music, other conversations and even if the speaker has a speech defect such as a stammer.

If a word is not fully comprehensible, a person is still able to complete the sentence, perhaps not correctly but at least plausibly. The problem of developing a model which can eventually learn to separate foreground from background noise and complete partial input in a credible manner are problems which occur in all perception – vision, for example. This is a difficult problem which would not be tackled in the initial stages of the model's development but nevertheless is a point to consider.

Comprehension

It is difficult to ascertain the process of comprehension. Swinney (1979) suggests that a procedure is followed whereby the meanings of a word are assessed, regardless of favouritism prior to the complete perception of the stimulus word. Contextual pressure to finalise the meaning operates very quickly, an inappropriate meaning being inhibited after about a few hundred milliseconds.

This gives a picture of comprehension as a bottom-up, automatic, process which is initially context-independent. To begin with, the lexical meanings are considered in isolation, then an assessment is made of the suitability of the choice given the top-down contextual information.

This however only takes into account the meanings of the individual words. Also to be considered is the meaning of a sentence taken as a whole. When a word starts to be recognised, and lexical meanings are activated before the full sensory input is processed, so too is a sentence tentatively processed before it is completely understood. In this way, processing of the sentence, what is said and the interpretation run in parallel, being completed almost simultaneously.

It also seems plausible to assume that the less favourable initial interpretations for the meaning of a sentence are not lost. For example, consider a joke, irony etc. a process which humans develop in the later stages of language acquisition. Swinney makes the observation that: *"the unfavourable interpretation can...be quickly recovered at the end, which shows that it must have been activated and preserved, in spite of contextual pressure against it"*. In this way another stab at the interpretation can be tried.

Once the meaning for a word has been accessed the context of the sentence may lead to a redetermination of that meaning. For example, the following sentence is given as a good example of something that has to be scanned more than once before the meaning is properly determined.

The old dog the footsteps of the young.

Apparently the reason why this sentence is so difficult to understand is because the word *old* is usually taken as an adjective to mean aged. The noun interpretation of elderly is far less frequently used. So from the beginning you are making wrong assumptions about adjectives, verbs and nouns. An adjective is usually followed by a noun so the dog must be the animal version, not the verb. It is not until you get to the rest of the sentence that you realise something is not right.

The highlight of this example is that the most frequently used version of a word tends to dominate in our initial interpretation.

Role assignment

McClelland and Kawamoto (1986a) discuss role assignment in sentence processing. They point out that: *"no-one disputes that various factors influence the final reading that is assigned to a sentence. However, there are various views of the ways in which these factors are taken into account online"*. They look specifically at word order and semantic constraints within a sentence.

We will look at their model later in the text.

Word representation

Models in the past have sometimes taken a node in a neural network to represent a whole word and to then set up inhibitions between these nodes and the letters which comprise the words. So that, for example, if the first letter of the word was S, this would cause the supression of all words which did not start with the letter S.

It is the general opinion now that words are not represented by nodes (Stone et al.,1989) and on the whole a more distributed approach is taken towards their representation, being achieved by a pattern of activity across the units.

One major drawback of having words represented by nodes was that the inhibitive effect described above tended to make the retrieval of partial or noisy data impossible.

Using the Delta Rule – Ambiguous Words

The goal of Kawamoto's (1988) network is to show that an arrangement of simple interconnected processing units are able to learn the meaning of ambiguous words by adjusting the connection strengths between the units.

Once trained, the effect of context and the relevant dominance of one particular meaning for a word over another meaning will be simulated and assessed. Previous models such as those by McClelland and Rumelhart (1981), and Cotterill (1984), used a local representation scheme to encode a word, this model using a distributed representation.

The idea of distribution facilitates learning within the network and also enables multiple activation and competition among alternatives.

Architecture

The network comprises 48 graphemic features representing the spelling of the word, 48 phonemic features representing its pronunciation, 24 syntactic features representing the type of speech, eg. noun, verb etc., and 96 semantic features representing the meaning of the word.

There are two layers of units, with 216 units in each layer, representing these graphemic (48), phonemic (48), syntactic (24) and semantic (96) features. In the first layer, the auto-associative units receive input from an external source and also from other units in the same layer. The second layer, the buffer layer, receives input from the auto-associative units and acts as a memory which retains a copy of the most recent word. There are connections from the syntactic elements in the buffer layer back to the corresponding units in the previous layer.

The input pattern is in the form of the spelling of the word and is applied initially to the auto-associative units. Each element in this layer forms connections to every other element in the layer to form an auto-associative network representing the spelling, pronunciation, type of speech and semantic features of the word. This information is then transmitted to the corresponding elements in the buffer layer which retains a copy of the word. Connections from the buffer layer speech type area back to the auto-associative layer allow word transition if this is demanded by the subsequent context of the sentence. For example, consider the two sentences below:

The boy fishes off the pier.

The boy fishes for praise.

The interpretation of the word *fishes* may initially be as a noun, but obviously in the second sentence, the context implies that this initial judgement is incorrect and the word is a verb. Hence the transition must be made from a verb to a noun.

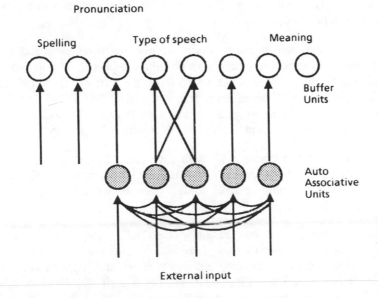

Fig.19.1.The 216 autoassociative units receive external input and also input from within the layer. The buffer units in the next layer receive input from the autoassociative units. This buffer layer is made up of 48 spelling, 48 pronounciation, 24 types of speech and 96 meaning units. The buffer layer stores the most recent word, the only feedback to the autoassociative layer is from the type of speech units.

Training

The network was trained using 12 pairs of words with four letters and ambiguous meanings. These being:

ACID   a chemical or a drug
FINE   adequate or, for example, a parking fine

FLAT	a surface or an apartment
LEAD	a metal or a direction to follow
ROSE	a flower or a direction of movement
WIND	a gust of air or to encircle
BLUE	a colour or a mood
COLD	a temperature or an attitude
DOVE	a bird or a joint
KNOB	a round handle or round mount
LONG	a distance or an emotion
RING	jewellery or a sound

These meanings together with the pronunciation were coded and each word defined as being a noun, verb or adjective.

In addition to this each pair of words was given a value to represent the frequency with which one could expect that particular definition to occur, in comparison with the alternative definition. For example, for WIND, the *gust of air* definition had a frequency of 4, the *encircle* definition a frequency of 3. For RING, the *jewellery* definition had a value of 6, the *sound* definition a value of 1. These values are really for testing and should not be taken as absolute, or accurate in any way.

A total of 800 learning trials were used, with each pair of words being presented to the network about 67 times, according to the ratios of frequency as defined. During this learning process the only changes to the network were the adjusting of the strengths of the connections.

The learning algorithm used was basically the Delta rule, with the additional amendment of something referred to as *habituation*. This enables instability of the network to be overcome by introducing a decay term which is applied to the units in the auto-associative layer when these elements reach their maximum or minimum values and the pattern of activity is no longer changing. A situation which implies that once the network converges onto a solution it will stay there even if that solution turns out to be contextually incorrect.

Initially the connection strengths are all set to 0. When a word is presented to the network the spelling of the word is initially activated, then after one time step activity spreads throughout the network via the connections. An example given showed that 16 iterations through the network for a particular input pattern would cause all the necessary information to be retrieved. In order to simulate context, the spelling together with parts of the semantic or syntactic fields are presented.

Results

It was found that for the words which had a frequency ratio of 6:1, the most dominant was retrieved in every case. However, for the 3:4 ratio, the less dominant meaning was retrieved 25% of the time. This can be interpreted in terms of Hopfield's bumpy ball in that the network will have stable states and the activity of the network will tend towards a local energy minimum. In this case the landscape looks like a ridge, either side representing one or other of the meanings of the word.

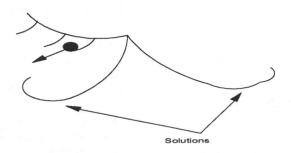

Solutions

Fig.19.2: The shape of the ridge is determined by the frequency. The starting point on the ridge is determined by the context.

When a single word is presented to the network, the starting point of the ball, in terms of which side of the ridge it is located, will determine where its final resting place will be. In the case of the frequencies which are very different, this starting point seems to always err towards the most likely outcome.

The effects of frequency and context are important in this model and the model has been designed in order to reflect that fact. Context will determine the starting point in the landscape and the frequencies will determine what the landscape looks like. With no context, the ball starts on the top of the ridge, equally likely to roll either way.

Although the network ends up by only looking at the context, evidence shows that both senses are activated initially. Evidence also showed that both meanings of the text were initially activated. Initially the response from a unit was the sum of its weighted connections until one unit reached either its maximum value (became *saturated*) or its minimum value. Once this occurred competition between the units was initiated until one meaning becomes minimised and the other is maximised. Without this element of competion both meanings would increase, though probably at different rates.

Results have been shown to be consistent with psycholinguistic data showing that people are more likely to produce a less likely meaning for a word if the previous context points to it.

The Boltzmann machine exhibits similar behaviour to this model in terms of the energy landscape and energy minima.

Word transition

The word transition process showed how the current word effects the processing of a subsequent word in a sentence. In order to include this in the model the second set of units, the buffers, were used to store the most recently accessed word.

Once the habituation process has been carried out the solution is transferred to the buffer units, overwriting any previous contents, and enabling a contextual constraint to be available for the next word. This of course means that context is only taken into account between successive pairs of words in a sentence, but it does allow the implications of context to be observed to some extent. The feedback from the buffer units enables the speech type of a word to be changed if it is later found to be inappropriate.

Conclusion

The network seems to support the view that frequency and context play a major role in the determination of a meaning for a word and that initially all meanings seem to be activated, the most dominant eventually supressing the others.

In a local model, this competition is achieved by establishing inhibitions between different senses. In the distributed model, the competition and inhibition only become involved after a unit has reached a maximum or minimum value. This model has shown how a distributed representation can capture the effects of frequency and context quite naturally.

Role Processing in Sentences

McClelland et al., (1986a) developed quite a different model in the sense that the goal was to provide a mechanism that could account for the joint roles of word order and semantic constraints on role assignments when processing sentences. By the role of parts of a sentence, we really mean the way in which parts of the sentence relate depending upon the effect that is had by one part on another. Let us look at some of the terminology:

Verb phrase (VP)	the verb part
Noun phrase (NP)	the noun part
Prepositional phrase (PP)	the second part of a phrase defined as following *with*
Agent	the part carrying out the action
Patient	the part receiving the action
Instrument	the part being used for the action
Modifier	a part of the PP which causes the first NP to be changed through context
Subject NP	
Object NP	

For example:

    1) *The dog ate the bone*
    2) *The dog ate the bone with his teeth*
    3) *The bone was eaten*
    4) *The dog ate the bone with a friend*

In 1), dog is the first NP, the Agent; bone is the second NP and is the Patient.

In 2), dog is the first NP, the Agent; bone is the second NP and is the Patient; teeth is the NP in the PP (after *with*) and is the Instrument.

In 3), bone is the NP, the Patient.

In 4), dog is the first NP, the Agent; bone is the second NP and is the Patient; friend is the NP in the PP (after *with*) and is a Modifier of the second NP.

Sentence test data

The sentences used with the model can consist of between one and three NPs, together with a verb.

There will always be a Subject NP, and there may be an Object NP as well. For example, in the following sentences, *door* is the Subject NP in 1) and the Object NP in 2).

1) *The door opened*

2) *The boy slammed the door*

If the sentence has an Object NP, it may also then have a *with-NP*, for example *foot* is the *with-NP* in 3) below.

3) *The boy closed the door with his foot*

The sentences are presented to the system as a canonical representation of the constituent structure of speech, in other words, it is coded to represent the relations which exist within the sentence.

The features are identified according to a set of definitions concerning the realtionships between the parts of the sentence. For example, a verb will have a code to say whether or not an Agent is present; whether or not the Agent, Instrument or both touched the Patient; and the nature of change that takes place in the Patient, given as pieces, shreds, chemical, none or unused. The noun can take a definition of human, softness, gender, volume, form, pointedness, breakability or object type. Each verb or noun can have only one option for each of these feature active in its definition, represented by a 1, all other options then taking a value of 0. These features were selected to describe what was felt to be the: *"important dimensions of semantic variation in the meanings of words".* It is emphasised that this is by no means a full set of definitions.

So a sentence may be presented in a coded form which can be interpreted by the model.

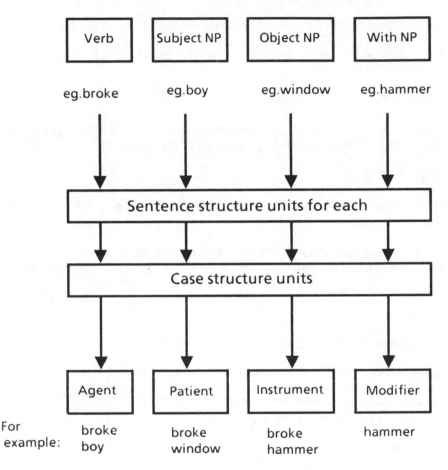

Microfeatures

Fig.19.3: The features of a sentence are input in terms of verb, subject NP, object NP and with-NP (broke, boy, window, hammer). These represent the SS units in this simplified diagram. The model then creates the sentence structure using the case structure units Agent, Patient, Instrument and Modifier.

Model

The model is made up of sentence-structure units arranged in four roughly triangular formations, with each unit representing a pair of features. The four triangles correspond to the Verb, Subject-NP, Object-Np and With-Np within a sentence. The model could have been set up so that a unit would only be activated if both the features it represented were active, which would enable the model to be finely tuned to microfeatures of the structure. One goal of the model was, however, to see how it would respond to noisy data, so the units were set to come on with a probability of 0.85 when both inputs were active, 0.15 when neither were active. In this way each feature of the input is represented in the activation of many of the SS units, none of which are crucial.

After the SS units, the model then creates the sentence pattern across four blocks of case-structure units for the Agent, Patient, Instrument and Modifier. Thus the model activates the noun features for the input it has received. For example, if the features are input for broke, boy, window and hammer in terms of noun and verb characteristics and relationships, in the sentence *The boy broke the window with the hammer*, the output will be in the form (broke, Agent, boy), (broke, Patient, window), (broke, Instrument, hammer) and (hammer,Modifier,-), where – indicates that no modification is necessary. This is an extremely simplistic representation of the actual procedure but serves to show the general principles.

Training and Learning

The learning algorithm used is equivalent to the perceptron convergence procedure. A sentence is presented and activates the sentence-structure units based on the information given in the feature definitions of the sentences. Each unit is activated probabilistically and the case-structure units are subsequently activated. The result is then compared to the required output and the connection strengths adjusted to minimise the error. Basically, if a unit is not active and it should be, all the weights on the active input lines are increased and the threshold is decreased, a similar process, in reverse, is used if a unit is active when it should not be.

Results

The main project involved the generation of sentences from a group of allowable sentence frames used in training. For example, *the eater ate the edible thing*. Using the features given for each word it should be possible to then generate sentences which fit into such frameworks. After 50 cycles of training, the model was tested on both learnt and new sentences. On average the model was turning on 85 out of 100 of the microfeatures that should be active and about 15 out of the 2400 that should be off. A very good result.

Further tests showed that the model was able to complete plausibly a partial sentence such as *the boy ate.*

With regards ambiguity, the model is able to distinguish very well provided the features are clearly enough defined. As far as this is concerned, two words that look and sound the same to us, will appear to be very different to the model as it only sees them in terms of features.

Shades of Meaning

This is quite an important and interesting emergent feature of the model concerning its ability to amend the information it is given in line with the knowledge it has accumulated from past experience.

The model was given the sentence *the ball broke the vase.* Now, the only information it had previously been given about the hardness or otherwise of a ball was that it was soft. In this context, however, the ball is the breaking agent and the model strongly activates the *hard* feature for the ball. Now this could be considered to be wrong given the learning experienced. Then again it could be a pretty astute assumption on the part of the model.

Generalisations

It was found that the model could deal with new words and place them contextually with errors only tending to appear in the Volume and Form dimensions. It could cope provided their definitions fell at least in part, within the space defined by an existing word that it knew.

Conclusion

The model deals very well with the objectives it was designed to meet, exhibiting some very interesting additional properties. The problem highlighted here, which seems to be common to most such models, is the difficulty of representation. This model is very limited in what it can deal with in terms of sentence construction, noun features and verb associations. It also has a very limited vocabulary.

It is interesting to note that the model picks up the strongest regularities first, according to the frequency concept of Kawamoto's model. The model has three basic properties: the ability to exploit multiple, simultaneous constraints; the ability to represent continuous gradations in meaning; and the ability to learn gradually without forming specific rules but picking up on the first major regularities. This is representative of parallel distributed models and applicable to all aspects of cognition.

An interesting question raised by McClelland et al. is whether or not words have literal meanings, that is, whether or not the meaning for a particular word is ever fixed and unambiguous. They come to the conclusion, based on observations of their model, that words are in fact clues to scenarios. No one word has an absolute meaning but all words working together to provide an explanation, or just clues, to the meaning of a sentence. No single word completely or uniquely determes the interpretation of the sentence.

The view was taken that this model is by no means complete but that PDP models, perhaps interfaced with a conventional word interpreter or parser, would be a natural and useful extension to consider.

NETTALK and DECTALK

DECTALK is a very impressive model developed by DEC which reads English characters and produces, with a 95% accuracy, the correct pronunciation for an input word or text pattern. The system uses a list of rules, derived by a team of linguists and contains a large dictionary of exceptions. The system uses a method of *looking the word up*, in a table or list, to find if it is an exception. If it is, the correct pronunciation can be located. If the word is not among the list of exceptions the linguistic rules are applied. DECTALK is an expert system which took 20 years to finalise.

Over one summer vacation, Terence Sejnowski put together a system called NETTALK (Sejnowski & Rosenburg 1987), a neural network which was to carry out the same task as the DECTALK system. After 16 hours of training the system could read a 100-word sample text with 98% accuracy!

The model

NETTALK is a simulation on a microcomputer which uses a hypothetical analog learning circuit. The model uses 309 units with 18,629 weighted connections and 80 hidden units. There are 55 output units, one for each phoneme. The model is described as being very crude compared to the behaviour of real neurons. It learns to match the letters it sees with the phonemes it hears, both being represented in terms of a series of 0s and 1s.

The system considers the words in terms of blocks of seven letters and moves this window across the text in order to apply context to the letter in the centre. In this way it is able to match the sounds with the letters and associated contextual forms. Once the output pattern has been determined, this is fed into a sound synthesiser, which enables the output to be heard.

Learning and testing

The learning algorithm used is back-propagation of errors and the system learns by being presented with the written words while also being presented with the sounds for those words. In this way, as it moves its window through the text, the hidden units build up associations and generalise regularities. Initially the system starts with random weights and to begin with the output from the voice synthesiser during training is unintelligable. Eventually the words start to take shape, and although the sounds have a distinctly childish flavour to them as the synthesiser had been purposely set to sound like a child in terms of pitch, the words begin to be correctly formed.

After being trained on 1,000 words, NETTALK achieved 91% correct phonemes when tested on the training set and 80% when tested on 1,000 different words. With 15,000 words in each set a success rate of 88% was achieved for the training set, 86% on the test set.

Analysis

The model was able to deal with new words using the generalisations it had built up. A cognitive map of the system showed that the network had formed a model of the vowel sounds simply from the repeated presentation of words and their pronunciations.

TRACE

This is a model (McClelland et al.,1986) of speech perception based on the principle of interactive activation, so called because the processing units form a dynamic structure called *the Trace* which provides the processing mechanism and the memory for the model.

The TRACE model uses the method whereby the perceptual system uses information from context in order to adjust connections, the mechanism then being able to tune into the perception as it goes. Other models were considered but this one was seen to be the one which offered the most potential towards solving some of the more tricky problems that McClelland identified.

The model consists of a very large number of units organised into three layers: the *feature, phoneme* and *word* levels. Each unit represents a particular hypothesis about a particular perceptual object at some point in time relative to the starting point of the utterance..

There are banks of feature detectors corresponding to speech sounds, such as acuteness, diffuseness and vocalic. These are split into time slices and each ranges from high to low activity. There is a phoneme detector for each phoneme. These span six time slices and are arranged in pairs to overlap. There are detectors for each word, the time slice covering the length of the word, again arranged in pairs to overlap.

Fig.19.4 is a much simplified version of that given by McClelland et al. to demonstrate the general features.

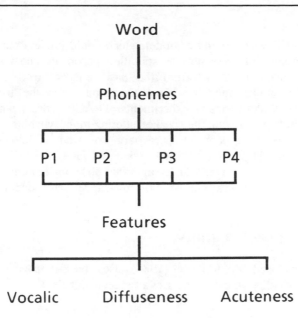

Fig.19.4: A simplified version of the Trace model

The input is presented to the feature detectors as a pattern of activity and is split into time slices to represent continuous speech. As such it moves through creating what could be thought of as a wave form of the sounds. The input is then applied to successive slices of the network as time evolves, with new input arriving as the previous input moves through the layers. Hence the output is a trace of the analysis of the input at each of the layers.

The processing and memory are integrated because of the continuing processing of the old time slices as new ones are input to the system. This continuation allows the model to interpret context and to retain information in what could be thought of as short-term memory in order to consolidate data items.

The units in TRACE have excitatory and inhibitory effects with units on different levels, which are mutually consistent, having mutually excitatory connections. Units on the same layer which are inconsistent have mutually inhibitory connections and there are no inhibitory connections between the layers. You would think that if the first recognisable phoneme was v, this would inhibit all words not starting with v. However, although this was used in earlier models it was found to interfere with the successful completion of partial information. All connections which do exist are bi-directional.

Connections between the feature and phoneme levels determine which features are most likely to activate which phonemes. The model then adjusts the connections from feature to phoneme as a function of phoneme activation at previous and subsequent time slices.

The idea of TRACE was to build a model which could process real speech. There was considerable concern about how to split the speech up, and which features to look for. This tended to detract from the basic concern over the fundamental properties of the model and its ability to account for the basic aspects of psychological data found in many experiments. TRACE I deals with recogniszing phonemes from real speech, with the speaker uttering monosyllables. TRACE II deals with lexical influences on phoneme perception for what is known about online recognition of words. This is a simplified version of TRACE I, using mock speech, consisting of overlapping but contextually invariant phoneme features. So some of the issues are avoided but it is easier to see how the model can account for many other aspects.

Features in speech signals

This model, developed by Rohwer (1988) uses back-propagation for labeling spectograms and identifying useful features in speech signals.

Model

The model has 200 input nodes representing 20 audiory parameters over 10 time steps, plus 10 hidden units and 11 output units. There are no direct connections between the inputs and output and the hidden nodes act as feature detectors, a quite small number being sufficient for the problem.

Learning

The learning data involved the recorded input of the words *eight, five* and *nine* four times from two male and two female speakers. The variation in responses from the speakers for this data is described as being *"comfortably small"*.

Training uses gradient descent which minimises the errors for the network between the actual and required output values.

Testing

The model was tested with an additional recording of each word from each speaker. A similar 300-28-19 network was also trained with seven utterances from two male speakers, and testing carried out with an extra two recordings from each person.

Results

It was found that individual nodes did not respond to specific words, but responded in a specific way for each word with the network finding its own criteria for distinguishing the words. The network seemed to be adequate for the task but there were problems with stability. The network was also slow to develop representations of the training patterns.

With feedback the model develops unbounded and unstable behaviour and is difficult to train. A back-propagation type algorithm (Almeida 1987) was tried but failed completely if any instabilities were encountered during training. An iterative scheme was used to stabilise the model by decreasing the size of the weights linking unstable nodes until those nodes stabilised. This was accomplished by sacrificing the monotonic decrease in the error.

Conclusion

Another method of the back-propagation learning algorithm was developed which overcame the problems. This method was not completely general, with feedback being allowed everywhere except between the hidden nodes and other hidden nodes. This version still has the problem that stability is not assured although the stable states of the network need not be known during training and the target states are guaranteed to be fixed points.

Word perception model

Rumelhart and McClelland (1986) put forward a model to represent the role of familiarity in perception. The units within the model represent letter recognition in four-letter words, with four position detectors to identify the position of a letter within a word, and detectors for the words themselves. They also gave the constraint that a letter can be in only one position at any given time.

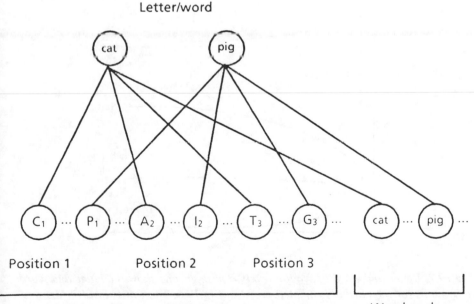

Fig.19.5: The letter nodes are only activated if they relate to the word node, in the specified position.

The activation value for a unit will depend upon whether or not the unit under consideration (i.e. letter) could possibly, perception-wise, represent what seems to be present. In other words, whether or not the letter under consideration could possibly complete the word.

They used as demonstration, partially obscured words. This is quite an interesting process because when you look at the example, you will in principle carry out the same mental considerations that the model demonstrates. Consider the following partially hidden word:

Fig.19.6: This word has been partially obscured.

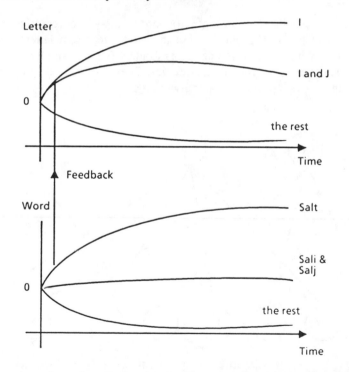

Fig.19.7: Letter and word activation levels. These graphs show the letter and word activations for the partially complete word in Fig.19.6. The words SALI, SALJ and SALT are initially activated as shown in the lower graph but SALT quickly dominates being the only recognisable word. This is fed back to the letter activations causing T to dominate, I and J to be suppressed.

The model activates all words whose first three letters are SAL and then looks at possibilities for the fourth letter. This letter may be I, J or T. All other letters, if we take 0 as the mid-point, are inhibited, and fall below 0 as shown on the graph. I,J and T are all excited as they are possibilities.

Initially the possible letters I,J and T are all activated. The words then become activated and SALT will quickly dominate being the only familiar solution, SALI and SALJ being rejected. This information is then fed back to the letters. After feedback from the word forms, T is further excited and dominates, I and J being supressed.

In the case where the word is unknown, for example:

Fig.19.8: This partially obscurred word could be SARN but this word is not recognised so alternatives such as EARN may be considered.

The only possibility is SARN, a word which is not recognised. In a case like this the model will consider EARN, BARN and other near misses. All these possibilities are partially activated but none of them actually dominate. This being the case there is no feedback from the words to reinforce any of the letters. The model finally settles on N as being the most likely.

This sort of simple interaction between processing units demonstrates human behaviour with respect to perception through familiarity in accordance with general principles. However, it does not comply exactly with linguistics rules (Chomsky and Halle 1968; Venesky 1970) or psychologists (Spoehr and Smith 1975). However, it has been said that although these only approximate human behaviour (Smith and Baker 1976) this sort of model may well be more accurate than a set of rules representing human competence in some areas.

Conclusion

Neural network models perform the task of speech perception very well and in the case of NETTALK, with a minimum of development time being spent on them. As we noted at the start of this chapter, the emphasis on these models is to discover more about how the brain processes speech, not just to produce a model that does the job.

The models tend to have different objectives and as such have been generalised to reflect those objectives. Trying to cope with the complexities of language is an awesome task but it does seem to be apparent that the simplest of models tend to provide the emergent features of those which attempt to create complex relations and definitions of word associations. One point of view is that it is better to leave the definitions to the model, the hidden units having been shown to create such models for word sounds, and that perhaps this would also apply to sentence processing.

It has been shown that (Elman,J.L., Zipser,D. 1988) the PDP models together with the back–propagation learning algorithm can provide a powerful tool for application in the domain of speech processing. The models are able to correctly categorise a number of highly confusable phonetic segments and are able to generalise to deal with new data. An important feature is that they are beginning to shed new light on how the brain processes language.

Dr David Touretzky (Personal communication) makes a very interesting observation when he says that: We don't know where noun phrases (for example) reside in the brain or how they are encoded. It's not even clear if there really are such things as noun phrases in the brain; perhaps they exist only in the imaginings of linguists.

The point that he is making here is not detrimental to linguists in any way. He is saying that the study of language can be carried out by experts in the field excellently given the definitions and representations available. For example, the role of a word and the relationships between words within a sentence, whether a word is a verb, noun, subject or object, whether or not we are using the past simple or past participle form of a verb etc. However, we have no evidence to support the fact that the brain uses the same representations and relationships used by linguists, if indeed it uses any at all.

20

Image

"The visual system of a single human being does more image processing than does the entire world's supply of supercomputers". (Mead, 1989)

The differences between the functioning of conventional digital computer systems and the brain are diverse and fundamentally irreconcilable. In fact, it has been said that digital computing simply serves to show us how neural computation is *not* done.

Vision is one of the most challenging potential application problems. Contributing to this is the fact that we now have quite a store of information about how the eye and brain process images. At a low level there are problems such as the removal of noise, deblurring, contrast enhancement, and boundary fining. These are solved with fairly standard algorithms essentially local in the 2-d topology of the image. They can be implemented on dedicated parallel hardware, using conventional silicon or more advanced optical techniques. At a higher level there is more of a challenge in the form of object location and recognition.

Research projects are numerous and diverse. For example, there are at least six approaches to character recognition problems (Bienenstock 1989). However, each particular model is designed to solve a specific problem and will inevitably turn out to perform poorly when applied to a different setting. The developments are far from universal and there is no general central theme or representative definition.

Brains can adapt instantly to visual input and make use of past experience and shrewd guesswork to identify images which are partially obscurred or ambiguous. There are cases when an object cannot be identified from any of its constituent parts and has to be seen completely before it can be identified. To deal with this, high-level tasks often need the introduction of long-range interactions in the image, that is, pixels which are a long way apart have to interact. A collective interpretation has to be found. Many neural models exhibit this sort of behaviour. Incorporated into the model should also be some kind of knowledge about the shapes and properties of classes of objects and images.

Interactions which go on in the brain are hard to understand and to formalise mathematically. It is thought that higher level knowledge is of a symbolic rather than numerical nature, meaning that a central concept must exist that is independent of rotation, angle, lighting etc. If this is the case there exists an interfacing problem between this symbolic high level with low-level image processing.

There are many examples of image processing distributed throughout the text. Here, a few examples have been selected which may give some overview of the research being carried out. Other examples are ALVINN (Chapter 21) which uses a camera and lasar unit to determine depth and environment in order to drive a vehicle along a road, the silicon retina developed by Carver Mead (Chapter 17) and the robot HERMIES (Chapter 21).

Considerations

One step towards the solution of visual problems is to construct an explicit representation of the image. Recognition can then be based on extracted features which are less sensitive to orientation, perspective of the viewer and lighting conditions (Kersten et al.,1987).

Another aim of research has been to form a global representation for an object which takes into account such things as orientation, curvature, depth and reflectivity. This is obtained from a variety of sources such as stereo, motion and colour. These *intrinsic images* are different from more abstract interpretations because they provide spatial details.

The problem of determining the identity of an object in a scene has been approached using *image segmentation* (Bilbro 1989). This method can be used to carry out the automatic understanding of images, particularly non-biological ones such as range or synthetic aperture radar. A pixel image can be understood when the objects are recognised or at least characterised. This characterisation is in terms of segments of the image, such a segment being a pixel group satisfying certain conditions of adjacency and similarity. In this example a Boltzmann machine type model was used which gave encouraging results.

A model (Korn 1989) has been developed to deal with the problem of intensity variations. The goal was to relate responses of a filter bank of different gradient filters to the structure of the picture determined by the physics of the image generation process. The picture was segmented, by close contour lines, into regions to form a representation, paying particular attention to outlines or edges as their role in shape definition is important. The property, extent and shape of the image is then compared to the outputs from various filters. This model is seen as a step towards bringing together various approaches in edge detection and segmentation.

The *stimulus equivalence* problem was recognised early on in neural network research and has not as yet been completely solved even using multi-layer systems. For example, people are able to recognise a character despite its size and orientation Marr (1979), and Neisser (1967) put forward the view that it is natural to assume that the input image is compared to some stored image. A conventional computer system would carry out this process by normalising the input image, that is, turn it around and make it a standard size, then compare it to stored images until a match is, or is not, found. Fukishima (1982) has carried out some interesting research to deal with this very problem, and has had very encouraging results with his model the Neocognitron. See later in this chapter.

The problem with the perceptron and more recent models is that they are unable to focus on an image in parts and then to look at the whole thing. Hinton (1987) developed a model which activated all posssibilities and then homed in on the correct one, carrying out the processing in parallel.

Developing models of these processes has proved to be extremely difficult, one reason being the lack of clarity of the problems involved. There are simply too many ways in which a given image can be incorporated into a complete scene.

One solution to this is to use a MAP estimation which finds the most likely image. This is looked at next and we will see how it can be used in a number of applications.

MAP Estimation

Given a scene it is possible to formally generate an image from it. The reverse of this is not so easy because there need not be a unique scene for any one image. For example, if you look at a picture you may be able to identify a circle and a square. However, if a group of 20 people are asked to create a picture containing these two images, it is highly unlikely they will all produce the same picture even if we specify size, colour and orientation.

One solution is to use *maximum a posteriori* (MAP) estimation which will compute the most probable scene. In the three examples which follow, learning is achieved by using the Widrow-Hoff error correction procedure.

This method is used by Kersten et al. (1987) to solve a number of problems namely optic flow measurement, shape from shading and stereo.

Motion Measurement

By taking local measurements of an object's motion, a velocity can be assigned to that object. An initial problem is the difficulty of sorting out in which direction an object is actually travelling because a motion reading is only taken in a direction which is perpendicular to the object.

In the brain, certain specialised groups of neurons in the striate cortex deal with orientation and speed of components of an image. This area sends a map to another area which has larger receptive fields and looks at speed and direction for the pattern as a whole. In the model the neurons were tuned to respond to particular speeds and directions thus the changing velocity of a pattern resulted in changing node activity.

For the simulation these selective units were placed at 15° intervals each covering a band of 90°. The response of a neuron depended on where within this bandwidth the image occurred, being strongest in the centre and tapering down to 0 at the sides. A total of 136 neurons were used at each location to cover 17 directions and 7 speeds. Two such sets of component detector units were used, together with one set of global detectors, the latter acting as pattern selective output units. The system was trained on 50 patterns. After 15 iterations through the learning procedure the system was found to be stable and was tested on the test patterns and 50 new ones.

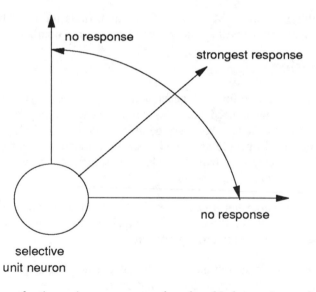

Fig.20.1: The selective unit neurons are placed at 15 degree intervals to cover a span of 90 degrees. This diagram shows a single neuron responding most strongly in a particular direction, the responses fading to zero as this region is moved away from.

The average error in direction was found to be 3.0° for the set of test patterns and 4.2° for the new patterns. For the speed, the average error was 1.1°/s for test patterns and 1.6°/s for the new patterns. For planar motion this was judged to be a fairly good result. Extensions to the model include 3-d motion and multiple objects.

Shape from shading

Without the shading information from boundaries, objects appear to be flat. Shading is used by the brain to turn a planar 2-d shape into a 3-d image. The aim of Kersten et al. (1987) was to develop a model to deduce the shape of an object soley from the information given by shading. Shading is defined as being a *"pattern of luminance reflected from a surface to the viewer"*. If we ignore the effect of shadows this will be determined by the shape of the object, the lighting, and the viewer's perspective. How does a person separate all these factors in the processing of an image?

The first step in the model is to somehow determine what the possible surface could be. It is thought that if a training set exists which will enable the model to learn about surfaces, no previous inbuilt knowledge needs to be stored in the system. The surfaces are assumed to be constrained by their overall structure, in a statistical sense, and an associative learning procedure is applied in order that the model can learn to assign shape to structure. For simplicity the model is deliberately limited to a subset of possible surfaces. White noise is filtered in such a way that an array of surface depths is available to the model.

A linear model is studied for this example. Although it can be said that such a model will perform poorly at boundaries and areas of shadow because of the sudden changes in image, this representing a nonlinearity, some interesting points will be observed which can give some ideas towards the formulation of a nonlinear version.

The Widrow-Hoff error correction learning rule was used to train the network to associate shapes with shading patterns. An nxn image was defined by identifying a set of points on the surface of the image, including the luminance contrast values for each point to indicate the shading at that point. A set of 800 29x29 pixel surfaces was artificially generated together with their depth images. It was found that the model makes a *"significant psychological predication: the slant bias and low-frequency undulations are lost in the reconstruction"*. The slant bias refers to the angle of the projected source of light. The fact that this is lost has the advantage that changes caused by such a bias can be attributed to changes in the surface or the intensity of the light source. Low frequency changes in shape being lost is due to the way in which the surfaces are originally defined and so is a problem which could be overcome.

The shape from shading problem is also approached by Sejnowski et al.(1987) and illustrated later in this chapter.

Stereo

The fact that we have two eyes plays an important role when we are determining the depth and shape of a visual image. Traditionally this problem has been approached in two parts, involving pairing up points which correspond to the image as seen by both eyes. Simple mathematics can then be used to determine depth.

Marr and Poggio (1976, 1979) developed a model for stereo vision which was able to solve a reasonably large range of random-dot stereograms (Julesz, 1960), these being computer generated images defining the depth of an image. To deal with a wider range of input, more complex constraints are needed. Marr and Poggio defined some constraints, developing an algorithm to eliminate false matches using uniqueness, continuity and compatibility.

The approach of the model described here, directly relates the objects on the two retinas to the way in which the scene is changing with respect to some local fixed point. False matches are actually considered to play a useful role in determining the true depth properties of a surface. This is because for a surface which has no depth changes, false matches will be found which can determine that no change in intensity exists. When there is a depth change a pattern of activity across the cells, at a variety of locations, will indicate edge locations.

Associative learning allows features for the input patterns to develop. The input patterns are generated such that the probability of a point being at a particular depth depends upon the neighbouring points. The surface images are made in a natural way in that two focal points converge onto a fixed position. The samples for the two will not necessarily be the same, due to the different angles that the eyes make with the surface. So an activation function is used.

A small bank of cells is located at each point in the image and the output is a map of the depth changes found in the surface. Learning was carried out using the Widrow-Hoff rule and 400 surfaces. Testing involved presenting 30 new images to the model and the judgement was that the model produced a *"good performance"*.

This problem has been solved either by limiting the range of input patterns or allowing any patterns to be used but rigorously defined using parameters and constraints. Neither is very satisfactory, both being a comprimise of one form or another. It was concluded that an interesting point would be to discover which sets of images or surfaces the brain groups together.

Cognitron and Neocognitron

In 1975 Fukishima put forward the following hypothesis of learning:

The synaptic connection from cell x to cell y is reinforced if and only if the following two conditions are true:

❑ presynaptic cell x fires

❑ None of the postsynaptic cells situated near cell y fires stronger (or brisker) than y

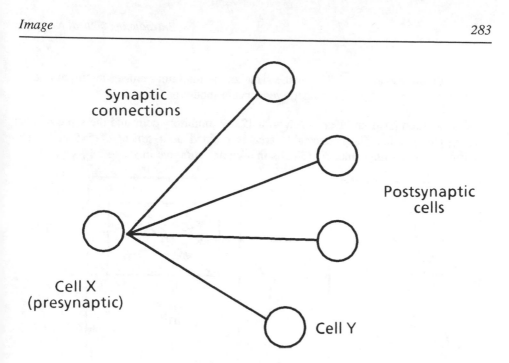

Fig.20.2: *The connection between x and y is strengthened if the response of y to cell x firing is the strongest of all the cells.*

Now this is basically the competitive learning principle (see Chapter 12) and was introduced to effectively organise a multi-layered network.

Fukishima developed a model which he called the *Cognitron* as a successor to the perceptron which was able to recognise symbols from any alphabet after training. This simply involved presenting the symbols to the model. However one drawback of the Cognitron was that it couldn't deal with orientation or distortion so, as a new improved version, he developed the *Neocognitron* which we will look at later.

Cognitron

The Cognitron is a self-organising multi-layer neural network whose basic form is very like our general model described previously except that Fukishima talks about *cascades* of layers. His cells receive input from defined areas of the previous layer and also from units within its own area. The neural elements for input and output can take the form of positive analog values which are proportional to the pulse densities of firing biological neurons. The cells use a mechanism of *shunting inhibition*, that is, a cell is bounded in terms of a maximum and minimum activity and is driven towards those extremeties. The model was simulated on a digital computer.

There are a couple of terms which need to be defined:

Connectable area: This is the area from which a cell receives input.

Vicinity area: This is the same as the inhibitory cluster in our simple competitive learning model of Chapter 12.

The simulation has four layers, each with 12x12 inhibitory cells and the same number of excitatory cells. The connectable area is defined as a square of 5x5 cells. The vicinity area is a little smaller, 13 cells in area and rhombic in shape.

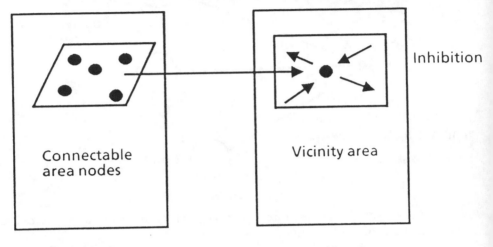

Layer U_1 Layer U_1 + 1

Fig.20.3: One node will receive input from its connectable area in the previous layers, and lies within an inhibitory cluster of 25 cells called a "vicinity area".

Because the connectable areas for cells in the same vicinity area are defined to overlap, but not to be exactly the same, once a slight difference appears between the cells this will be reinforced so the gap becomes more apparent. In this way each cell is encouraged to develop its own characteristics.

Fukishima looked at a variety of methods of determining the connectable area for each cell, this being the area from which it receives input. He found that using a probabalistic distribution for the destination of each branch enables the whole of the first layer to be adequately represented in the last layer, without having to increase the number of layers too much or making the areas too big. Other methods seemed to end up with one or only a few cells in the last layer firing, which seemed to Fukishima to contradict the general idea of a concept being represented as a pattern of activity across a number of cells.

Training

Five stimulus patterns were repeatedly presented to the first layer. Fukishima found that after the 20th cycle the Cognitron was organised in such a way that each pattern generated a response pattern in each layer, most cells, particularly in the last layer, responding only to a selective group of patterns.

The model progresses well without a teacher, that is, there are no instructions given which determine how the individual cells will respond. An advantage of this is that sophisticated initial connections are not necessary.

Conclusion

For the Cognitron, the relationship between input and output uses the same expression as that used to approximate the nonlinear input to output relations of the sensory receptors eg. cones. This is used in neurophysiology and psychology. As this bears such a close resemblance to the natural characteristics of a biological neuron, Fukishima says it is well suited for various kinds of visual and auditory information processing systems.

The conclusion is that the model is similar to an animal's brain in many ways. It has a multi-layer structure so there is more capacity for information processing than in previous models. This is not intended to be a complete system, additional units being needed at the input for initially getting the sensory input, and at the output to act as a decision maker, judging the results. Improvements could be made if the layers were modified eg. back coupling between cells of different layers or cross coupling between cells of the same layer. In either case the algorithm would still be valid. Finally, Fukishima points out that perhaps the organisation of other synapses is governed by other rules - it seems unlikely that the brain would use a single global process.

Neocognitron

Improvements to the Cognitron, in the form of the Neocognitron, were brought out by Fukishima and Miyake (1982) to overcome the problem that the Cognitron could not deal with changes in shift and orientation of letters. The new model uses the same algorithm but can now recognise patterns which are position-shifted or shape-distorted. The Cognitron would have seen these as different patterns. The model uses two main types of cells: S-cells and C-cells. These are analog type in that the input and output signals are positive analog values and defined as follows:

S-Cell: Trained to respond to certain features in the previous layer.
C-Cell: Allows for spatial displacement.

The input layer is a photoreceptor array device which holds the image as a 19x19 binary representation. After this layer there follows a cascade of a number of modular structures. Each module is made up of two layers, one composed of S-Cells, the other of C-cells, learning layers interleaved with non-learning layers. Only the input to the S-cells can be modified, all others are fixed.

Each unit *looks* at a 3x3 square in the previous layer. The C units will look at the preceding S layer and respond if there is an active unit in their window. They have the effect of *spreading* a feature, demonstrated in Fig.20.5..

Input
layer

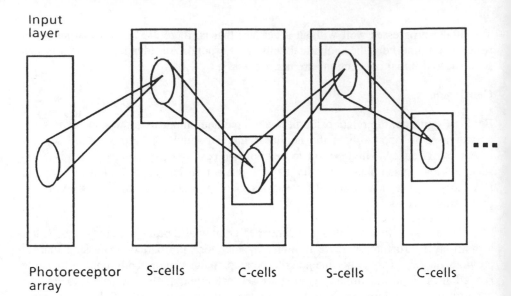

Photoreceptor   S-cells   C-cells   S-cells   C-cells
array

Fig.20.4: Neocognitron model. The circles show the connectable areas for the cell on each layer. The squares denote the group of feature detectors to which the cell belongs. There will be many more than in each area than the single one shown.

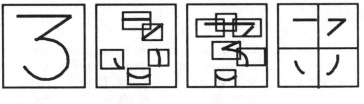

Input   C-cell   C-cell   C-cell
                         layer 1   layer 2   layer 3

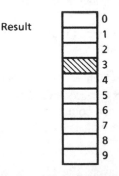

Result

Fig.20.5: Spreading effect. The units in a Neocognitron have the effect of splitting and spreading an image until a result emerges.

The S units look for combinations of selected features in the previous C layer, perhaps horizontal or vertical bars. Fukishima went on to develop his model so that it could deal with selective attention which we will look at next. This is the ability to cope with an image which contains more than one letter and recognises each by focusing on them in turn.

Selective Attention

Fukishima's (1986) model can carry out segmentation and pattern recognition from a composite stimulus, containing two or more patterns. The model will focus on one pattern, segment it from the others and then recognise it. Attention is then switched to another pattern and the process repeated. The model is able to recognise an imperfect pattern and recall the complete pattern with the defects and noise removed. This can be done even if the image is deformed in shape or shifted in position. This model is a multi-layered network like the Neocognitron in that layers of S and C cells are arranged alternately. However, this version includes additional backward connections between the layers. The process is as shown in Fig.20.6:

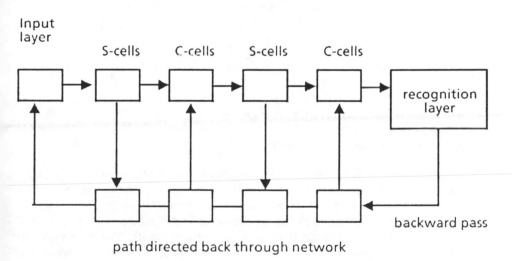

Fig.20.6: The selective attention model is similar to a Neocognitron with alternate layers of S and C cells. However, the results of the recognition layer are fed back through the network.

The S-cells are feature extractors with the features that they respond to being determined during the training process. During this learning it is only the S-cells with the maximum outputs which have their connections strengthened. The C-cells again detect the spatial positioning of an image.

The output of the final layer, the recognition layer, is sent back through the network tracing the same path as the forward signal until reaching the recall layer (identifiable with the input layer).

When there is more than one pattern in the image, the backward pass causes signals for the identified pattern to be strengthened until the other pattern signals become insignificant. So attention has been selectively focused on one pattern.

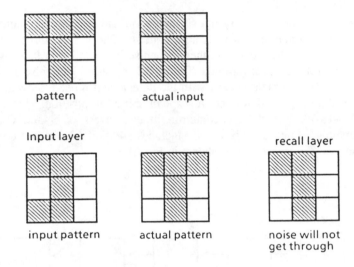

Fig.20.7: The pattern which is input to the model contains noise. During the path back through the model, the noise is prevented from getting through and is filtered out of the final image at the recall layer.

The image of the identified pattern at the recognition layer will be seen at the recall layer because the backward signals will arrive at the same positions as the pattern, guided by the forward signals. If there is more than one pattern in the image, this will cause segmentation as only one pattern will respond. If the pattern is deformed it will be initially segmented at the recall layer in its deformed state. The backward pass having failed to get through all the paths because of this deformation, will try to find the missing features. No noise or blemished will be included because the backward pass would have failed to get through at those points. We can demonstrate the principle in an extremely symbolic way, in the figure below.

Results

The model was simulated and training carried out by repeatedly presenting *standard* and *non-deformed* patterns of the characters 0, 1, 2, 3, 4 and 5. The model was then able to deal with examples like those shown in Fig.20.8.

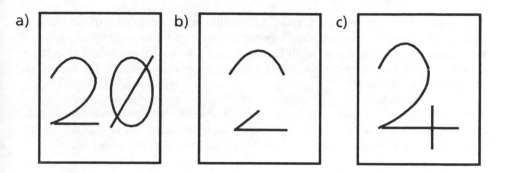

a) b) c)

Fig.20.8: Examples of the model's response to incomplete patterns and those with more than one image.

Shape from Shading

This is another *shape from shading* model (Sejnowski and Lekhy 1987) in order to simulate the complex problem of how the eye extracts information about the curvature of a 3-dimensional object from the light cast upon it - an impression of depth from changing shades of grey.

Model

The architecture used a three-layer network with 122 input units, 27 hidden units and 24 output units. Each unit is connected to every unit in the next layer.

The input units have a circular receptive field arranged so that they are similar to cells found in the retina, overlapping as shown in Fig.20.9. This type of overlapping configuration is referred to as *coarse coding*.

Receptive fields

Shape of
complete array

Fig.20.9: The circular receptive fields overlap, a similar design to that found in the retina.

The input units are of two types: *on-centre*, which have an excitatory centre and inhibitory surround, and *off-centre* which have an inhibitory centre and excitatory surround. The input is sampled by both arrays of these units.

The output units were tuned to respond to magnitude and orientation of the curvature at a specified point of the surface. They are arranged in a 4x6 rectangular array with the 6 columns corresponding to different peaks. The rows correspond to different curvature sizes, the top two rows coding the maximum curvature and the bottom two the minimum curvature.

This model has an ambiguity problem in that it is difficult to tell whether a shape is concave or convex and various images could lead to the same response. This could be overcome with a larger network with units representing different spatial scales.

Learning and Training

The back–propagation learning algorithm is used to minimise the error between the pattern and the firing rates from the output units.

2,000 images were used to train the network, each being different in terms of size and orientation of the two principle curvatures, in the direction of the illumination and the location of the image within the input field. The general type of shape was a parabolic 3-dimensional curve as shown in Fig.20.10.

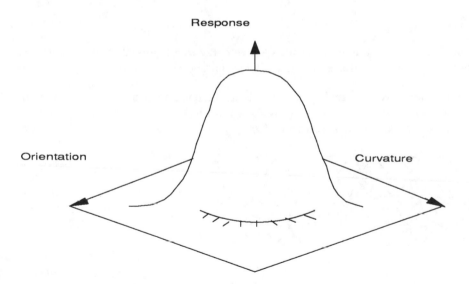

Fig.20.10: An example of a typical shape used to train the network with parameter values for orientation, curvature and response.

The input image causes activity in the 3x9 array of hidden units which in turn projects to the output units.

After 40,000 training patterns had been presented to the network the correlation between the correct and actual outputs reached a plateau at 0.88, and the network was able to generalise for new patterns.

The network was trained to extract curvature given an input of activity much like that which would be seen in the eye of a cat. However, on investigation, the units were found to have acquired properties very like those of the simple cells of the visual cortex. It was found that the hidden units were providing the output units with information about the orientation, convexity and concavity, and magnitude of an image. The hidden units seemed to be either acting as filters giving values for the parameters they represented, or behaving as feature detectors, discriminating between alternatives. Some of the hidden units were difficult to classify and four of them did not develop large weights at all.

This model only uses one feature of detecting curvature; we tend to use other clues such as noting the direction of the light or moving our heads to get a different perspective of an object. As such this may be considered as a module in an array of detecting facilities.

Bars and Edges

This model (Moorhead et al.,1989) was developed in order to gain some understanding of the representations derived by multi-layer networks and to relate the results to the neurophysiological characteristics of the visual pathway.

The network was trained to recognise patterns of bars and edges by drawing some comparisons with the extensive data which exists concerning actual cell responses to such stimuli. Learning was carried out with a back-propagation algorithm using filtered computer-generated images as input. The associated output patterns consisted of specifications of the orientation and contrast tuning.

Training

The training set consisted of computer-generated bars, with defined edges and potential noise. Each was in the form of 21x21 pixel square, the width of the bars being kept at a constant 2 pixels and all bars and edges passing through the centre of the image. The orientation varied from 0 to 360 degrees in steps of 15 degrees and there were 9 contrast values, with a fixed background colour.

These combinations gave 255 images and the addition of 3 blank images gave a result divisible by four, a requirement of the back-propagation with transputers, the architecture used for the simulation.

The model had either 4 or 8 output units depending on whether the response was to be geared towards edges, bars or perhaps both. The model was trained not to respond to blank images or noisy images.

Conclusion

Image is a very tricky problem. The process is highly computationally intensive and requires a large number of features to be identified. Models tend to concentrate on a single issue, or group of related issue in order to try to introduce as much simplicity into a problem as possible. Perhaps it will be found that these models form subsystems of the whole picture.

Beroule (1989) states that the problem of perception should not be approached in a hybrid way but as a whole. Not only should the problems of perception be taken into consideration but also higher level tasks such as movement generation, and any process involved in communication.

21

Robotics

Robotic systems have a number of requirements which seem to be applicable to so many different types of processing. This could be standard digital computations to make rapid and accurate calculations and implement overall system control; AI features to carry out decision making and real-time planning; and neural networks to provide an interface to the outside world and solve optimisation problems. For battlefield robots further complexity is necessary. Threat assessment, threat avoidance, threat to weapons allocation, reducing the enemy's tank (as opposed to your own tank) to ashes etc. Recently the emphasis has been on including learning capabilities in robotics. This is not just to build environmental models from sensory information but also to be able to control sensor allocation for optimal tracking of positions, courses, identities of potential obstacles or threats.

Navigation

Oak Ridge National Laboratory is using neural networks implemented on parallel machines applied to the problem of autonomous robots (Barhen 1987). This particular area of study is aimed at assessing the application of neural networks to combinatorial optimisation, robot navigation and multi-sensor intergration. The design of the systems is intended to be based on evolutionary principles.

Conventional computer systems find navigation in unfamiliar environments extremely difficult because of their lack of flexibilty and inability to process incoming perceptions. A neural network is being used for the model because they are highly suited to this sort of task – the rapid processing of continuous perceptions. The algorithms under study are implemented on a general purpose concurrent computer with a 64-node hypercube architecture and a 2-processor distributed system which serves as an *evolution machine* for the optimisation of neural network parameters. Basically what this does is to evolve the test machine and refine it according to results of previous experiments.

The hypercube architecture is developed by the NCUBE Corporation (Beaverton, Oregon). This enables 1,024 processors to be utilised in a space which is about 0.5m^3. Each processor has a computational power of about 2 million instructions per second (MIPS).

The neural network controls a mobile robot called Hermies (Hostile Environment Robotic Machine Interactive Series) – a self powered device which manoeuvres about on wheels. It has a directionally controlled sensor platform, two appendages (arms) and an onboard distributed processor (a 16-node hypercube multi-processor) fully software compatible with the model machine.

The aim is to minimise the overall execution time by spreading tasks between processors and minimising processor communications. Problems may arise if tasks are waiting for other tasks to complete, or if the number of tasks is greater than the number of available processors. Deducing optimal schedules for task control is difficult if not imposssible.

The asynchronous neural network is used as an effective computational tool. Each neuron is regarded as a computing process and interconnections as *virtual* communications links embedded in the hypercube. Neurons have an associated decision algorithm in order that their next state can be determined with the synaptic strengths being updated dynamically using feedback terms. The model uses an asynchronous, stochastic algorithm, which allows for escape from local minima. The stability and capacity of the network depends nearly entirely on a postsynaptic firing rate function.

Tests are carried out by simulating the environment and allowing Hermies to explore. Location uncertainties are stored in the network using a modified Hebbian learning rule applied such that the room's volume is partitioned.

After learning a series of potential rooms from slightly different positions, the robot is given a particular sensor graph which is a view of a particular unidentified room. Threshold-limited associative-recall criteria cause a best fit reconstruction of parts of the room which are out of the line of sight in order that a potential path between two given points can be planned. Neural states can be defined in terms of how certain the system is that 3-d obstacles are present in a room type environment using phased-array sonar.

The neural network calculates likely room pattern matches by sending a sonar *line-of-sight* distance vector simultaneously to lots of nodes. Each node carries out a best fit and sends the result to the controller, the interface between the robot and the external processor. The node thresholds are then increased until just one pattern dominates which will be the most likely solution. At the same time, a second set of nodes names the pattern and informs the expert system CLIPS used to control the higher-order robot planning under a rule based system. CLIPS will hold information about the room and will be able to determine a path.

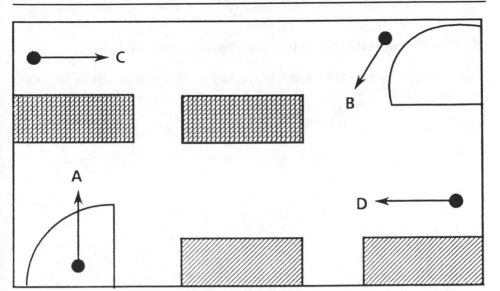

Fig.21.1: The training set for a room may be as shown with a number of views being presented. Fig.21.2 is a floor plan showing obstacles and views taken by the training patterns.

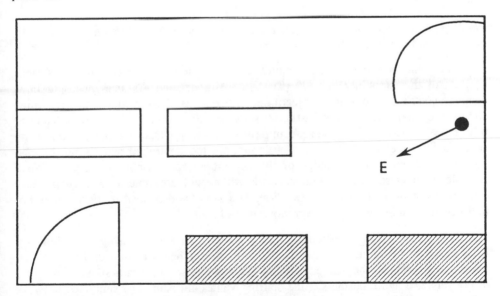

Fig.21.2: Given a view of the room described for our training set, the system should be able to deduce the obstacles which are out of sight, depicted here with dotted lines.

Robot motor control – precise movement of limbs

This model (Ritter et al.1989) concentrates on training a robotic arm to be able to position its end effector at a certain point on a 2-d plane.

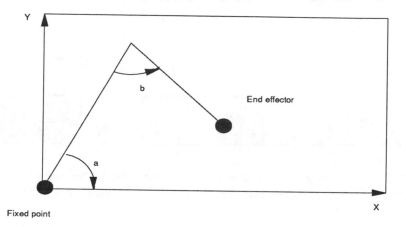

Fig.21.3: A combination of the angles a and b will cause the end effectors to be placed at different points (x,y) of the plane.

Limb movements and responses cannot be hard-wired, as it were, into a system because of the variability in body parts. In addition, such a system needs to have adaptive control and to be able to learn new movements. A robot may also have limbs changed or adjusted. The ballistic movements of a multi-jointed robot can be physically carried out using torque impulses on the joints. Such pulses cannot be controlled by feeding back sensory information, the controlled actions need to be known in advance. A knowledge of the necessary action can be acquired using a suitable learning rule in a neural network which will associate a required position with a movement to achieve that position. The example described is for a simple but non-trivial 2-jointed arm which can move in a plane.

Learning is based on Kohonen's algorithm and enables a relationship to be built up between series of torques and the desired response. When a neuron updates its own tensor, its neighbours help in adjustment. This cooperation gives a significant speed of convergence and robustness if the starting values are poor. The simulated network comprised 100 units in a 10x10 grid. After 3,000 learning cycles the model found a satisfactory mapping between the location of the end effectors of the arm and the series of torques necessary to achieve those positions. The units responsible for the execution of movements learnt to respond quite accurately to the test movement required.

ALVINN the Road Tracker

Essentially this is a chapter about using perceptions of the surrounding environment to control hardware. If we are thinking about robotics, this usually involves moving the robot from A to B without it bumping into anything and without having the route preprogrammed.

The *Autonomous Land Vehicle in a Neural Network* (ALVINN) developed by D. Pomerleau (1989) is a neural network which controls a vehicle and drives it down a winding road with trees on either side. The only information the network has been previously given is in the form of being shown pictures or images of the road and being told the best route in terms of direction to take.

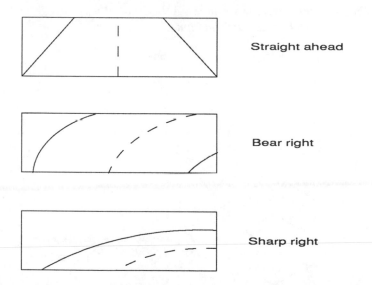

Straight ahead

Bear right

Sharp right

Fig.21.4: The system learns to associate input with direction.

ALVINN drives the NAVLAB, a test vehicle equipped with a video camera and laser range finder both used to give information to ALVINN about the oncoming scene.

The video camera sends a 30x32 pixel image, with each pixel corresponding to an input unit in ALVINN's *input retina*. The brighter the image the more a unit is activated. The laser range finder sends an 8x32 pixel image to ALVINN's *range retina* which indicates the distance from given objects in the line of sight, units being activated according to these distances. So the network is equipped with information about scene image and depth of field.

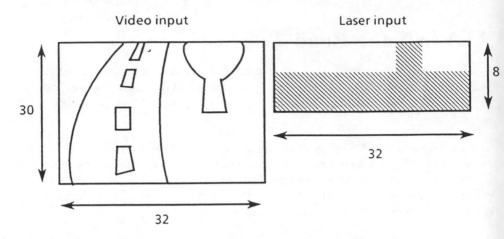

Fig.21.5. ALVINN receives input from two sources. A 32x30 pixel video image and a 32x8 pixel laser image for depth of field information

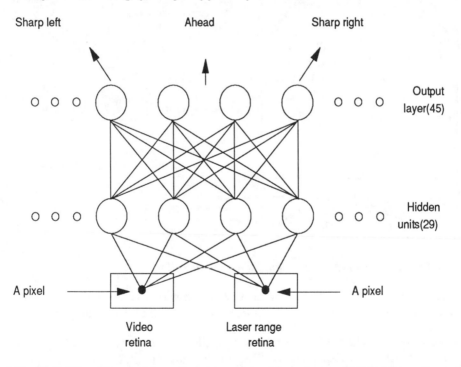

Fig.21.6: The video and laser input is received by a layer of 29 hidden units and then passed to the output layer. The output layer determines the direction of travel as indicated in the diagram

The two input retinas send the information received to a layer of 29 hidden units. These are in turn connected to a layer of 45 output units which determine the direction in which the vehicle should be guided, only one being activated at any one time. The unit in the centre corresponds to *go straight ahead*, ranging gradually down to a *sharp left* instruction from the left-hand unit and *sharp right* from the right-hand unit. There is full connectivity between the layers. This means that each of the 32 pixels in the 30 rows of the video retina connect to every one of the units in the hidden layer, and similarly for the laser range retina pixels. A simple representation of the architecture shown in Fig.21.6.

Training

The model is described as being difficult to train. The process was carried out by presenting 1,200 simulated road images for different parts of the road in a variety of lighting conditions and from a number of perspectives. Each was shown to the network 40 times and the weights were adjusted using error back-propagation.

Results

It was found that the hidden layers developed interesting internal representations. If the training images showed a road of fixed width the hidden units acted like detectors for particular stretches of road. If the roads were varied in width the hidden units became detectors for the edges of the road, each looking at either the left or the right side, but not both.

ALVINN was able to drive the test vehicle nearly twice as fast as a non-neural network algorithm used on the same vehicle, and ALVINN managed 3.5 (three and a half) miles per hour. This is not an impressive speed but we must put the project into perspective. It is a tremendous achievment that the vehicle can be manoeuvered at all considering it relies exclusively on interpreting data from image and depth compared with learned experiences.

22

Consciousness

Throughout history there have been theories and hypotheses put forward to explain the functioning of the brain, the mind and the Universe. In so many cases consciousness has been excluded from the reasoning. It cannot be explained using mathematics, physics or logic and has been considered to be of little importance in man's efforts to determine his world.

As Laplace said when asked of the place of God in his deterministic model of the universe: *"I have no need for that hypothesis"*.

No Place for Consciousness

The difficulty of defining anything as intangible as consciousness presents a problem which has been dealt with in a number of ways. Neurophysiology leaves no place in the brain for the existence of the mind, many scientists saying that it does not exist as a separate entity but is an integral part of the functioning of the brain itself. Psychology and psychiatry also have no framework in which to explain and investigate consciousness. (Fenwick and Lorimer 1989).

Reductionist science made no further headway, and left no space for consciousness either, everything counld be defined in terms of logical processes. Bertrand Russell called bundles of perceptions sensibilia and argued that mind and matter were merely logical constructions out of these sensibilia. AI also excludes consciousness, and so do neural networks. Cognitive and computer scientists seldom investigate consciousness, simply because there is no need for it in the models being developed. All that can be done is to model what is known. Some scientists say that the mind can be explained by the electrochemical processes in the brain which is possible as we do not fully understand how they operate. Perhaps it is hoped that consciousness will be an emergent property of a collective neural network.

William James came up with his idea of the solution to everything which he referred to as the *stream of consciousness*. This existed between mental substances and bundles of perceptions and ensured continuity of exeprience. However, this does not explain such things as sleep and comas. How can people endure such periods of unconsciousness?

Bold attempts have been made to understand biology as a physical phenomenon. None have succeeded though having said that, none should be discounted. We know too little and the subject is too vast.

Not a Separate Entity

Attempts to understand have involved physicists who face the task of explaining our inner thoughts in terms of the equations of physics, an awesome task which has understandably been avoided or skirted around. The idea of consciousness as a separate entity has been continually pushed out by science which determined that: *"man was not a subject suitable to mathematical study hardly more than a bundle of secondary qualities"* (E.A.Burtt). Newton supported the abandoning of causality and purpose in his Rules of Reasoning being concerned with how, not why.

However, can we separate the subjective from the objective as all these past theories have done? Quantum mechanics has shown that this is not feasible because the observer and the observation are intimately related and so cannot be separated. For example, unless observed, a particle has no precise location. Stephen Hawking (1988. P58.) cites some examples of other such particles which seem to be defying the laws they are supposed to adhere to. An experiment was carried out using a beam of light which was split to pass through two slits in a screen. However, when the beam was reduced to a single electron, it still passed through both slits! There is a huge joke here somewhere and I just wish we all knew how to share it.

Not to be found

In 19th century came the understanding that the brain was responsible for the appearance of consciousness. Neural study was fully expected to give all the answers to the questions of the location of consciousness within the brain, but it seems to have given us precious little to go on.

Sherrington (1942) had reasoned that the brain functioned as a whole: *"where it is a question of mind the nervous system does not integrate itself by centralising upon one superpontifical cell. Rather it elaborates a millionfold democracy whose each unit is a cell"*. This was his *enchanted loom* analogy for the brain which was very astute but did not satisfy him as an explanation of consciousness.

Physics and the Universe

Physics in the 20th century brought about the development of laws for the very large and very small and some hoped that consciousness would be lurking in some far-flung corner of the Universe. Is consciousness a gift? Part of some higher entity with our brains simply controlling the material body in which we reside? The big bang theory suggested that the precision required for the first few moments of the Universe would have had to have been precisely chosen for it to have been created. In fact, it is believed that directly preceding the creation, the laws of physics break down; something which is called a singularity occurs. Some are of the opinion that this could not have happened by chance. As Einstein said: *"God does not play dice"*.

Anthropic principle

The idea of our existence being a deliberate act is maintained by the reasoning of the anthropic principle. The chance of life forming is pretty slim and has been likened to the probability of two snooker balls colliding which are rolling across a snooker table the size of the Sahara. The anthropic principle states that the Universe is tailor-made for human observers (Rees 87), thus eliminating the chance factor: were we designed to be here? Consider the tree falling in a desert, if there is no-one there to see it does it make a sound? No it can't, because sound is only vibrations hitting our ear drums. Could we extend this notion to all perceptions? In which case our view of the Universe simply exists because we are there to see it. On the other hand, one could also say that if the Universe had not evolved against such enormous odds there would be no-one to stand around and say how amazing and unlikely it all is.

Modern theories have managed to close a few more of the gaps which allow for consciousness as a separate entity. A variation of the above suggests that the Universe evolved by chance or simply because it was the best option available at the time. Are we then to assume consciousness only exists if we believe there is some divine creative force driving everything?

It doesn't go away

Subjective experiences of the world, love, beauty, compassion etc. are generally termed consciousness; those things which we know exist and yet cannot explain even through neuroscience. However, even if science cannot explain it, unfortunately for many it would seem, it just will not go away. Consciousness is an acceptable and self-evident fact of life in humans as well as animals. And what about plants? It has been shown that they carry electrical pulses and can react to stimuli. The Mimosa and Venus Fly Trap are two excellent examples of this. We can explain away the physical reactions of our bodies but there is a quality we cannot define so easily. This is beautifully expressed in the following extract:

"For instance, a star which we perceive. The energy scheme deals with it, describes the passing of radiation thence into the eye, the little light image of it formed at the bottom of the retina, the trains of action potentials travelling along the nerve to the brain...as to the perceiving of it by the mind, the scheme puts its finger to its lips, and is silent". Sherrington (1942)

Consciousness as Neural Activity

The models of the brain we have looked at rely on external input or control to explain the functioning of the brain. Physiologists and psychologists say that this does not reflect the way the brain works or how the models are built, which is a valid comment and a view generally shared by the developers of the models themselves. However, they describe perception as being generated internally which prepares the organism to seek outside stimulus in the future. The brain actively grasps out into the environment for the consequences of an action. This is what distinguishes looking from seeing and listening from hearing and is an essential part of our experience of consciousness.

"It is the continual readjustment of self and the world in experience". (Dewey 86)

There is much research being carried out in an effort to understand consciousness globally by examining its emergence from a network of neurological interactions. Freeman (1989) has discussed the role of consciousness and his comments are for the most part representative of this approach.

"Consciousness arises from the interactions of immense numbers of nerve cells that individually act in a thousandth of a second, but that, taken as a whole, produce an evolving sequence of patterns much more slowly, as we well know from introspection. Within each pattern lies the seed of a bodily action that at once grows form a preceding pattern-and-action pair and prepares for the one to follow". (Freeman 1989)

Freemans deductions are from work he has carried out on the theory of chaos (see Chapter 16) which gives an interesting insight into the functioning of the brain. He suggests that the world is built on ordered patterns generated by chaos within the brain which manifests itself in the form of nerve cell activity. Chaos is a characteristic of the brain as a whole and can create information as well as destroy it. For example, a certain type of epilepsy in humans results in a temporary loss of memory. The victim completely loses awareness and contact with the outside world but will maintain posture and react to physical stimulus, for example, backing away from a hand in the face. This person is no longer goal-orientated, the flow of consciousness has been interrupted. Freeman goes on to say that consciousness depends on the proper functioning of the physiological reflexive system, not just on anatomical integrity. It will be maintained providing the *"neural connections remain in reasonably active condition"*. Alzheimer's disease, where the connections start to perish, particularly between the hippocampus and the entorhinal cortex, leads to a profound memory loss and deteriorisation of consciousness. The reflex neural machinery remains but again the goal-directed self-organising behaviour, characteristic of consciousness, is gone.

> *"Consciousness is an intrinsic and essential attribute of a functioning brain operating in a responsive body"*. (Freeman 1989)

As far as disembodied existence is concerned, such as out of body experiences and the like Freeman says that; *"neural mechanisms appear to be necessary for consciousness to exist. Since all neural mechanisms cease functioning entirely after death, consciousness probably ceases too"*.

He also says that: *"consciousness depends upon the body only as long as the person is in it and is liberated by death, a position supported by the near-dead. But such evidence can also be explained as faulty perceptions in a faulty nervous system"*.

So what about a report from the actually dead?

Brain Death and Consciousness

Brain death is defined as the condition when there is absolutely no activity from the brain. The neurons are not functioning at all. Now read the following passage taken from Colin Wilson, 1988.

> *"As the surgeon forced his mouth open and inserted an air tube down his throat, Jack Seale thought, 'Thank God, thank God....' Then he died. (It was later discovered that the snake had injected enough venom to kill fifty men) A few hours later he returned to consciousness to hear a harsh rasping sound and 'peep, peep, peep' noise: it gradually dawned on him that he was listening to his own breathing and heartbeat. When he tried to move he discovered he was completely paralysed. The monitors showed that his brain was dead; they failed to record the fact that consciousness had returned.*
>
> *For the next eight days Jack Seale remained completely paralysed, yet able to hear everything that went on. When two young nurses inserted a catheter he heard one of them remark that he had the smallest dick she'd ever seen: she was much embarassed when he reminded her of this later. A doctor shone a torch into his eye and expressed the opinion that he had been brain damaged. ....on the third day he heard the doctor say, 'That poor woman (his wife) is going to be stuck with a vegetable for the rest of her life. The best thing we can do is to pull the plug....' After further discussion they decided to leave him on the machine because the case was clinically interesting"*.

When he finally mangaged to move a finger to indicate he was alive, he said that his normal consciousness returned layer by layer.

As Wilson says:

> *"Medically speaking this only proves that consciousness can remain intact when the body is clinically dead. Yet for those who insist that life is inseparably connected with the body there remains the puzzle of how Jack remained conscious when monitors indicated brain death".*

If we dwell on our own consciousness, we know that there is far more to it than can be explained in logical terms of any description. Perhaps the point is that we do not know for sure how to define it.

We can look in wonder at a painting, read a moving poem or listen to one of the great composers. Could we build a machine to create all these things? Some people obviously believe it is possible, perhaps it is, who can tell?

> *"If the doors of perception were cleansed, everything would appear to man as it is, infinite".* (William Blake).

The Future

Initially this chapter was to contain details of systems which are being used commercially, how many neural networks have been developed and what they are being used for. There would be little point to such a list. If you require details like this Hecht-Nielsen (1989) gives lots of information. Basically there are about 14 commercially available neural network systems and an ever-increasing number for PC simulation.

The future of these systems seems assured because they fill a gap that cannot be closed using existing techniques - mainly all problems that deal with the processing and interpretation of perceptions.

The question concerns the thinking machine. Is the term neural networks a good description of what is being developed? Are these networks anything like the brain?

Sixth Generation Hybrid systems

The first four generations of computers can be defined by hardware, being the use of vacuum tubes, transistor, integrated circuitry and VLSI respectively. Fifth generation computer systems were defined as knowledge bases, designed originally to accept sensory input. These combined AI software and parallel hardware for logical inference and data retrieval, involving very traditional logic programming.

Arbib (1988) and many others, see the sixth generation as an integration of insights from cognitive science and neuroscience into computer design and programming; the development of perceptual robots carrying out problem solving using a neural network and not a serial machine. Schema theory will provide the specification language for computers configured as networks of interactive subsystems. They will learn in a constrained way and be made efficient. The future is not seen as the development of huge homogenous networks according to some one-learning rule, but a cooperative computation that integrates different subsystems, each quite specialised in structure. The brain has been described as a house with many rooms and this is the principle that will be applied with adaptive network methods being used to tune specific subsystems. We will still need to know how complex tasks are most effectively decomposed; it is a question of interfacing with a complex and dynamic environment.

Many also see the future as hybrid architectures which combine both the conventional and neural aspects of computing. There could be a sensory neural layer which processes speech and vision. This layer would have no learning taking place but would help the task of learning in a cognitive net. These could be connected to a digital processing and checking system for high-speed calculations.

Sensory Systems

There can be no doubt that pattern recognition or artificial perception is most certainly the best area of application for neural nets. For example, remote sensing, medical image analysis, industrial computer vision and input devices for computers.

Many such systems have already been developed; for example, for the segmentation and classification of regions from images, recognition of handwritten charaters and text, speech recognition and processing, restoration of noisy pictures to name a few. All these are dedicated to the solution of a particular problem. The future will need to see work put into the development of complete systems for image analysis, image understanding and speech understanding.

The ultimate goal is defined by v.d.Malsberg (1989) as the: *"construction of flexible robots, based on massively parallel structures and on self-organisation"* which includes the construction of a generalised scene. Some of the sub-issues of such a system have been dealt with but this architecture has to be further developed. Major issues are a reduction in learning times, integration of subsystems and the introduction of syntactical structure.

The development of such systems will need a sound base on which to build. This can be seen as taking place at this current time, but how good are our foundations?

How Valid are Models?

Modeling is an important process in development. Through trying to emulate conceptual issues in information processing carried out by the brain, new phenomena can be discovered. Things can be done that cannot be done with living tissues, actions can be made accessible. By expressing the chemical and electrical signals used in the brain in computational terms the abstract algebra can be explained.

The problem is that we are trying to model something about which very little is known. As such the models tend to be simplified to such an extent that some would say they are invalid. There are a number of differences between the brain and current models apart from the obvious one of connectivity and the sheer numbers of neurons.

The separation of dendrites from axon (input and output) is grossly oversimplified in models. Some cells have no axon but can in fact both receive and transmit. As well as chemical synapses there are electrical synapses, which communicate using graded electrical signals. The process of integrating the signals has been very simplified, it is possible that each part of the dendrite acts as a processing unit. If this is the case then a considerable amount of processing is possible. Not only are we oversimplifying the physical appearance of the brain, we are also, it seems, completely underestimating the processing power of the neurons themselves. There is also the problem of interpreting a model once it has been developed.

There are currently two classes of models which use computer simulation techniques. First there are those which present a very simplified view of the structure in order that the properties of the model can be seen and made technically avaialable. This may take the form of an array of neurons, possibly with connective symmetry which we know is a poor representation of the brain. The second class of simulations are those which attempt to be faithful representations of the brain, in which case they are by definition very complex and practically impossible to analyse.

General Issues

General issues have been raised concerning the validity of connectionist models. Arbib (1990) asks the questions of whether or not there is enough complexity in the models to enable solutions for the general case to be coded, whether the models can achieve a solution in a practical time and how a solution can be defined in terms of usefulness.

Rumelhart and McClelland (1986) tackle many of the questions posed with reference to their PDP models. We can also draw attention to other types of models in order to develop a discussion for neural network research in general.

The Models are Too Weak

There is the continuing comment concerning the comments of Minsky and Papert that perceptron type models were unable to solve any interesting computations. This criticism has persevered and in cases has been justified. The barrier of developing learning algorithms for a multi-layer perceptron has now been overcome and so the repertoire of examples tackled by such models is expanding. The so-called hard-learning problems have been overcome and research is now concentrating on further issues such as stability and generality.

Problem of Stimulus Equivalence

The problem of recognising a shape despite its orientation or size requires some method of normalisation of the input plus an attention mechanism which can focus on part of an image and then back to the whole.

Models tend to lack the attention mechanism and although it is said that in principle the stimulus equivalence problem can be solved, it has not been accomplished in practice.

However, competitive learning models such as the Neocognitron deal successfully with this very problem. See Chapter 20.

Recursion

If a model lacks recursive facilities it has been said that it will be unable to provide mechanisms for processing sentences and other recursively defined structures. Of course, recursive networks exist and learning algorithms have been developed for them. However, this criticism was levelled particularly at PDP models. Rumelhart and McClelland argue that they have not produced recursive processing mechanisms simply because they are not of the opinion that such capabilities are the essence of human computation. What is needed instead is a model which simultaneously considers large numbers of mutual and interrelated constraints. The challenge, they say, is to show those processes others have chosen to implement using recursive systems are better explained using natural PDP processes.

Models are not cognitive

The general basis of neural network models is that behaviour is not necessarily rule-driven. Features can emerge from models rather than forcing higher-order structures.

This view has been described as being in opposition to cognition. Equally one could say that it is the very essence of cognition, the application of a rule being no more cognitive than the activity of a unit.

Rumelhart and McClelland say that cognitive science is the strive towards explaining mental phenomena through an understanding of the mechanisms which underlie those phenomena.

The Oxford Dictionary definition for cognition is:

> *"knowing, perceiving, or conceiving as an act of faculty distinct from emotion and volition"*

Can we dismiss people's ideas or concepts as being wrong or ill informed simply because they do not agree with our own? If someone could stand up and prove that the brain carries out symbol processing for one function, uses strictly logical rule-driven computations for another and a connectionist approach for something else then all would be clear. At the moment it is a matter of bite it and see.

The models are at the wrong level of analysis

From a psychological point of view there are three levels of analysis:

❑ **Computational theory:**   The goal of the computation, why it is appropriate and the logic of the strategy used to carry it out

❑ **Representation and algorithm:**   Implementation of computational theory. Representation of input and output, transformation algorithm

❑ **Hardware implementation:**   Physical realisation of the representation and algorithm

The view of phsychologists is that the models are implemented at the final level - the implementation level, and as such are irrelevant because the assumptions made about distributed memory are only meaningful at the first or computational level.

The response is that neural network models should be considered as competing with other models as a means of explaining psychological data.

Reductionist and Emergent properties

The criticism here is that models tend to be reductionist in that psychology is reduced to neurophysiology and eventually physics. By reducing a system to units and connections the very basis of cognition is being avoided.

The response is that by studying the interactions of connected units an understanding of cognition may emerge.

Not enough is known

A valid criticism of any model is that not enough is actually known about the functioning of the brain to develop models which claim to represent those functions. On the whole it has been stressed in most research papers that the model under discussion is neurally inspired and not neurally loyal. There are claims, as there probably always will be when a result is particularly exciting or new, that a particular development will lead to a breakthrough in our understanding of the cognitive functioning of the brain.

Most models tend to take the most obvious features that can be discovered about the brain and use these in a model in some attempt to start somewhere. The basic considerations are that neurons are slow, they are connected to many other neurons and they all operate in parallel. There is some method by which those neurons can assess their own input and decide whether or not to then produce an output. Information is continuously available and there is no central control.

The associated criticism that models lack neural realism is in part true. In another way, it is not true. It is difficult to preserve the integrity of a structure about which so little is known.

Nativism vs. Empiricism

The nativism view is that all the connections within the brain are genetically determined at birth and develop through maturity. It has been suggested that this infers that such a system would be then capable of performing any function which a brain could do. Neural network models seem to agree with this.

The empiricist view, on the other hand, suggests that no predefinition of the connections exist and that they are determined by experience. Neural network models seem to conform with this view as well.

Some middle path between the two extreme views seems to suit all requirements because some characteristics must be genetically inherited and we must be able to also learn from experience in order to survive.

Are rats as clever as us?

Apart from the obvious fact that we have more cortex than a rat, given that the architecture and methodology behind the functioning of the brains is the same, this is a valid question.

One could put it down to our environment and our having evolved within it, or perhaps the human brain has a greater capacity for establishing the kind of neural connections that enable intelligent thought. Rats and other animals are not incapable of intelligent thought: my cat will simply place its food bowl in front of me when it is hungry.

> *"At least for the time being we will not be able to emulate the 'technology' of the nervous system in any literal sense".* (v.d.Malsberg 1989)

So what is needed in order that these models can be of more use?

What is needed?

Understanding is a point which features highly on our list of needs. In terms of perceptions, this involves more knowledge about how the brain deals with the intrinsic properties of the input of natural pattern primitives, for example, lines, edges, curvature, visual information describing surface curvature and cusps, phonological invariants in speech etc.

The number of papers published on pattern recognition currently stands at about 30,000. So it would seem that research must have covered everything that requires a straightforward solution and yet the performance of the networks still leaves a lot to be desired. However, the scale of the problem being tackled has to be remembered.

Pattern recognition and perception, as we have seen, discuss concepts in terms of representations. However, Freeman and Skarda (1987), through their study of brain patterns, have a different view of the role of patterns and representations in the brain.

Are Representations Helpful?

> *"Biologists have shown no lack of hubris in pontificating about the properties of the brain supporting mental functions"*. (Freeman & Skarda 1987)

As we have seen, there is a humble lack of understanding expressed in this field. Constantly throughout the text we have been reminded how little we know about the brain. Yet biologist books belie this. With the advent of digital systems, manipulation of symbols became the predominant trend. Now the role of the brain is to incorporate features of the outside world and make internal syntactical representations of these data, which together constitute a world model that serves to control motor output.

Freeman proposes that physiologists use these terms because of this lack of understanding. Representation and associated terms are used to hide this fact. He says that the term *representation* is unnecessary and seriously impedes any progress towards real understanding.

Much work has been carried out by Freeman (see Chaos Chapter 16) on the brain activity of rabbits when presented with different smells. This cannot be equated with internal representations because simply presenting the rabbit with a smell does not form a pattern. It is only when the smell is reinforced and leads to a change in behaviour that you get patterns of neural activity. Smell-specific activity patterns are dependent on bahavioural response. When the reinforcement is changed the pattern changes. Perhaps the activity being studied does not refer to the smell at all but to the behaviour in some way. Patterned neural activity is also context dependent. A new smell will lead to changes in all previously learned patterns. If patterns of activity are seen as internal representations, this has got to be a misinterpretation of the data.

"patterned neural activity correlates best with reliable forms of interaction in a context that is behaviourally and environmentally co-defined....(as) a dialectic....(there is) nothing intrinsically representative about this dynamic process until the observer intrudes....It is the experimenter who infers what the observed activity patterns represent to or in a subject, in order to explain the results to himself". (Werner 87, Dreyfus and Dreyfus 1986).

It is all down to interpretation which depends on the interpreter.

Representation has the commonly accepted meaning of a rule-driven symbol manipulation. Dreyfus & Dreyfus regard intelligence as being dynamic. Before 1940 representation meant the undefinable relationship between brain activity (mental content) and the outside world (imagination is close enough).

Neural patterns were not viewed as representations, other questions needed to be asked. Mathematical, statistical and electronic models have been developed to explain the neural dynamics of pattern generation which have caused changes to many views on brain operations. They are seen more as physiochemical systems that largely organise themselves, rather than reacting to and being determined by external input. Each brain has a history, formed from within not imposed from the outside, as is supposed under sensory stimulation. An essential condition for patterns to appear is the existence of what appears to be noise but which is chaos. New forms of order within the brain need old ones to collapse into a chaotic state before they can appear.

Two main assumptions have been challenged here. Firstly, the theory that the complete information is introduced and is then degenerated by noise. This has been likened to the disorganisation of the universe, chaos. However, chaotic systems like the brain operate far from equilibrium and create information internally. Secondly, signals embedded in noise is not appropriate. The same neural system that generates the signals also generates the background chaos, or noise. When a switch is made from chaos to burst activity, the signal stops and another signal starts. Up to that point there is chaos and no annealing takes place because the selection has already happened.

Many reports of neural networks take the term representation for granted. They are also discussing machines and not brains. Back–propagation does not exist in biology and even though this claim has never been made, it rather defeats the principles of the process in the first place. We are back to Turing's definition really. Although people talk about neural networks, they are really talking about machine intelligence. You can get it to read and sound like a child, but it has no understanding of what it is saying.

Theories of best match and error detection are machine cognition, not neural cognition. Freeman states that physiologists do not need representations, and that those wishing to find algorithms for the brain should also avoid the term. This definition is desperately needed by functionalist philosophers, computer scientists and cognitive psychologists but it is unnecessary for brain dynamics, being totally misleading and impeding progress. He says that these brain function definitions avoid the problems of *"what neurons do and seduce us into concentrating on relatively easy problems of determining what our computers can or might do"*.

A neural structure uses information to create its own internal states which then acquire meaning. The internal states are the neuronal system's own symbols. Once symbols can be viewed as the system's own creations any reference to representations becomes superfluous. This idea of getting rid of symbolic representation has been described as something which will:

> *"...unburden us of the Trojan horse that was smuggled from the land of Artificial Intelligence into Neuroscience. Perhaps the protestations that representations exist only in the minds of the observer who jointly beholds an environment will at last be heard"*. (Maturana & Varela 1980)

Perhaps we do need representations and symbols in order to discuss what we have found. The unfortunate point of this work seems to point towards a pattern as having no meaning. If this is the case, neural network models will need to think again.

Further Research Views

The brain is a biological device which has not evolved overnight. *"In biological sensory systems, a very thorough and multilevel optimization of the information processing functions and resources has been achieved during evolution"*. (Kohonen 1989). We have a number of years catching up to do.

Kohonen goes on to say that the analytical definition of mappings of input data seems hopeless. The only possibility is to provide models with *"adaptive properties which optimise their network structure as well as their tuning"*. There is also the problem of invariance with respect to various transformations and how to take general context into consideration.

An alternative view is given by Feldman (1989) who says that: *"positive results will be based on existing knowledge of computational structures, not on mystical emergent properties of unstructured networks"*.

Feldman points out that a critical issue is the role of learning. A notion that a general learning scheme will get rid of the need for neuroscience, psychophysics, perceptual psychology and computer vision research disappears as soon as the vision problem is taken seriously. There is no reason to believe that other perceptions such as language etc. are any simpler or less structured. The systems will need to be programmed, the behaviour understood and adaptions controlled. These are major continuing concerns expressed very clearly in a reference by Zuse (1989) to the *Devil's Wire*.

The Devil's Wire

Zuse says that developers of computer systems could be thought of as representatives of our cultural society. Typical scientists and researchers. Such people have the mentality of Faust in that they regard themselves as idealists, striving for the fulfilment of good and providing growth for mankind. But their souls are in the hands of the devil. Is the computer a work of Mephistopheles?

Feedback is seen a critical step and has perhaps deliberately been avoided in early computers. This Devil's Wire means that we cannot keep the development under control, *"the devil is in the nuts and bolts"*. We can already see this in problems with things like data protection. How would we fare if a thinking machine had the power to launch nuclear missiles? It is not inconceivable. The potentially frightening thing is that we have no choice, the onward search will have to continue because *"humanity and society cannot exist without Faust's technology or without the computer. Future problems of the West cannot be solved without the computer"*.

Summary

There is not a research facility in the world which is not working on neural networks. It is the fastest area of research in computing at the moment (Aleksander 1990a). We have seen examples throughout this text of the potential applications which could possibly touch every aspect of our lives. The opinion of the popular press could be summarised in the following extract:

> *"The Neural micro of the near future....(has) no need for a keyboard because you communicate with each other using normal spoken language. Nobody programmed your micro, it learned to live with you. It can even predict your wants and needs. As a friend and teacher, your micro is interconnected with every aspect of both your personal life and environment. Science fiction? Not any more"*. (Haines, Commodore User,1990)

This is a wonderful thought but in reality, how accurate is it? It is easy to overestimate the developments that have taken place because there have been some remarkable achievements and no doubt further very valid and useful applications will be developed. But let's not get too enthusiastic because we are well aware of the limitations of these systems. To compare them to people (a friend and teacher) and imply that they have human level intelligence is simply not true and is totally misleading.

> *"(the) approach has not yet provided significant results in solving real world problems, compared with the established methodology...(there is a) difficulty for it to come apart from the tools already developed in the algorithmic approach to pattern recognition"*. (Beroule 1989)

"A house fly has a million neurons, far more than have ever been simulated on a computer. A cockroach, with its intricate sensory and motor apparatus and flexible goal seeking behaviour, is as superior to one of our artificial neural networks as humans are to cockroaches. There isn't a scientist alive who understands how a cockroach works. Insects are just too complex....Please explain to readers that these (developments such as the famous NETTALK, or the road follower ALVINN) are just simple pattern recognition devices; they are no closer to artificial brains than is an IBM PC". (Touretzky 1990)

Touretzky goes on to say:

"What I am trying to say is this: neural networks are an emotionally-charged topic, besause they combine the mysteries of the brain with the thrill of a new technology and a host of ancient philosophical questions about the nature of the mind. It's hard to maintain one's balance in such a heady environment. But one thing the field doesn't need right now is another 'gee-whiz' popularisation...don't just uncritically pass on all the 'dawn of a new age' drivel that's been showing up in the popular press".

Strong words perhaps but absolutely accurate, expressing the view held by researchers who know what is actually happening. Feldman (1989) states that this current explosion of neural networks is based on scientific and economic expectations, some of which are unreasonable. These systems will not replace conventional systems, get rid of programming or unravel the mysteries of the mind. Research will eventually lead to a better understanding of the brain but only through interaction with other approaches. Formalisms must provide a basis for theoretical systems neuroscience and enable experimental predictions to be carried out. A scientific language is needed which will also describe the higher levels of cognition. A direct mapping to neural structures is here deferred, perhaps indefinitely.

So what future do these systems have? Feldman (1989) sees their use in computationally intensive areas that have not yet been tackled. Areas which involve human-like capabilities such as perception, language or inference, traditionally seen as the realm of AI. If these processes depend on intelligent activity we will be back to studying scientific issues. However, if it is found that symbolic formalisms exist at a higher level then it is unlikcly that neuro-computers will be needed.

As far as hardware is concerned, the connectivity of the brain cannot currently be achieved in silicon although a compromise may be made by trading speed of processing for number of elements. Within a decade or two it is likely that we will see an increase in the use of neural networks and the implementation of fully parallelised neural computers. This may be using optical computing or on membranous or molecular structures.

We are still very far from this goal and as long as developments are still in an evolutionary state, is it a good idea to fuse systems to hardware anyway? In the coming years, research should concentrate on using simulations and flexible control in order to learn more about the brain.

None of the systems come close to supporting the range of computation that is already known to be needed and we are only at the beginning of knowing what we need. Neural network studies can without doubt lead to important practical and scientific advances, but will require basic research in several areas and a thorough integration with many disciplines.

It is a cynical though unfortunately valid opinion that research is stimulated by funding from military sources. Morally this is a sad but true fact of life. We only have to think of the mad rush of technological developments which take place when countries are at war with each other. It would be so convenient to be able to send robotic troops in which could recognise and destroy the enemy and selected targets. With the advent of environmental awareness, it is more commercially viable for financiers to put their money into *green* developments and systems which appeal to the consumer. Something which may lead to a lack of resources for future neural network research.

We will undoubtedly see the development of speech driven systems, image recognition devices and the like. However, without research going ahead at full speed, it is difficult to envisage the development of any machine with human-level intelligence in the near (in terms of tens of decades) future.

A machine with machine-level intelligence aims to achieve a different set of objectives and to some extent these have already been met in a number of examples that we have seen. There has been, and still is, confusion between machine and human intelligence. The process of discovering what a computer can do has unfortunately been wrongly interpreted as what a brain can do. There is little comparison and provided we remember this we can clearly and correcty assess developments in this field.

References

Abu-Mostafa, & Psaltis, D. 1987. Optical Neural Computers. *Scientific American*, March 87, vol. 255, no. 3.

Ackley, D. H. 1987. *Stochastic Iterated genetic hill-climbing.* PhD thesis, Carnegie-Mellon University, Pittsburgh PA.

Albus, J. S. 1971. *Math. Biosci*, 10, 25-61.

Aleksander, I. 1990. *An introduction to neural computing.* North Oxford Academic Press (UK), MIT Press (USA).

Almeida, L., 1987. A Learning Rule for Asynchronous Perceptrons with Feedback in a Combinatorial Environment, *Proc. IEEE International Conf. on Neural Networks*, San Diego, June 1987.

Almeida, L. B. 1989. Backpropagation in perceptrons with feedback. *Neural Computers: Proc NATO Adv. Research Workshop* 1987 (R. Eckmiller & C. v. d. Malsburg eds.) Springer-Verlag.

Alspector, J. & R. B. Allen. 1987. A Neuromorphic VLSI Learning System. *Advanced Research in VLSI: Procs. 1987 Stanford Conf.* (Loseleben, P. ed.), MIT Press, Cambridge, Mass.

Alspector, J. & R. B. Allen. 1988. A VLSI model of neural nets, *Bellcore technical memorandum TM ARH002688.*

Amari, S. 1988. Dynamic Stability of Formation of cortical maps. *Dynamic Interactions in Neural Networks: Models and Data,* (M. A. Arbib & S. Amari eds.), Springer Verlag.

Anderson, D. Z. 1986. Coherent optical eigenstate memory. *Opt. Lett.*, 10: 98.

Anderson, D. Z. & M. C. Erie. 1987. Resonator memories and optical novelty filters. *Opt. Eng.*, 26: 434.

Anderson, D. Z. 1988. Material demand for optical neural networks. *MRS bulletin*, Aug. 88.

Anderson, J. A. (1973). A Theory for the recognition of items from short memorised lists. *Psychological Review*, 80, 417-438.

Anderson, J. A., J. W. Silverstein, S. A. Ritz & R. S. Jones. 1977. Distinctive features, categorical perception, and probability learning: some applications of a neural model. *Psychological Review*. 84: 413-451.

Anderson, J. A. & M. C. Mozer. 1981. Categorization and selective neurons. In *Parallel Models of Associative Memory*. (G. E. Hinton & J. A. Anderson eds.) Hillsdale, N. J: Erbaum Associates.

Anderson, J. A. , 1983. Cognitive and psychological computation with neural models. *IEEE Transactions systems, Man and Cybernetics* SMC-13: 799-815.

Anderson, J. A. , Silverstein, J. W. and Ritz, S. A. Distinctive Features, categorical perception and probability learning: Some applications of a Neural Model, *Psychological Review*, 84: 413-451.

Anderson. J. A. , M. T. Getel, P. A. Pen, D. R. Collins, 1990, Radar Signal Categorisation using a Neural Network, *IEEE Procs. Special Neural Network Issue*, Sept. 1990.

Arbib, M. A., 1964, *Brains, Machines and Mathematics*. New York: McGraw-Hill.

Arbib, M. A., 1985, *In Search of the Person: Philosophical Explorations in Cognitive Science*, Univ. of Mass. Press.

Arbib, M. A., 1987. *Brains, Machines and Mathematics, 2nd edition*. Springer-Verlag.

Arbib, M. A & S. Amari, 1988. *Dynamic Interactions in Neural Networks: Models and Data*. Springer Verlag.

Arbib, M. A. 1989 *The Metaphorical Brain 2: Neural Networks and Beyond*, Wiley.

Arbib, M. A., E. J. Conklin, & J. C. Hill. 1987. *From schema theory to language*. Oxford Univ. Press.

Arbib, M. A. Interacting Subsystems for Depth behaviour and Detour Behaviour. *Dynamic Interactions in Neural Networks: Models and Data*. (M. A. Arbib & S. Amari eds.) Springer Verlag.

Baer, J., 1988. Making machines that think, *The Futurist*, Feb. 88.

Barhen, J., W. B. Dress, C. C. Jorgensen. 1989. Applications of concurrent neuromorphic algorithms for autonomous robots. *Neural Computers: Proc NATO Adv. Research Workshop 1987* (R. Eckmiller & C. v. d. Malsburg eds.) Springer-Verlag.

Barto, A. G. & P. Anandan. 1985. Pattern recognising stochastic learning automata. *IEEE trans. on Systems, man and cybernetics*. 15: 360-375.

Bekey, G. A. 1989. Robotics research at USC, *Computer*, March 89.

Beroule, D. 1989. The never-ending learning. In *Neural Computers: Proc NATO Adv. Research Workshop 1987* (R. Eckmiller & C. v. d. Malsburg eds.) Springer-Verlag.

Bienenstock E. L., L. N. Cooper & P. W. Munro. 1982. Theory for the development of neuron selectivity: orientation specificity and binocular interaction in visual cortex. *J. Neuroscience* 2: 32-48.

Bienenstock, E. 1989. Relational models in natural and artificial vision. In *Neural Computers: Proc NATO Adv. Research Workshop 1987* (R. Eckmiller & C. v. d. Malsburg eds.) Springer-Verlag.

Bilbro, G. L. M. White & W. Snyder. 1989. Image Segmentation with Neurocomputers. In *Neural Computers: Proc NATO Adv. Research Workshop 1987* (R. Eckmiller & C. v. d. Malsburg eds.) Springer-Verlag.

Bliss, T. V. P. & T. Lomo, 1973, *T. Physiol*, 233: 331-356.

Bounds, D. G., P. L. Lloyd, (1988). A multi-layered perceptron network for the diagnosis of low back pain. *Proc. IEEE 2nd Int. Conf. on Neural Networks*, San Diego, July 1988, Vol. II, p 481.

Brady, R. M. 1985. Optimisation strategies gleaned from biological evolution. *Nature*. 317: 804-806.

Brierly & Kidd, 1986. Transputing across the buses. *Microsystems Design*, Oct. 1986.

Brug, A. et al., 1986. The taming of R1, *IEEE Expert*, Vol. 1, No. 3.

Bullock, T. H. 1985. Re-examination of some common properties in the brain analysis of communicative signals: Representations and evolution. In *Common Principles of Electric and Acoustic Communication*. (H. Zakon, W. Wilczynski, G. Pollak, eds.)

Carling, A. 1988. *Parallel processing: The Transputer and Occam*. Sigma Press.

Carpenter, G. A. 1989. Neural network models for pattern recognition and associative memory. *Neural Networks*, Vol. 2: 243-257.

Carpenter, G. A. & S. Grossberg, 1989, ART 3 Hierarchical Search, May 1989, *Neural Networks*.

Chomsky, N. 1968. Recent contributions to the theory of innate ideas. In *Boston studies in the philosophy of science*. Vol. 3: 81-107.

Collett, T & S. Udin. 1983. The role of the toad's nucleus isthmi in prey-catching behaviour. In *Procs. 2nd workshop on visumotor coordination in frog and toad: Models and Experiments*. (R. Lara & M. A. Arbib eds.) COINS-Tech. report 83-19, Univ. of Mass. Amherst, MA.

Cotterill, R. 1986. The brain: An intriguing piece of condensed matter. *Physica scripta*, T 13: 161-168.

Cottrell, G. W., 1984, A model of lexical access of ambiguous words. *Procs. 4th Int. Conf. AI. : 61-67. Austin*, Texas. Los Altos: Morgan Kaufmann.

Dascal, M., 1989. On the Roles of Context and Literal Meaning in Understanding, *Cognitive Science*, 13: 253-257.

Davis, L. (ed.) 1987. *Genetic algorithms and simulated annealing*. Pitman. London.

Dejerine, J, 1892. Contribution a l'etude anatomo-pathologique et clinique des differentes varietes de cecite verbale, *Memoires Societe Biologique, 4*.

Didday, R. L., 1970. A Model of Visuomotor Mechanisms in the Frog Optic Tectum., *Math. Biosci*. 30: 169-180.

Divko, R. & K. Schulten. 1986. Stochastic spin models for pattern recognition. In *Neural networks for computing, AIP conf. procs.* , 151: 129-134 (J. S. Denker ed.) New York: American Inst. of Physics.

Dreyfus, H. L. & S. E. Dreyfus. 1986. *Mind over machine. The power of human intuition and expertise in the era of the computer*. New York, Free Press.

Elman, J. L., D. Zipser, 1988. Learning the Hidden Structure of Speech, *J. Acoust. Soc. Am.* 83 (4), April 88.

Erman, L. , & V. R. Lesser, 1980. The HEARSAY II system: A tutorial. *Trends in Speech recognition.* (W. A. Lea, ed.) : 361-381. Prentice-Hall.

Farley B. G & K. A. Clark, 1954. Simulation of Self-Organising Systems by Digital Computers. *IEE Trans. Inf. Theor.* 4: 76.

Feldman, J. A. 1982. Dynamic connections in neural networks. *Biological Cybernetics,* 46, 27-39.

Feldman, J. 1989. Structured Neural Networks in nature and in computer science. *Neural Computers: Proc NATO Adv. Research Workshop 1987* (R. Eckmiller & C. v. d. Malsburg eds.) Springer-Verlag.

Feldman, A. G. & D. H. Ballard. 1982. Connectionist Models and their Properties. *Cognitive Science* 6: 205-254.

Fenwick, P. & D. Lorimer. 1989. Can brains be conscious? *New Scientist.* 5 Aug. 89.

Freeman, W. & C. Skarda. 1987. Representations: Who needs them? *3rd conf. on neurobiology of learning and memory.* Oct 87.

Freeman, W. J. 1989. On the fallacy of assigning an origin to consciousness. *Int. Conf. on advanced methods in neuroscience.* Havana, Cuba: 25-27.

Freeman, W. 1989. Perceptual coding in Olfaction and Vision. In *Scientific American.*

Freeman, W. J. 1989. Perceptual coding in olfaction and vision. *Scientific American.*

Fukishima, K. 1989. A hierarchical neural network model for selective attention. In *Neural Computers: Proc NATO Adv. Research Workshop 1987* (R. Eckmiller and C. v. d. Malsburg eds.) Springer Verlag

Fukishima, K. 1975, Cognitron: A self-organising multilayered neural network. *Biological Cybernetics,* 20: 121-136

Fukishima, K. 1980, Neocognitron: A self-organising neural network model for a mechanism of pattern recognition unaffected by shifts in position. *Biol. cybernetics,* 36[4]: 193-202

Fukishima, K., 1988, A Neural Network for Visual Pattern Recognition, *Computer,* March 88.

Fukishima, K. & Miyake, S. 1982. Neocognitron: A new algorithm for pattern recognition tolerant of deformations and shifts in position. In *Pattern Recognition,* 15: 455-469.

Gabor, D. 1969. *IBM Journal Res. Dev.* 13: 156.

Gardener, E., N. Stroud, & D. J. Wallace. 1989. Training with noise: Application to word and text storage. In *Neural Computers: Proc NATO Adv. Research Workshop 1987,* (R. Eckmiller & C. v. d. Malsburg eds.) Springer-Verlag.

Gazzaniga, M. S. 1984. Advances in Cognitive neurosciences: The problem of information storage in the human brain. *Neurobiology of Learning and Memory,* (G. S. Lynch, J. L. McGaugh, N. M. Weinberger eds.), New York: Guildford Press.

Geman, S., & D. Geman. 1984. Stochastic relaxation, Gibbs distributions, and the Baysian restoration of images, *IEEE Trans. Pattern Analysis and Machine Intelligence.,* 3: 79-92.

Getting, P. A. *J. Neurophysiol.* 49: 1017.

Gilmore. J. F. 1987. Survey of diagnostic expert systems. *Proc. IEEE Conf. Applications of AI V*, IEEE Computer Society, Calif.

Goldman, P. S., Rakic, *Annu. Rev. Neurosci.* 11: 137.

Grossberg, S. 1976. Adaptive Pattern Classification and universal recoding I: Parallel development and coding of natural feature detectors. *Biological Cybernetics*, 23: 121-134.

Grossberg, S. 1976a. Adaptive Pattern Classification and universal recoding II: Feedback, expectation, olfaction, and illusions. *Biological Cybernetics*, 23: 187-202.

Grossberg, S. 1990. ART3: Hierarchical search using chemical transmitters in self-organising pattern recognition architecturs. *Neural Networks*. In press.

Grossberg, S. 1982. *Studies of Mind and Brain: Neural principles of learning, perception, development, cognition, and motor control.* Boston. Reidel/Kluwer.

Hampson, S. E. & D. J. Volper. 1988. *Dynamic Interactions in Neural Networks: Models and Data.* (M. A. Arbib & S. Amari. eds.), Springer Verlag.

Head. H. , & G. Holmes. 1911. Sensory disturbances from cerebral lesions. *Brain.*, 34: 102-254

Hebb, D. O. 1949. *The Organisation of Behavior.* New York, Wiley.

Hecht-Nielsen 1989. Neurocomputer applications. *Neural Computers: Proc NATO Adv. Research Workshop 1987* (R. Eckmiller & C. v. d. Malsburg eds.), Springer-Verlag

Hillis, W. D. 1987. The connection machine. *Trends in computing.* June 87.

Hinton, G. E. 1981. Learning translation invariant recognition in massively parallel hardware. *Parallel models of Associative memory,* (Hinton, G. E. & Anderson J. A. eds.), Erlbaum, Hillsdale, NJ.

Hinton, G. E., 1987. Connectionist Learning Procedures, Artificial Intelligence.

Hinton, G. E. , D. H. Ackley, & T. J. Sejnowski. 1985. A Learning Algorithm for Boltzmann Machines. *Cognitive Science*, 9: 147-169

Hinton, G. E. , & T. J. Sejnowski. 1986. Learning and Relearning in Boltzmann Machines. In Rumelhart, D. E. , McClelland, J. L. , and the PDP Research Group, (eds.) *Parallel Distributed Processing: Equations in the Microstructure of Cognition. Volume I Foundations,* MIT Press, Cambridge, MA.

Holland, J. H. 1975. *Adaptation in neural and artificial systems.* Univ. of Michigan Press.

Hopfield, J. J., 1982. Neural networks and physical systems with emergent collective computational abilities, *Procs. National Academy of Sciences USA*, 79: 2554-2558.

Hopfield, J. J., 1984. *Proc. Nat. Acad. Sci. , USA*, 81: 3088-3092.

Hopfield, J. J., 1986. Physics, Biological Computation and Complementarity. In *The lesson of quantum theory.* (J. de Boer, E. Dal, O. Ulfbeck eds.) Elsevier Science Publishers, B. V.

Hopfield, J. J. & D. W. Tank, 1985. *Biol Cyber.* , 52: 141-152.

Hopfield, J. J. & D. W. Tank, 1986. Computing with neural circuits: A model. *Science*, 233: 625-633.

Hopfield, J. J. & D. W. Tank. 1987. Collective computation in neuron-like circuits, *Trends in Computing*, Dec. 87: 54.

Hubel, D. H. &T. N. Wiesel. 1962. Receptive fields, binocular and functional architecture in the cat's visual cortex. *J. Physiol.* 160: 106-154.

Jarosh, J. 1989. Get smart!, *Automotive Industries*, Feb. 89.

Johnson, R. C. 1988. *Cognizers: Neural networks and machines that think.* Wiley.

Johnson, R. C. , 1990. Artificial Intelligence. *Omni,* Feb. : 28.

Jordan, M. , 1989. Serial Order: A Parallel Distributed Approach., *Advances. in Connectionist Theory: Speech. Hillsdale,* (J. L. Elman & D. E. Rumelhart Eds.), NJ. : Erlbaum.

Julesz, B. 1960. Binocular depth perception of computer-generated patterns. *Bell Syst. Tech. J,* 39: 1125.

Kawamoto, A. H., 1988. Distributed Representations of Ambiguous Words and Their Resolution in a Connectionist Network, in *Lexical Ambiguity Resolution: Perspectives from Psycholinguistics, Neurophysiology, and Artifical Intelligence.* (S. Small, G. Cottrell & M. Tanenhaus, Eds.), Morgan Kaufmann Inc. , San Mateo, CA.

Kersten, D. A. J. O'Toole, M. E. Sereno, D. C. Knill, J. A. Anderson,1987. Associative learning of scene parameters from images. *Applied Optics*, vol. 26: 4999, Dec. 87.

Kienker P. K., T. J. Sejnowski, G. E. Hinton & L. E. Schumacher, 1986. Separating figure from ground with a parallel network, *Perception* 15: 197-216.

Kohonen, T., 1977, *Associative memory: A system theoretical approach* (Springer-Verlag, Berlin).

Kohonen, T. 1982. Clustering, taxonomy, and topological maps of patterns. *Procs. of the 6th Int. Conf. on Pattern Recognition,* IEEE Computer Society Press, (Lang, M., ed.), Silver Spring, MD.

Kohonen, T. 1988. *Neural Networks* 1, 3.

Kohonen, T. 1984. *Self-organisation and associative memory,* New York, Springer-Verlag.

Kohonen, T. 1989. The Role of Adaptive and Associative Circuits in Future Computer Designs. In *Neural Computers: Proc NATO Adv. Research Workshop 1987* (R. Eckmiller & C. v. d. Malsburg eds.) Springer-Verlag.

Kohonen, T. 1977. *Associative memory.* Berlin: Springer.

Kohonen, T 1980. *Content addressable memories.* New York: Springer.

Korn, A. F. 1989. Towards a primal sketch of real world scenes in early vision. In *Neural Computers: Proc NATO Adv. Research Workshop 1987* (R. Eckmiller & C. v. d. Malsburg eds.) Springer-Verlag.

Lang, K. J. & M. J. Witbrock, 1988, Learning to Tell the Two Spirals Apart. *Procs. of the 1988 Connectionist Models Summer School,* (D. S. Touretzky, G. E. Hinton & J. Sejnowski, eds.) San Mateo, CA: Morgan Kaufmann Publishers, 1988.

Lashley, K. S. 1951. The problem of serial order in behaviour. *Cerebral mechanisms in behaviour: The Hixon symposium* (L. Jeffress ed.) : 112-136, Wiley.

Lettvin, J. T. H., Maturana, W. S. McCulloch, Pitts, W. H. 1959. What the frog's eye tells the frog's brain. *Proc. IRE* 47: 1940-1951.

Lorenz. K. Z. 1981. *The Foundations of Ethology.* New York: Springer-Verlag.

Longstaff, I. D & Cross, J. F. 1986. *Royal Signals and Radar Establishment (Malvern) memo,* 3936.

Lynch, G. J. L. McGaugh & N. M. Weinberger, 1984. (eds.) *Neurobiology of learning & memory.* Guildford.

Mackie, S. , H. P. Graf & D. B. Schwartz. 1989. Implementation of neural network models in silicon. In *Neural Computers: Proc NATO Adv. Research Workshop 1987* (R. Eckmiller and C. v. d. Malsburg eds.) Springer-Verlag.

Malsburg, C. v. d 1989. Goal and Architecture of Neural Computers. In *Neural Computers: Proc NATO Adv. Research Workshop 1987* (R. Eckmiller & C. v. d. Malsburg eds.) Springer-Verlag.

Marr D & G. Poggio. 1976. Cooperative computation of stereo disparity. *Science* 194: 283-287.

Marr, D. 1969, *J. Physiol.* 202: 437-470.

Marr, D. & T. Poggio. 1976. Cooperative computation of stereo disparity. *Science* 194: 283.

Marr, D. & T. Poggio. 1979. A computational theory of human stereo vision. *Proc. R. Soc. London Ser. B* 204: 301.

May, D., & R. Shepherd. 1989. The Transputer. In *Neural Computers: Proc NATO Adv. Research Workshop 1987* (R. Eckmiller & C. v. d. Malsburg eds.) Springer-Verlag.

McAuliffe, K., 1990, Get Smart: Controlling Chaos. *OMNI*, Feb. 1990: 43.

McCarthy, J. 1989. Approaches to artificial intelligence. *Computing Futures*, Inaugural Issue.

McCulloch, W. S. & Pitts, W. 1943. *Bull Math. Biophysics* 5: 115-133.

McClelland J. L., D. E. Rumelhart & the PDP Research Group. 1986. *Parallel Distributed Processing*, Vol. 1. MIT Press.

McClelland, J. L & A. H. Kawamoto, 1986, *Mechanisms of Sentence Processing: Assigning Roles to Constituents of Sentences.* in R&M.

McClelland, J. L & A. H. Kawamoto, 1986, Mechanisms of Sentence Processing: Assigning Rules to Constituents, *Parallel Distributed Processing,* (McClelland, Rumelhart, and the PDP Research Group, Eds.), vol. 2, MIT Press, Cambridge.

McClelland, J. L & D. E. Rumelhart, 1981, An interactive activation model of context effects in letter perception: Part 1. An account of basic findings. *Psychological Review* 88: 375-407.

McClelland, J. L., & J. L. Elman, 1986, Interactive processing in speech perception: The TRACE model. *Parallel Distributed Processing,* (McClelland, Rumelhart and the PDP Research Group, Eds.), vol. 2, MIT Press, Cambridge.

McClelland, J. L., & J. L. Elman, 1986. The TRACE model of speech perception, *Cognitive Psychology*, 18, 1986.

McCulloch, W. S. & W. Pitts. 1943. A logical calculus of the ideas immanent in nervous activity. *Bulletin of mathematical biophysics.* 9: 127-147.

Mead, C. 1989. *Analog VLSI & Neural Systems*, Addison-Wesley.

Minsky, M. L. 1954. *Theory of neural-analog reinforcement systems and its application to the brain model problem.* PhD. Dissertation. Princeton Univ.

Minsky. M. 1975. *A framework for representing knowledge.* The psychology of computer vision. (P. H. Winston ed.) 211-277. New York. McGraw-Hill.

Minsky, M. L. and S. Papert. 1969. *Perceptrons, an essay in computational geometry.* The MIT Press.

Moorhead, I. R., N. D. Haig, R. A. Clement, 1989. An Investigation of Trained Neural Networks from a Neurophysiological perspective. *Perception*, 1989, vol 18: 793-803.

Mozer, M. C., 1988, *The Perception of Multiple Objects: A Parallel Distributed Processing Approach*, April 1988. ICS Report 8803.

Neisser, U. 1976. *Cognition and reality: Principles and implications of cognitive psychology.* W. H. Freeman.

Neisser. U & P. Weene. 1962. Hierarchies in concept attainment. *J. Exp. Psychol.* 64: 640-645.

Palm, G. 1979. On representation and approximation of nonlinear systems, Part II: Discrete time, *Biological Cybernetics*, 34: 49-52.

Parker, D. B. , 1985. MIT, Sloan School of Management Technical Report Tr-47.

Pearlmutter, B. A. & G. E. Hinton. 1986. G-Maximisation: An unsupervised learning procedure for discovering regularities, *Neural networks for computing*, (J. S. Denker ed.) New York: American Inst. of Physics. 333-338.

Pelionisz, A. & R. Llinas. 1985. Tensor network theory of the metaorganisation of functional geometries in the central nervous system. *Neuroscience*, 16: 245-274.

Penfield, W. & T. Rasmussen. 1952. *The cerebral cortex of man.* New York: Macmillan.

Percival, I., 1989. Chaos: A Science for the Real World, *New Scientist*, October 1989.

Phillips, W. A. 1988. Human Cognition & neural computation. In *Neural Network from Models to applications.* E. S. P. C. I., Paris, 1988, I. D. S. E. T. , Paris, 1989 (Personnaz, L. & G. Dreyfus eds.)

Piaget J., 1980 *Structuralism.* Basic Books.

Piaget, J., 1971. *Biology and Knowledge*, Edinburgh Univ. Press.

Pineda, F. 1987, Generalisation of Back Propagation to recurrent neural networks, *Phys. Rev. Lett.* 59, p. 2229.

Pomerleau, D. A, 1989. ALVINN: An autonomous land vehicle in a neural network. In *Advances in neural information processing systems I.* (D. S. Touretzky ed.) San Mateo, CA: Morgan Kaufmann Publishers.

Prager, R. W., T. D. Harrison & F. Fallside. 1986. Boltzmann machines for speech recognition, *Computer Speech and Language.* 1: 3-27.

Psaltis, D. 1989. Optoelectronic Implementations of Neural Networks. *IEEE Communications Magazine*, Vol. 27, No. 11, Nov. 1989.

Psaltis, D. 1990. Holography in Artificial Neural Networks, *Nature*, vol. 343: 25. Jan. 1990.

Rall, W. 1970. Dendritic neuron theory and dendrodendritic synapses in a simple cortical system. *The Neurosciences: Second Study Program* (F. O. Schmitt ed.): 552-565, Rockerfeller Univ. Press.

Rashevsky, N. 1938. *Principles of Neurodynamics.* Washington DC: Spartan Books.

Recce, M. & P. C. Treleaven. 1989. Parallel architectures for neural computers. In *Neural Computers: Proc NATO Adv. Research Workshop 1987,* (R. Eckmiller & C. v. d. Malsburg eds.) Springer-Verlag.

Rees, M. 1987. The anthropic principle. *New Scientist,* 6 Aug. 87.

Ritter, H., K. Schulten. 1989. Extending Kohonen's self-organising mapping algorithm to learn ballistic movements. In *Neural Computers: Proc NATO Adv. Research Workshop 1987* (R. Eckmiller & C. v. d. Malsburg eds.) Springer-Verlag.

Rohwer, R., 1988. *Connectionist Methods in Speech Recognition, Procs.* Speech 88, Institute of Acoustics.

Rosenblatt, F. 1958. The Perceptron: A probabilistic model for information storage and organisation in the brain. *Psychological Review.* 65: 386-408.

Rosenblatt, F., 1962. *Principles of neurodynamics.* Spartan.

Rumelhart, D. E. & D. Zipser. 1985. Feature discovery by competitive learning. *Cognitive Science* 9: 75-112.

Rumelhart. D. E. 1977. Understanding and summarising brief stories. *Basic processes in reading: Perception and comprehension.* (D. LaBerge & S. J. Samuels eds.), 265-303, Hillsdale, NJ: Erlbaum.

Rumelhart, Hinton & Williams, 1985. Learning Internal Representations by Error Propagation, Parallel Distributed Processing: Explorations in the Microstructure of Cognition. Vol. 1: Foundation, (Rumelhart, D. E. & McClelland, J. L. eds.), Cambridge, MA: Bradford Books/MIT Press.

Rumelhart, Hinton & Williams, 1986. Learning Internal Representations by Back-Propagating Errors, *Nature* 323: 533-536.

Rumelhart, D. E., G. E. Hinton and R. J. Williams, 1986, Learning Internal Representations by Error Propagation *Parallel Distributed Processing: Explorations in the microstructure of Cognition,* vol. 1., Foundations, MIT Pres, pp 318-362.

Rumelhart, D. E., G. E. Hinton and R. J. Williams, 1986, On Learning the Past Tenses of English Verbs. *Parallel Distributed Processing* (McClelland, Rumelhart, and the PDP Research Group, Eds.), vol. 2, MIT Press, Cambridge, pp. 216-271.

Rumelhart, D. E., G. E. Hinton and R. J. Williams, 1986, Learning internal representations by error propagation. *Parallel Distributed Processing* (McClelland, Rumelhart and the PDP Research Group, Eds.), vol. 1, MIT Press, Cambridge.

Rumelhart, D. E. & J. L. McClelland. 1986. *PDP models and general issues in cognitive science.* ICS report 8602.

Rumelhart, D. E. & J. L. McClelland. 1986a. On learning the past tense of English verbs. *Parallel Distributed Processing: Explorations in the microstructure of cognition* (D. E. Rumelhart & J. L. McClelland eds.), vol. 2: 216-271. The MIT Press/Bradford Books.

Rumelhart, D. E. & D. Zipser. 1985. Feature discovery by competitive learning, *Cognitive Science,* 9, 75-112.

Schmajuk, N. A. 1988. The Hippocampus and the Control of Information Storage in the Brain. in *Dynamic Interactions in Neural Networks: Models and Data*. (M. A. Arbib & S. Amari eds.) Springer Verlag.

Sejnowski, T. J. 1981. Skeleton filters in the brain. *Parallel models of associative memory*. (G. E. Hinton & J. A. Anderson eds.) Hillsdale, N. J: Erbaum Associates.

Sejnowski, T. J. 1989. Neural network learning algorithms. *Neural Computers: Proc NATO Adv. Research Workshop 1987*, (R. Eckmiller & C. v. d. Malsburg eds.) Springer-Verlag.

Sejnowsky, T. J. & S. R. Lehky. 1987. Neural network models of visual processing. *1987 short course on computational neuroscience*. (M. A. Arbib & S. A. George eds.) Society for neuroscience.

Sejnowski, T. J. & G. E. Hinton. 1987. Separating figure from ground with a Boltzmann machine, *Vision, brain & Cooperative Computation*, (M. A. Arbib & A. R, Hanson eds.) MIT Press, Cambridge.

Sejnowski, T. J. & C. R. Rosenburg, 1987. Parallel Networks that Learn to Pronounce English Text. *Complex Systems*, 1: 145-168.

Shannon C. E & W. Weaver, 1949. *The Mathematical Theory of Communications*. Urbana, Illinois: Univ. of Illinois Press.

Shepherd, G. 1979. *The Synaptic Organisation of the brain*. 2nd edition. New York; Oxford Univ. Press.

Sherrington- 1906. *The Integrative Action of the Central Nervous System*. New York. Scriber.

Skarda, A. & W. Freeman. 1987. How brains make chaos in order to make sense of the world. In *Behavioral and brain sciences*. Vol. 10 no. 2, June 87.

Stewart, I. 1989. Portraits of Chaos, *New Scientist*, 4 November 1989.

Stone, G. O. & G. C. Van Orden, 1989. Are Words Represented by Nodes?, *Memory and Cognition*, 17 (5): 511-524.

Sutton, R. S., 1987. *Learning to predict by the method of temporal differences*. Technical report, GTE Labs. tech, report TR87-509. 1.

Swinney, D. A., 1979. Lexical access during sentence comprehension: (Re)consideration of context effects, *Journal of Verbal Learning and Verbal Behaviour*, 18: 645-659.

Thatacher, M. L. & P. S. Sastry. 1985. Learning optimal discriminant functions through a cooperative game of automata. Tech. Report EE/64/1985, Dept. Elec. Eng., *Indian Inst. of Science*, Bangalore-560012, India.

Touretzky, D. S., G. E. Hinton & T. J. Sejnowski, (eds.) 1988. San Mateo, CA: Morgan Kaufmann Publishers.

Touretzky, D. S. & D. A. Pomerleau. 1989. What's hidden in the hidden layers? *BYTE*, Aug. 89: 227-232.

Turing, A. M. 1950. Computing machinery and intelligence. *Mind* 59: 433-460.

Turing, A. 1936. On the computability of numbers. *Proc. London Math. Soc.* 42: 230.

Vivaldi, F. An Experiment With Mathematics, *New Scientist*, 28 October 1989.

v. d. Malsburg, C 1973, Self-organisation of orientation sensitive cells in striate cortex. *Kybernetik*, 14: 85-100.

von Neuman, J. 1948, *Collected Works*, Vol. 5, ed. A. H. Taub. Pergamon Press, New York, published 1963: 304.

von Neumann, J. 1951. The general and logical theory of automata.*Cerebral mechanisms in behaviour: The Hixon symposium* (L. A. Jeffress ed.), 1-32. Wiley.

von Neumann, J. 1956. Probabilistic logics and the syntheses of reliable organisms from unreliable components. *Automata studies* (C. E. Shannon & J. McCarthy, eds.): 43-98. Princeton Univ. Press.

von Neumann, J. 1966. *Theory of self-reproducing automata* (A. W. Burks ed.) Univ. of Illinois Press.

Wallace, D. J., 1987. Neural network models: A physicist's primer. *Proc. 32nd Scottish Summer School in Physics*, Edinburgh Univ. Press.

Werner, G., 1987. Five decades on the path to naturalising epistemology. Chapter to appear in: *The Neural basis of sensory processes*.

Widrow, G. & M. D. Hoff. 1960. *Adaptive switching circuits*. 1960 *IRE WESCON Convention Record*, Part 4: 96-104.

Widrow, B. & S. D. Stearns. 1985. *Adaptive Signal Processing*. Prentice-Hall.

Widrow B. 1962. Generalisation and information storage in networks of ADALINE neurons. In: *Self organising systems* (Yovitts GT, ed.) Spartan books.

Widrow, G. & M. E. Hoff. 1960. Adaptive switching circuits. 1960 *IRE WESCON Convention Record*, Part 4: 96-104.

Wiener, N. 1948. *Cybernetics*. New York: John Wiley and Sons.

Wiener 1948 *Cybernetics, or Control and Communications in the Animal and the Machine*. Cambridge MIT press.

Williams, R. J. & Zipser, D., A Learning Algorithm for Fully Recurrent Neural Networks, Oct. 1988. *ICS Report 8805*.

Wilson, C. 1988. *Beyond the Occult*. Guild Publishing London.

Y. Le Cun, 1985. *Procs. of Cognitiva* 85, Paris, 1985.

Zipser, D. 1986. A model of Hippocampal learning during classic conditioning. *Behavioural neuroscience*. Vol. 100, no. 5: 764-776.

Zuse, C. 1989. Faust, Mephistopheles and Computer. *Neural Computers*: Proc NATO Adv. Research Workshop 1987 (R. Eckmiller & C. v. d. Malsburg eds.) Springer-Verlag.

INDEX